THE SHAPING OF CZARDOM

THE SHAPING OF CZARDOM

UNDER IVAN GROZNYJ

By

BJARNE NØRRETRANDERS

VARIORUM REPRINTS
London 1971

SBN 902089 12 9

Published in Great Britain by

VARIORUM REPRINTS

21a Pembridge Mews London W11 3EQ

Printed in Switzerland by

REDA SA

1225 Chêne-Bourg Geneva

Reprint of the 1964 Copenhagen edition

VARIORUM REPRINT S4

To Yvonne

Acknowledgements

On the occasion of the publication of this work, I take the opportunity to thank the staffs of The Royal Library, Copenhagen and The University Library, Helsinki, for their unstinted assistance and helpfulness while I was working on the book, and I am grateful, also, to the Committee of the Jens Lomand Rasmussen Fund, whose grant enabled me to spend a period studying at Helsinki.

To Colonel Harold Young, who has translated the work from Danish, I am very grateful for his ready understanding and for inspiring discussions. To my teacher, emeritus Professor Anton Karlgren, and his successor, Professor Carl Stief, I owe the encouragement without which this work would hardly have been brought to a conclusion.

It is with great regret that I must point out that A. A. Zimin's book, "Opričnina Ivana Groznogo", which has just been published, did not reach me until the present work had gone to press, and consequently could not there take what would otherwise have been its natural place.

B. N.

Contents

Preface to the 1971 Reprint

The original edition of the present book, published in 1964, went out of print within three years. For some time this did not concern me too much. I felt I had made some contribution to research in the field of Muscovite political thought and practices three hundred years ago, and noted with satisfaction that research had gone further and past my book, not only with Zimin's admirable study mentioned in the acknowledgements in the 1964 edition, but also with a whole number of new contributions published over the following years.

On the other hand I have been receiving an increasing number of requests for a reprint. So it seems that the book may still be useful to students in this field, however much I am aware of the points of criticism which can be levelled against it. The attention of the reader should be drawn to reviews such as that of J..S. Lur'je *Istorija SSSR*, Moscow 1966, pp. 200-204. However the fact that I remain convinced of the essential correctness of my analysis, and that I still feel the need to convince others, makes me a willing victim to the temptation of presenting this study once again, in a reprint.

B.N.

I

Introduction

In his book on political thought in the 16th Century, J. W. Allen wrote that men are constantly engaged in an, on the whole, highly successful effort to adjust their ideas to circumstance and, also, in an effort, very much less successful, to adjust circumstance to their ideas (1). A study of the field, which Allen did not include in his book, of Russian developments in the same period, would undoubtedly have confirmed him in this view. Ideas and circumstances in Russia differed in many ways from those in Western Europe, but here, too, efforts were made in both these directions, certainly with varying degrees of success. And here one is sharply brought up against the problem—clearly insoluble, but equally clearly, fascinating—of where runs the boundary between the lordships of ideas and of circumstances.

The Czarist autocracy, as it was formed and confirmed under Ivan Groznyj on the basis of previous tendencies in the grand duchy of Moscow, made its appearance in the historical development of Russia in a peculiarly ambivalent manner. On the one hand, it was undoubtedly the product of general economic, social and cultural development in the course of the previous century, particularly under Grand Duke Ivan III Velikij. And from this point of view it might well seem justifiable to call the formation of Czardom the result of a successful effort to adjust ideas to circumstances. On the other hand, however, the change of system that took place under Ivan Groznyj was so eruptive that consideration of it frequently compels the question whether ideas and not circumstances supplied the decisive motive and stimulus underlying the acts themselves.

It is not easy to find answers to such questions, since at that time there was no well defined relation between political ideology and practical politics, as two separate fields, such as may—with a certain amount of luck—be discerned in later periods, and which is found to some extent in Western Europe even in the 16th century. In Moscow, this boundary was undefined. And so it has remained in the view of subsequent generations, though less definite, perhaps, than is necessary. In the last few decades, a new approach to the political content of the ideology and publicistics of the period has

---

1. *J. W. Allen: A History of Political Thought in the Sixteenth Century* (London 1928) p. xvii.

been made by a number of Soviet historians, notably *J. S. Lur'je* and *A. A. Zimin,* but the relation of ideology to practical politics has attracted less attention. This is undoubtedly due to the fact that Soviet historical research works on the basis of historical materialism.

From the fundamental viewpoint of historical materialism, it is inevitable to prefer an interpretation that deduces all ideological and politico-cultural statements from the contemporary economic and social conditions (2). On this interpretation, ideology is a secondary, politico-cultural superstructure, determined by the economic-social conditions of the real world. And since the development is dialectical, there is, it is true, a connexion between ideology and practice, but the regularly determined development of the economic-social plane can never be definitively changed by arbitrary inter-ference from the politico-cultural plane. The contrary, however, must in-evitably happen.

There is much to justify this point of view, which gives many fruitful im-pulses, as an essential element in it is the sound common sense that also led Allen to observe—though in rather more cautious terms—how much easier it usually is to adjust ideas to circumstances than to do the opposite. Con-sequently, it is obvious that the Soviet researchers' description of political events and ideological tendencies in Ivan Groznyj's period as the expression of the replacement of a decentralized system by a centralized government is a formula that is both useful and correct, taken as the framework of a description in a long perspective (3). And yet, in many cases, one feels con-stricted by too tight a scheme, which does not permit full freedom of move-ment in coming to a conclusion about concrete questions of motivation and cause.

Naturally, these hesitations present themselves first and foremost in con-nexion with the volcanic events of the Czarist change of system, rather than with the long-term economic-social tendencies. Here it is often tempting to apply quite another point of view, and to interpret acts as the result of arbitrary intervention determined by personal choice. This implies, there-fore, the absence of a necessary regularity such as is assumed by historical materialism, since a personal choice may, of course, be conceived as having epoch-making historical significance, whatever may have been the motives for the choice.

From this point of view, the motives might well consist of ideas that have no objective justification in the prevailing economic or social conditions or laws. It is conceivable that the choice that is made may lead an idea to victory over the circumstances—or, in other words, that an ideologically

---

2. See for example *Osnovy marksistskoj filosofii* (Moscow 1959) pp. 352 ff., 431 ff.

3. *Očerki*, pp. 218, 901.

determined act decisively alters the course of social and economic development. Before the Revolution, this point of view was taken by certain Russian historians, since from a Slavophile standpoint, they saw Ivan Groznyj's organization of the central government and of his autocracy as the forcible imposition of an idea that was quite contrary to ancient Russian custom and brought catastrophic consequences, both economic and social, for the Russian peasant class in subsequent centuries (4).

From this point of view, however, the motives that determine the concrete acts need no more be ideological than they need be objective economic and social laws. There are cases where Groznyj's view of and exercise of his power as Czar is viewed as the expression of a peculiarly Russian mentality —often called "the Russian soul"—that is taken to give the life of the Russian community its special character (5). Finally, the Russian historians have very often chosen to explain Ivan Groznyj's way of acting as the result of special personal conditions, either dependence on bad advisers, or pronounced neurasthenia or merely the desire for personal power without regard to the conditions for this, but with the use of the most suitable ideological reasons (6).

Seen in relation to the point of view of historical materialism, these views —however much they may differ from one another—may all be said to take their starting point in a development that admittedly leads to a centralization of power in the Czar, based on ideological principles of a religious and nationalist character, but which in its actual course is determined primarily by that person's utilization of these ideological principles and of the resources available to him. This antithesis to historical materialism might be called historical idealism. At any rate, this term finds support in Marxist terminology.

It is not immediately obvious, however, why one of these views should be particularly marked by materialism, or the other by idealism. Were it not for accepted convention, the two terms could very well be exchanged without causing any confusion in ideas. And so the terms should be used with a clear sense of the irony in the fate that can overtake words and terms.

The characteristic element in historical materialism is that it claims that objective laws are the cause of every development, the actual course of which is only in appearance determined by "subjective" acts. Every act that is contrary to these objective laws will fail, in one way or another, and so brings its own punishment. In order, however, to keep this theory intact through every analysis, one is reduced to using such a complicated set of

4. *K. S. Aksakov: Polnoje sobranije sočinenij* t. I (Moscow 1889) pp. 143, 154, 164, 162.

5. *H. von Eckardt: Iwan der Schreckliche* (Frankfurt a. M. 1947) pp. 22, 32, 386.

6. *Karamzin* t. IX, pp. 432 ff., *V. O. Kl'učevskij: Sočinenija* t. II (Moscow 1957) pp. 187–199, *P. I. Kovalevskij: Ioann Groznyj i jego duševnoje sostojanije* (Kharkov 1893).

qualifications and implications, that the objective laws assume the character of a rather abstract idea. There is no possibility of direct and exact testing or demonstration of error in the particular case. An attempt to perform an historical act that by definition is in accordance with the objective laws— and consequently with the prevailing material conditions—may fail; or, on the contrary, an act may succeed under material conditions that, according to the objective laws should have been so unfavourable that it must necessarily have failed. In such cases, it may seem that historical materialism is making a great effort to adjust the concrete conditions in history to its ideas of historical necessity.

In such cases, historical idealism will say that the "objective" laws that posterity believes it has observed behind historical developments, are in the last resort the result of subjective acts—that is, those acts that actually come to determine developments, or that it is desired to interpret as decisive. History is written by the victors, and historical laws are decreed by their heirs, it will come to be said, perhaps. But this criticism of historical materialism does not imply that ideas have necessarily determined historical acts, any more than abstract rules can be deduced from the course of history. It is rather that acts and the course of development are reduced by this type of analysis to playing quite arbitrarily for political power and financial gain, and consequently to materially determined opportunism.

Here it is not the intention to argue for the acceptance of either of these points of view. The historical evaluation of Ivan Groznyj's system of government has—as already indicated—in many cases suffered from the unreasonably strong influence of these very standpoints. This influence is so strong and enduring that it may be called a tradition in the writing of history in Russia.

A more detailed account and an analysis of this tradition has been attempted elsewhere (7). Here it is only necessary to recall that one of the most distinguished of Russian historians, *S. F. Platonov,* consciously freed himself from the influence of this tradition and showed its unfortunate effects. Platonov gave an untendentious approach and an understanding of the period as the two most important requirements for research on Ivan Groznyj as an historical person—no trivial requirements, indeed. For the same reason, however, it is difficult to agree with Platonov when he describes the historical study of the governmental system of Ivan Groznyj as a victory for the scientific approach, won by a constantly refined historical method, and sees in this a contrast to the literary and artistic treatments of the subject (8). In reality, historians and novelists agreed again and again in

7. B. Nørretranders: *Ivan den Skrækkelige i russisk tradition* – Studier fra Sprog- og Oldtids-forskning, nr. 230 (København 1956), Summary in English in *Excerpta Historica Nordica,* ed. *Povl Bagge,* Vol. III (Copenhagen 1962) pp. 19 f.

8. *S. F. Platonov: Ivan Groznyj 1530–1584* (Pbg. 1923) pp. 5, 24.

approaching the subject in equal dependence on tendencies, and equally engaged in the problematics of their day.

That something similar has also applied in the writing of history in Russia after Platonov's day, should also be mentioned, for the sake of completeness. Platonov lived long enough to dissociate himself, discreetly, from a book on Ivan Groznyj, in which, with patriotic enthusiasm, he is pictured as a sort of superman, the most distinguished diplomat and statesman of his time. This did not, however, prevent its being reprinted as part of an international information campaign after the second world war (9). This book corresponded more closely, at the time, to the contemporary signals than did Platonov's monograph.

Platonov did not engage in any personality cult of Ivan Groznyj. He neither overlooked nor defended his acts of terrorism, but explained them as being due to Ivan's being burdened with a number of psychological difficulties in consequence of his unhappy upbringing, or as being forced upon him by the need to be ruthless in order to carry through his policy against the will of the opposition. Platonov maintained that Ivan Groznyj was not mad, and that his writings, right up to his death, showed masterly judgement, and that his policy was a logical and consistent attempt to resolve a clash of interests that had long afflicted Russia: it was a means by which to overcome feudal divisions and to facilitate further development towards centralized administration of the state (10). He kept his portrait of Ivan Groznyj, within this framework, better balanced than those of his predecessors.

It can hardly be doubted that this feat was possible only by virtue of his liberation from contemporary interests and loyalities. Individual traits and actions had formerly been emphasised and exaggerated to serve as confirmation of a preconceived opinion. Those historians to whom the Czardom was holy and sacrosanct, necessarily described Ivan Groznyj as an aberration from the normal Czarist rule and explain the aberration as due to personal unhingement. Conversely, his attempt to create a new political system against hard and compact opposition, but in conformity with ruling tendencies in the development of society, could inspire reformist historians to describe him as the clearsighted, revolutionary individualist. The first claimed that he misused ideas to secure power, the latter that he secured power in order to realise ideas.

In spite of all his reservations, Platonov inclined rather to the latter view —and perhaps more than is justifiable. It is characteristic that in later years, Soviet historians have criticized Platonov for interpreting Ivan's *opričnina*

---

9. *R. Wipper: Ivan Groznyj* (3rd edn, Moscow 1947), cf. *Platonov op. cit.* p. 24 and *S. M. Dubrovskij* in *Voprosy Istorii* 1956/8 pp. 121 ff., *Zimin Ref.* p. 45.

10. *Platonov: op. cit.* pp. 132, 155 ff., 97, 104, 122.

one-sidedly as a political instrument for achieving his aims, while ignoring the role of this institution as a means of economic exploitation of the peasants (11). It should be noted, then, that even Platonov's balanced characterization of Ivan Groznyj seems to imply a certain distortion in regard to the evaluation of his political outlook, his motives and his decisions.

The reason for this distortion is probably to be found not so much in the Russian historiographical tradition previously mentioned, and from which Platonov himself had largely freed himself, as in another circumstance of a fundamental character. Platonov's views of Groznyj's system of government have this much in common with the others mentioned above, that he started with what may be called an anachronistic view of the formation of political ideas.

When Platonov attributes to Ivan Groznyj a logical and consistent political programme, he is, in other words, assuming that Groznyj was fully aware of what he was doing—not only in regard to political practice and tactics, but also in regard to theory and ideology. This assumption naturally involves another—that Ivan Groznyj was conscious of a distinction between theory and practice, between idea and action, and that in a given situation he could, so to speak, check one against the other, i. e. see if an action was in accordance with the realisation of his programme or ran counter to it. To this belongs, moreover, the natural, or at all events, the related assumption that the distinction between ideology and the exercise of power existed not only in the consciousness of the person acting but also in that of those around him. And finally, from this assumption it is only an insignificant little step to the assumption that the origin of the ideology, the ideas or theories lay first and foremost in circles that were not primarily burdened with the actual work of exercising power, while on the other hand, the practical application of the theories—whether this meant violation or realisation of them—was the task of the Czar and his servants.

To assume this to the extent indicated here is synonymous with describing political conditions as we know them from the last few centuries in Western Europe. It cannot be taken for granted, however, that the same conditions prevailed in 16th Century Russia. If this were so, there should be a well defined set of political ideas, which, perhaps in competition with other ideologies, could form a programme for Ivan Groznyj's government, and there should be some form of public opinion that could call him to account in relation to this ideology by demonstrating violations or deviations, perhaps even call him politically to account by depriving him of the support necessary for the retention of power. If this were so, it should be possible—to some degree, at any rate—to decide the question of Ivan Groznyj's motives by a comparatively simple method, i. e. by deciding that his actions

---

11. *Očerki* pp. 213 ff.

were determined by ideas when contrary to obvious opportunist considerations, and determined by opportunism when they were in conflict with his set of ideas.

As stated above, it has proved difficult, not to say impossible, to reason in this manner without coming to conclusions that inevitably give rise to criticism. On this basis, it is considered justifiable to speak of an anachronistic view of the formation of political ideas. But this does not, on the other hand, imply that it can be taken for granted that none of the conditions mentioned existed in Groznyj's time, or that some of them did not prevail then—only that those that did exist did so to so small an extent that their effects cannot be described on the accepted lines.

It is well known that the Orthodox Church in Russia at that time was the bearer of a nationalist and political idea, which in the 16th Century was given its most distinctive formulation in the thesis that Moscow was the Third Rome, and which was intimately connected with the formation of Czardom. It is likewise well known that sectarian movements originating in western districts of Russia were sustained by currents of opinion with evident political aims, among hitherto unprivileged but increasingly important groups in the population, such as artisans and traders. And finally, it is well known that political publicistics begin to take form in Ivan Groznyj's time, especially with Ivan Peresvetov's tracts, the writings of Andrej Kurbskij, and the Czar's own manifestoes. The expressions of opinion mentioned here give collectively a fairly clear pattern of ideas and conflicts of opinion, but the crucial point, in this connexion, is that it is not possible to distinguish directly between the political and the religious threads in the pattern.

On the whole, we are dealing with the formation of political ideas at an embryonic stage. Ivan Peresvetov is probably the only known example of a political theoretician who at that time produced a set of ideas for the guidance of those in power without himself having any part in government. In general, it is impossible to distinguish between those without political responsibility who formulate the ideas and those who are responsible and must act as conditions allow. Nor can it be taken for granted that Ivan Groznyj united in his own person a clear-sighted political theoretician and a conscious political tactician and man of action. On the other hand, it may be assumed with a high degree of probability that he was at once theoretician, tactician and man of action, but without any conscious distinction between these, so that in present cases it is not possible to make an immediate distinction between ideology and exercise of power, or, between idealism and opportunism (12).

---

12. It is consequently not considered possible to distinguish between constitutional law, constitutional custom and publicistics as consistently as is proposed by *V. Val'denberg: Drevnerusskije učenija o predelax carskoj vlasti* (Pgr. 1916) p. 27.

To this argument also belongs the provisional assumption that it is not possible to attribute to Ivan Groznyj clearly and unambiguously either of these attitudes, to the exclusion of the other. To begin with, it will be necessary to consider theory and practice, ideology and the exercise of power, together as one, though at the same time one is compelled to recognise symptoms of the incipient independence of each of the two fields. But for this second point, it would be enough to aim at the most precise description possible of the course of events under Ivan Groznyj. As things are, however, it is not possible—with, e. g. the discouraging results of previous tendencies to analyse Ivan Groznyj's system of government according to principles, in mind—to refrain from at any rate an attempt to analyse the motives and the elements of this system of government, which in many ways is epoch-making.

It has been mentioned that a simple, chronological registration of the course of events would very easily take on the character of a purely anecdotic history from the point of view of what, for want of a better term, was called historical idealism. Events will then appear in unpredictable chaos, with the result—in itself a quite logical result—that the chief person behind the events either is seen as an arbitrary, unprincipled tyrant, or is described in the clinical case-sheet as mentally abnormal. And on the other hand, it has also been mentioned that such a registration would, oddly enough, from the point of view of historical materialism, be pressed into so tight a system of alleged regularity that it is impossible to see the motives, objectives and possibilities of choice that have given these events their unique human— some will say, all too human, and others, perhaps, inhuman—character.

But here a third element comes in—that in the attempt to abstract from these two views, one cannot but feel deeply dissatisfied with the skeleton of actions that is left when all the rest has been stripped away. One cannot help asking what play of circumstances and ideas lay behind the coronation of the sixteen year-old Grand Duke Ivan as the first Czar of Russia in 1547—the same year in which Moscow dramatically revealed that it was in an explosive condition of social tension. One is tempted to try to elucidate the forces behind the succession crisis of 1553, when the Czardom seemed about to die an early death along with the wearer of the imperial crown, though both, however, contrary to all expectations, survived. And one is compelled to look for signs of tactical calculation or of ambitious objectives behind the abdication crisis in the winter of 1564–65, the immediate result of which could have been chaos, and the actual result of which was the Czar's introduction of a private state within the state maintained by terror.

In the following pages, the attempt will be made to analyse, on this basis, the system of government erected on the foundation of Ivan Groznyj's aims and actions, and to find a method in what has traditionally been attributed to madness. And the search will also be for personal choice-situations and special conditions for the choices made, in what has been ascribed, just as traditionally, to the working of natural laws. With this in view, attention will first be directed to discovering what were Groznyj's political ideas and concepts.

II

Ivan Groznyj's Programme

When the question arises, whether Ivan Groznyj had an ideology of a political kind, or at any rate, a set of clearly defined axioms, on which he based his exercise of power, it is natural to seek the answer in his correspondence with Prince Andrej Kurbskij. This document is the richest source for the elucidation of the Czar's personality and his way of thinking and expressing himself, and perhaps also for a knowledge of his convictions and the development of his ideas, but in any case, for ascertaining what he wanted the rest of the world to know or to think were his beliefs and his views (1).

In this connexion, the most significant part of the correspondence is the first message to Kurbskij, obviously written in July 1564—a couple of months after Kurbskij had gone over to the Polish King (2) and six months before Groznyj's revolution. This paper, the prolixity of which provoked the receiver's scorn, resembles more a treatise then a letter. There has been some discussion on the question of whether the message was originally meant for Kurbskij alone or for a wider circle (3). In favour of the first view, there is its personal, often actually colloquial style: in favour of the second, its breadth and polemical aim. And yet it seems evident, even without deciding this question, that the message is the expression of a general clash and a programme with political aims (4)—a clash with hitherto powerful forces in the Russian czardom, forces that are symbolized in Kurbskij's defection, and a programme that portends an intensified struggle against these forces, the struggle that began at the turn of 1564.

It is thus not only the extent and copiousness of the message that makes it an invaluable means of coming *in medias res*. According to the traditional

---

1. *S. M. Dubrovskij* (*Voprosy Istorii* 1956/8, p. 123) has doubted whether the text is genuine, though without giving any other reason than that the original manuscripts are lacking. *J. S. Lur'je* (*TODRL* t. XV, 1958, pp. 505 ff.) in reply, has given representative expression for an otherwise unaminous acknowledgement of their genuineness.
2. See *Epstein* p. 23 with references.
3. *Lur'je* pp. 510 ff. and in *TODRL* t. XV (1958) pp. 507 f., *Posl. Grozn.* pp. 470 ff. Cf. below pp. 140–145.
4. Cf. *S. Ščeglova* in *Žurn. Min. Narodn. Prosvešč.* t. XXXII (1911) p. 136.

interpretations of earlier Russian historians, the years from 1560 to 1564 formed a fateful period in Groznyj's life, during which he underwent a metamorphosis from a just ruler to a tyrant, from normal to abnormal (5). In this connexion, it is useful to note that Ivan's first message to Kurbskij was written in the closing stage of this period of metamorphosis, and that, in taking this message as the main source for the elucidation of Groznyj's views and the development of his ideas, one feels on more or less safe ground with regard to the general value of this source for the subsequent years also. It does not originate from a sane person who later went mad. If it marks the end of an epoch, it gives, at any rate, just as clear warning of a new one. The inclusion of Groznyj's second letter to Kurbskij, written thirteen years later, serves as further confirmation, for, in spite of slight differences, it is a repetition of the first.

The theory that Ivan Groxnyj underwent a change in the course of those four years of crisis was first formulated by Andrej Kurbskij in the letter he sent to the Czar soon after his defection, which might be called a notice of renunciation of allegiance. It is addressed "To the Czar, exalted above all by God, and who appeared most illustrious, particularly in the Orthodox Faith, but who has now, in consequence of our sins, been found to be the contrary of this" (6). The rest of the letter is in the main only a justification of this contention that the Czar is changed, with particular emphasis on what, for Kurbskij, was the most important consequence of the change, Ivan's liquidation of his magnates and army leaders "whom God has given him". In other words, Kurbskij admits that the Czar sits on his throne by the Divine will, but indicates at the same time that the change in the monarch is such as to lose him the Divine benevolence, and that consequently his subjects must be entitled to regard him with aversion. Moreover, he manages to limit his admission of Groznyj's divine authority by inserting the remark about the magnates and army leaders being given to the Czar by God, just as the throne was. The Czar is therefore not justified in treating them in an ungodly way, he implies. And now that he has, according to the writer of the letter, turned to this way, this is a fall from grace, which justifies Kurbskij's defection. If this letter is taken as notice of renunciation of allegiance, the analogy with feudal custom in Europe can be taken further, and its content called a portrait of a *rex iniustus*.

---

5. *Kurbskij* col. 13–44 cf. 99–116, 12, 100. Here, and in what follows, the references are to this edition of *Istorija o Velikom Kn'aze Moskovskom* instead of to *RIB* t. XXXI, since it was possible to use the latter for a limited time only. The corresponding places in the text in *RIB* t. XXXI may be found by adding 160 to the number of the page referred to. Karamzin t. IX p. 149.

6. *Fennell* p. 2. For practical reasons, reference is made, here and subsequently, to this edition of the text, which also gives an English translation.

This was Groznyj's cue to define his attitude to this view of his authority, and in the moment of action, so to speak, to give his reply to posterity's theory of the change in him. It appears very clearly from Ivan's first letter, how anxious he was to repudiate and invalidate the allegation of a fall from grace.

In form, the introduction of the message is constructed in accordance with the scheme of the traditional intitulation and the devotional formula as it is found in the Czar's second letter to Kurbskij, and in most of his other letters (7). But it is quite obvious that the pattern is burst in the first message. The *dei gratia* of the devotional formula, usually expressed by *Boga milost'*, appears here in a couple of variants (*Božije izvolenije, Božije povelenije*) with an underlining of the Divine will and command, and as the framework of a full confession of faith, while the intitulation takes the form of a historical justification of the Czardom (8).

The bursting open of the introductory formula may probably be explained stylistically by the need for a fuller and more monumental exordium to this enormous letter than the usual one. This is scarcely an adequate explanation, however, in that it does not answer the far more important question of why the bounds of the epistolary style, as a whole, burst under the pressure of the content. The essential point, also in regard to the introduction, is undoubtedly an intention that exceeds the needs of the routine, official communication, and which, therefore, is not content with the conventional, official statement of the religious justification of the power of the Czar, but requires something more impressive and emphatic. The letter is a piece of psychological warfare. And since the war was about the very basis of the Czardom, Groznyj cannot be satisfied here with the official statement of this basis, but must plunge into defensive polemics at the very start.

In his introduction, Ivan attaches great importance to stressing that the Orthodox, well pleasing to God, dominion on earth begins with the Emperor Constantine the Great, and began in Russia with St. Vladimir when he Christianized the country. From that time, Ivan claims, the Orthodox autocracy was transmitted from monarch to monarch, and finally, by the will of God and by God's command—and thus not merely suffered to happen by God's grace or God's mercy—has been inherited by Ivan Groznyj himself. From this follows his claim that he exercises the autocracy, *samoderžanije,* by virtue of the Divine command and the right of inheritance. In other words, Groznyj repudiates the right of Kurbskij or anybody else to set up criteria by which the Czar's authority can be judged—it is nationally and religiously rooted—founded on the rocks of the nation and Orthodoxy,

---

7. *Ibid.* p. 186. *Posl. Grozn.* pp. 144, 148, 213, 241, 266, 275.
8. *Fennell* pp. 12–14, cf. 24.

and cannot be shaken. The Czardom is one and indivisible, beyond human caprice. The Czar is not responsible to man.

This emphasis on the Czardom as an unlimited autocracy by the grace of God, is repeated later in the message with greater precision. Ivan replies to Kurbskij's reproaches for having exterminated the country's magnates with the sarcastic remark that he does not know whom Kurbskij is talking about, since the Russian realm is governed by God's mercy and the grace of the most pure Mother of God, the prayers of all the Saints, the blessing of all his parents and finally by Ivan himself, its sovereign—but not by magnates and army leaders, of whom, for that matter, by the help of God he has enough, even without defecting traitors. Otherwise, he reserves to himself the right both to punish and to reward his servants (9). It is right that a master should correct his servants, but not that the servant should call his master to account. No-one dared to reprove the ungodly Emperor Theophilos, in ancient Byzantium, in the manner Kurbskij takes the liberty of reproaching a pious Czar—it is consequently not seemly for subjects to distinguish between just and unjust rulers. Even Constantine, most pious of Emperors, killed his own son for the sake of the Empire. The Czar will render his account only to God on the Day of Judgement, but in return he will also answer for the acts of his subjects, if any have sinned owing to the Czar's remissness (10). It is therefore impossible to accuse him, the Czar, of devising methods of torture against the Christian race, as Kurbskij claims he does. Ivan is ready to defend this people against all enemies, both with his blood and with his life (11). In other words, there is no basis for a right of resistance to the Czar: on the contrary, he is bound at peril of his salvation to prevent his subjects, whether they will or not, from going astray, and to keep the realm of Orthodoxy safe from enemies.

It is consequently not for his own pleasure that the Czar undertakes the punishment of disobedient servants. He must do so, since good must be rewarded with good and evil with evil. This does not mean that the Czar himself is without sin, for only God is without sin—all the more reason for subjects to avoid provoking the Czar to wrath, so that in his human weakness he might, perhaps, be led into sin. Such lapses on the part of the Czar, however, do not alter the main point, that God has enfeoffed him with the unlimited autocracy. It is precisely this that is the crucial difference between the truly Orthodox Russia and the impious nations—with which Kurbskij has been kind enough to compare the Czar—that these, characteristically enough, do not have rulers with sovereign power, but only monarchs who obey the orders of their servants (12). And, Groznyj adds,

---

9. *Ibid.* pp. 66, 106, 192.
10. *Ibid.* pp. 126–128, 38, 124.
11. *Ibid.* p. 152, cf. below pp. 44 ff.
12. *Ibid.* pp. 150, 152, 110, 26, cf. the challenge to Elisabeth *Posl. Grozn.* p. 142.

that just as the boyars and army leaders have no right to rebuke the Czar, neither have the clergy any such right. It is not the Lord's intention that priests should meddle with matters of government. It is one thing to save one's own soul, and quite another to have the responsibility for many souls and bodies. It is one thing to abide in fasting, but another to live in common with others. The spiritual authority of the church is one thing, to govern as Czar another. In communal life, there are supervision and rules and punishment, and if these are neglected, the life of the community breaks down (13).

According to Groznyj's definition, as it appears from the account given above, the ideal government—Orthodox Russia's *samoderžanije*—is a dominion exercised by the hereditary Czar over the subjects of the realm, without respect of persons, without responsibility to the church or any other earthly representative of the divine power, but responsible only to the Highest Judge at Doomsday. In life on earth, the Czar has the right and the authority to decide what is fidelity and what treason, good and evil, piety and sacrilege in relation to the Czardom.

It is obvious that this view of the state, in spite of its radical and sharp formulation, cannot be accepted as well defined without further consideration. It is so broad and so abstract in its formulation, that it is more axiomatic or dogmatic than definitive or of the nature of political science. Ivan's repudiation of Kurbskij's approach to the formulation of a right of resistance and renunciation of allegiance does not imply a clear position on the Czar's responsibility to the rules he has himself dictated. By laying it down that in communal life there must be rules that must be maintained to prevent the life of the community from sinking into chaos, he has debarred himself from claiming the right to break or change quite arbitrarily the rules he himself has made—a point which Kurbskij has also taken up, as will be seen later. And by claiming for the Czardom an exclusively religious legitimation, he has simultaneously undertaken to show, at any rate, a steadfastness in piety that does not seriously offend against the general notions of piety. To Kurbskij he curtly declared that he was and would remain pious, unlike his Byzantine predecessor Theophilos. But he was unable to draw the logical conclusion and state that in cases where the spiritual and the temporal clashed, it would be the temporal power that would decide what was true piety.

Seen against the background of this capacious axiom, it is not surprising that Ivan Groznyj had to support his view still further by a series of reasons or proofs of various types, primarily, of course, biblical reasons, a *scriptural justification*. In continuation of what might be called the extended devotional

---

13. *Fennell* pp. 26, 46, 58.

formula, and because the church was in principle declared incompetent in temporal matters, the Czar turned to the Bible itself as the unshakable foundation—and, one might add, the long-suffering instrument—for the temporal power's claim to religious legitimation. The Pauline formulation of a theory of the state (14), which in the course of the centuries has played a much more fatal role than the much criticized realism of Machiavelli, forms the corner-stone of Groznyj's argumentation (15), and lies so close alongside his way of thinking and expressing himself that the quotations merge into the context. The sword here is not merely legitimized, it is legitimation itself. This authoritarian justification of the autocracy naturally does not make it more explicit or concrete, rather it assumes, to an even higher degree, the character of an axiom, firmly founded on the inappellable revelation. What this involves for Ivan Groznyj's argumentation will be discussed later.

In connexion with his religious proofs, the Czar also gives a *historical justification,* as already foreshadowed in the introduction to the message. Because of the nature of the situation, it was very natural that Groznyj should replace the traditional intitulational list of the actual extent of his dominion by a list of the ancestral gallery of the Russian autocracy. Historically, of course, this was quite unjustifiable, since the autocracy in Groznyj's sense had not existed in previous centuries. It was a postulate, of the same kind as the genealogies by which the Russian royal house—like the other potentates of Europe at that time—claimed descent from Caesar Augustus (16). Groznyj, however, had a more concrete form of historical justification, reference to previous cases illustrating the consequence of strong or weak rule in the ancient states.

The Emperor Augustus, says Groznyj, ruled over the whole world: all states were under the same rule up to and including the first Christian ruler, Constantine the Great. But after Constantine's sons had divided the Empire between them, power began to be divided and weakened. Small princes and governors began to establish their own independent kingdoms—as the traitors to Ivan also dream of doing—and from that time order ceased in the Greek Empire, because every man interested himself only in power, glory and wealth, and it perished in political conflicts. Although the power of the Byzantine Empire steadily decayed, its magnates and councillors did not cease their egoistic intrigues and disruptive manoeuvres, but continued in their evil ways, closing their eyes to the threatening dangers. The end was inevitable under such conditions, and the unbeliever Mohammed destroyed the Greek Empire and like a storm-wind and a tempest, left no trace behind.

14. *Rom.* XIII, 1–7.
15. *Fennell* pp. 18, 40.
16. *Posl. Grozn.* pp. 158, 629 f., 200 f.

Which shows how ill it goes with that kingdom which is characterized by the Czar's obedience to his magnates and councillors (17).

It is obvious that with this argumentation, Groznyj has crossed the boundary between the axiom based on religion and political theory. From a historical point of view, the justification of the autocracy lies in its importance for the existence, undivided and unimpaired, of the kingdom. Autocracy means order—aristocracy, chaos. Nationally, therefore, the Czar has a duty to keep the magnates under control, just as much as it is his religious duty to do so.

In the last resort, Groznyj's theory of history is a means of supporting what is actually and essentially a *political justification*. We have already seen how the Czar distinguishes sharply between the tasks of the individual in respect of his spiritual life, and the tasks of the Czar as the guardian of society. Spiritual authority must require a mighty suppression of the tongue, of glory, of honour, of adornment, of supremacy, which are all things unbefitting monks. But the Czarist system is compelled to use terror, repression and coercion, even the most extreme oppression, corresponding to the madness of the most evil and cunning men. To the Czar, not even the scriptural command to turn to other cheek applies (18)—he must return the blow. If he does not, he will never be able to keep the kingdom safe, since without internal peace and order no kingdom can defend itself against external enemies, just as a tree cannot blossom if its roots are dry (19). In other words, the Czar's power rests not merely on divine grace, but also on the supreme *raison d'état*—not only on faith but also on reason.

It is not for his own pleasure or to enrich himself at the expense of his subjects that the Czar punishes and executes traitors. To wage effective war against the enemy, the Czar has need of many army leaders and assistants, and consequently no Czar in his right mind would begin to exterminate his assistants if it were not necessary. But traitors do get their well deserved punishment, as is the custom in other countries where government is not corrupted by the intrigues of the magnates (20). When Kurbskij had to reveal his traitorous sentiments, therefore, it did not surprise the Czar that he should choose to go over to the country hostile to Russia, where King Zygmunt August cannot exercise any rule, but is less then his lowest servant. It will soon appear that Kurbskij will find little comfort or support in such a place, where each thinks only of his own advantage (21). No, life must be lived in accordance with the requirements of the present day—for other-

17. *Fennell* pp. 48–56.
18. *Ibid.* p. 58.
19. *Ibid.* p. 84.
20. *Ibid.* p. 68.
21. *Ibid.* p. 154.

wise thieves and traitors will work their will and the kingdom perish in confusion, simply because its shepherd had no care for the disorders of his subjects (22). It is thus not merely the lessons of history that furnish the proofs of the indispensability of the autocracy for the kingdom and its vital interests, but also, unfortunately, the actual state of things.

It will be clear that while Groznyj is quite ready to accept the authority of the Bible when it is a question of the Pauline theory of the state, he did not consider the words of Jesus about turning the other cheek were of general application—the command does not apply to Czars. There are two necessities—one religious, one political. It might seem as though Groznyj was conscious of a choice between these two things should they come to clash—a choice which for him must quite obviously be the political necessity. He cannot declare himself clearly, and as a programme, on this point. This was partly because his period—in spite of approaches to political realism, such as Machiavelli's—was not favourable to secularization, and especially not in Orthodox Russia, and partly because Groznyj—bound as he was by the cultural situation in Russia—was scarcely able to make a fundamental analysis of this problem. None the less, there are certain hints in his polemical writing, besides those already mentioned, of what is perhaps an involuntary, perhaps actually unconscious, tendency to secularization.

One of Kurbskij's accusations, and the one to which Groznyj returns most frequently and with the greatest resentment, is that the change in him has caused him to forsake his former piety and to turn against the faith—that he has become "the opposite", *soprotiv* (23). It is obvious that Ivan feels the central significance of this accusation, and attaches corresponding importance to refuting it. It is quite extraordinarily striking, however, that though in his message he takes up this accusation no less than eleven times, he disputes against the word *soprotiv* in its original context, that is, with regard to orthodoxy, at only one of these places (24). In five other places, the connexion is not clear, though at any rate with more connexion with political than with religious questions (25). And finally, in the last five cases, he uses the word in a way quite different from Kurbskij's, in that he connects the word with the concept of reason, *razum,* instead of with orthodoxy, *pravoslavije* (26). In these last cases, he justifies his refutation clearly and unambiguously by political necessity and the Czar's responsibility for the unity and security of the kingdom. It is not contrary to reason that the Czar will

---

22. *Ibid.* pp. 36, 38.
23. *Ibid.* p. 2.
24. *Ibid.* p. 24 supra.
25. *Ibid.* pp. 26, 28, 64 102, 116.
26. *Ibid.* p. 24 infra, 38, 44, 90, 100. It has been preferred to seek a meaning in the text as it stands, rather than to assume misreading or slips of the pen, like *Stählin* p. 32.

not serve his servants, that he will rule as the time requires, that he will defend himself against opponents, that when he came of age he decided to make his formal mastery real, instead of allowing himself to be guided by the will of others.

In so central a question, then, Groznyj not only puts the main emphasis on interests of state and political motives when he wants to prove his adherence to the true faith, he actually, in the heat of action, makes a shift in his concepts, so that he comes to argue from a purely temporal criterion, that his actions are in agreement with political reason. It is difficult to explain this shift merely by the fact that Kurbskij in his letter brings in the concept of reason in the next sentence. Here it is a matter of such vital principles that Groznyj would hardly have made a contamination of the concepts unless he had had some deeper motive for doing so.

Further support is to be found for the conjecture that for Groznyj, the political motives dominated over the religious ones, by examining that part of his argument that may be called a *personal justification*. By this is meant his argumentation for his political views by means of examples from his personal experiences as ruler of the Muscovites—and they were abundant, since he succeeded to, or was put on, the throne at three years old, twenty-one years before he wrote his message to Kurbskij. This personal justification is a long, connected argument in the form of a sort of autobiography, and occupies a good fifth of the total text of the message (27). Here Ivan paints a sombre picture of political conditions after the death of Vasilij, that grew even worse after the death of his mother. The tendencies towards centralized government were energetically countered by the powerful boyar houses, which did not shrink even from attempting to promote their own interests by making agreements with the rulers of neighbouring countries. As to home politics, this was completely dominated by the struggle for power among the boyars, and their egoistic urge to enrich themselves. The regency during Ivan's minority assumes the character of a struggle, often bloody, with the supporters of the royal house. On several occasions, he saw these violent, and tumultuous events at close quarters, as when he was present at an attempt to murder one of his faithful boyars in the very dining chamber. In other ways, too, he could observe the hostility of the magnates and the regents, for both he and his brother were normally reduced to living as though they were foreigners or paltry serving boys. Irregular meals and inadequate clothing were the order of the day, just as the indignant boy had to look on while one of his regents sprawled comfortably on his late father's bed, without showing the boy prince either the kindness due to a child or the respect due to the sovereign of the country.

From his fifteenth year, the boy now tries to take control, but is met by

---

27. *Fennell* pp. 68–100.

intensified intrigues by the boyars, who, for example, try to exploit the great fire at Moscow to raise the people against the Grand Ducal house. And when the young Czar has taken his first steps in an independent exercise of government with the help of two new men in the administration, Aleksej Adašev and the priest Sil'vestr, he only finds that his two assistants ally themselves more and more closely with his enemies, and even that the priest, instead of devoting himself to the Czar's spiritual education, starts intriguing politically. Ivan is constantly excluded more and more from deliberations and decisions on matters of state. Should he contradict even an inferior servant, he is scolded for his bad behaviour, but if he himself was abused by a councillor, without respect or kindness, the councillor, on the other hand, is reckoned a pattern of good behaviour. Ivan's honourable supporters and followers are persecuted and martyred, but his enemies and opponents come to riches and honour. When he speaks, Adašev and Sil'vestr brush him aside with reproaches for his unreasonableness and his childishness—which he has in remembrance when he now reads Kurbskij's accusations (28).

The most incurable of the hurts in Groznyj's memories belong to his time of trial, when, in his twenty-third year, he lay on his death-bed, given up by all. His first and last thoughts were to secure the continuity of the Czardom, to prevent the work of reform he had started from coming to a stand-still, and to ensure the continuation of the consolidation of the kingdom externally, so well begun with the conquest of Kazan' some months previously. He demanded that the boyars should swear fealty to his infant son, and thus guarantee his succession while he himself still lived. Instead, they prepared to make his cousin, the insignificant Vladimir Starickij, Czar, so that they could have free scope in the future. This plan failed only because Groznyj, by the grace of God, survived the crisis. This, and many other plots, caused Groznyj to take measures against the boyars and the councillors. At the beginning of this purge, the Czar's wrath, *gnev,* was administered with mercy, *milost'*. Nobody was put to death, but the worst opponents were banished from the court and council, and others were ordered to hold no communication with them. Not until this order was disregarded, and every means used to intrigue again, did Groznyj turn to the sterner measures for which Kurbskij now attacks him.

This autobiographical account cannot, of course, on the face of it be considered to be more in accordance with the truth than his historical justification. That does not matter, however, in this connexion, where the object is to ascertain what are the Czar's views and arguments, not to verify his evidence. Yet it is natural to note here two confirmatory circumstances. First, there is a clear difference between the basis and premisses of the

---

28. *Ibid.* p. 140.

historical justification and the autobiographical one. The historical justification partakes largely of the character of a myth which serves to render intelligible the Czar's political doctrine. Groznyj writes Russian and world history from his present standpoint, and adjusts it to this, which was not out of keeping with the custom of the time. The history of his own life, however, was still too recent to mythologize it. Secondly, the principal motif of his autobiographical review, the fundamental conflict of interest between the boyars and the Czar, was real enough. It is unnecessary to resort to psychiatric or psycho-analytical explanations to find meaning in Groznyj's argumentation, however great a part his autobiographical statements may have played in posterity's judgement on his mental state and constitution.

With every conceivable exaggeration, aberration of memory, suppression and perversion of facts—some of these will be discussed later—the autobiography is something other and more than an illustration of Groznyj's general political justification. It is an account of an extremely concrete and direct experience of life, which could find adequate, theoretical expression only in Groznyj's political formulations. This does not, however, answer the question of whether Groznyj wanted to force the conditions to take form according to his ideas, or whether he wanted to do the opposite. But it is clear enough that he has not reconstructed the story of his life to make it fit his ideas. He has constructed his autobiography in polemical form, it is true. But the ideas were taken from experience, not the other way round.

In the previous pages, it has been argued that Groznyj's historical justification supports the political one, and that in the last resort, the political role plays a greater part for Groznyj than the religious one, at any rate, where the two clash. This last point seems to gain further confirmation from the study of Groznyj's personal justification, which to such a great extent centres in his experiences with his political opponents. His very sharp emphasis on the priest Sil'vestr's alleged misuse of his spiritual authority to meddle with temporal matters, and his disillusioned view of the ideal of piety of those around him as a cynical excuse for keeping him in tutelage—all this also points towards a tendency—conscious or unconscious—to *secularization* in Groznyj, simultaneously with his adherence to the axiom of Orthodoxy. This compound of religious dogmatism and political realism, of axiom and empiricism, must now be brought into the centre of observation, in the attempt to analyse the method in Groznyj's argumentation.

There may appear to be little justification for speaking of tendencies to secularization in Ivan Groznyj, when it is considered that he quotes from the Old and the New Testaments, the Church Fathers, and other Orthodox authorities to such an enormous extent that the quotations occupy about a quarter of the text. How quotations are used, however, is not without importance, a point of which Kurbskij also found occasion to make an acid comment (29).

In many places, it is striking to note with what casualness, almost even laxity, the Czar turns to account these ultimative sentences. We have already seen him appeal to St. Paul, where St. Paul's words fit a ruler's hand like a glove, but reject like a challenge and without hesitation, Jesus' injunction to exercise patience. And he himself declares that he shall not be called to account till Doomsday, but in response to Kurbskij's declaration that he will appeal to the Supreme Judge against Groznyj, he replies that that is to blaspheme against the very words of the Saviour, who said, "Let not the sun go down upon your wrath" (30). That the words are those of St. Paul is, of course, of less importance than the polemical aptness of the quotation in the debate. Kurbskij was not slow to make use of this weakness. When Groznyj wished to show that his defection was not only a betrayal of his fatherland but also a disregard of the words of Jesus—"If a kingdom be divided against itself, that kingdom cannot stand"—Kurbskij promptly replied with the just as authoritative "When they persecute you in one city, flee ye into another" (31).

It is a trite observation, that Kurbskij's obvious repugnance to this duel with quotations is due to his humanistic education, very different from Groznyj's traditional Byzantinism. From the point of view of style, Kurbskij shoots with whetted arrows, while Groznyj hurls granite boulders. To Kurbskij, a quotation is a means of expressing much in a few words, as he says in his criticism of Groznyj's style. Groznyj, on the other hand, quite obviously quoted in order to express one and the same thought through as many impressive authorities as possible. He underlines their weight with such phrases as "as Gregory who is called the Theologian said, writing with solemn words", or "as the divine Gregory (Nazianzen) said to those that have confidence in their youth, and who at all times presume to be teachers", or "this was said by the divine (Dionysios the Areopagite) in his epistle", or the like (32). Groznyj's aim is not to spit his opponent on a well directed point, but to crush him under the massive weight of his authorities. It did not worry him, therefore, that the quotations sometimes grew so long that the starting-point is forgotten before the end is reached. Groznyj's cultural orientation and ideal were rooted in the Russian literature of translation, and through this to the Byzantine classics. The quotations undoubtedly show that in this field he was well read. And yet it does not seem possible to explain the use of the quotations simply by reference to the type

29. *Ibid.* p. 180.
30. *Ibid.* p. 132. Cf. *Ephes.* IV, 26.
31. *Ibid.* pp. 82–84 cf. *Mark* III, 24; p. 206 cf. *Matth.* X, 23.
32. *Ibid.* pp. 106, 110, 126, 174, 142.

of education the Czar had received, so different from Kurbskij's. Many of the quotations look as if they had been stuck on afterwards, caught by an association of ideas, under the need to find polemical ammunition.

In one single case, the first quotation from the letter to the monk Demophilos, traditionally ascribed to Dionysios the Areopagite (33), it is perhaps possible actually to get an insight into Groznyj's technique in preparing his propaganda piece. The word for word quotation—about the vision of the Blessed Carpos—is followed by some concluding remarks to Kurbskij, after which several manuscripts have a colloquial paraphrase of the same account, but now ascribed to Bishop Polycarp instead of to Carpos, and this again is followed by approximately the same concluding remarks to Kurbskij. Earlier conjectures of two different but extremely homogeneous accounts must be rejected, as does *J. S. Lur'je*. Instead, we must assume a tautological error in editing, committed perhaps by Groznyj or his assistants while actually drafting the text (34). It is very natural to take this idea a stage further, and to assume that the second version is one, dictated from memory, of the quotation Groznyj wanted his chancellery to produce for him, but which, either by a lapse of memory or by a misunderstanding, was not removed from the fair copy. Obviously, no-one minded this visionary tautology. The more, the better.

The second, very long extract from the epistle to Demophilos (35) seems to have been seized on with joy in Groznyj's spiritual reading as a welcome proof of the universal validity of his idea of the state.

The gist of what is said here is that Demophilos has no moral or ecclesiastical right to exceed his competence by denouncing a superior in the ecclesiastical hierarchy. One cannot, on behalf of Our Lord, assume the right to change the divinely transmitted order. Disorder and laxity are aberrations from the divine commands and edicts. And apart from the fact that one cannot permit oneself to judge without having authority to do so, God's perfect justice will not tolerate that one should allow one's anger to infringe upon His clemency.

It is obvious that this quotation attracted Groznyj because of its emphasis on the unshakableness of authority. The requirement of clemency is one-sidedly thrown over on Kurbskij, without Groznyj's realising that it could come back like a boomerang. He has simply not been interested enough in this idea to consider its possible relation to himself. From the observation of this to the conjecture of what it is that particularly struck Groznyj in reading this passage and fixed it in his memory it is only a step—it must be just

---

33. *Ibid.* pp. 142–148 cf. *Migne gr.* t III, col. 1097 f.
34. *Fennell* p. 148, note, *Posl. Grozn.* pp. 608, 543. This hypothesis seems simpler than that proposed by *I. Dujčev*, see *TODRL* t. XV, 1958, pp. 172–176.
35. *Fennell* pp. 158–172 cf. *Migne gr.* t. III, col. 1088 ff.

the comparison with worldly conditions: "And if someone were to take upon himself the government of a people without being commanded to do so by a king, justly would he be tormented. And what if anyone present of those who are subjected to a prince should dare to criticize that prince when he was acquitting or condemning anyone, to say nothing of vituperating him and driving him from power?" (36). What is meant, in the epistle, to serve merely as an illustration of the spiritual order, to Groznyj is the main point, which is to be to confirmed by this spiritual authority—which thus furnishes one more argument for his *groznoje povelenije,* his "terrible fiat" (37).

This twisting of the real meaning of the quotations is revealed with absolutely sublime irony by the little quotation from St. John Chrysostom (38), where men are enjoined to refrain from strife: with men, one wins or loses on earth, with God one is in every case defeated. The quotation is aimed at Kurbskij, and is meant to prove to him that it is vain to resist Groznyj's spiritually and temporally rooted power, which, like the house Jesus spoke of, is founded upon a rock. Here the axiomatic compound of power and piety appears in its purest and clearest form, but expressed by the words of the very man whose efforts were concentrated on getting the theory of the state in the Epistle to the Romans accepted as meaning that though temporal authority as an institution (*to pragma*) was undoubtedly of God, the individual representatives of that authority (*hoi kath' ekaston arkhontes*) were not necessarily so (39)—and who cited Jesus' house that was founded upon a rock in defiance of the omnipotence of the Byzantine Emperor. Even if Groznyj had been able to realise this, he would certainly have been quite indifferent. Here, the object is not logical or dogmatic proof, not a linking of his own thoughts with those of others, but exclusively the exploitation of the thoughts of others for his own purposes.

This—to use a word that Groznyj can hardly have known, but which was beginning to be really topical in the Western Roman Catholic world—was *propaganda.* Propaganda not for the Faith, but for the supremacy of the Czar (40). That Groznyj devoted so much of his polemical tract to religious evidences, was primarily due to the fact that Orthodoxy was the only common and accepted ground for Ivan, Kurbskij and the Russian people. It was the medium, so to speak, in which an argument could be carried on. This is not meant to imply that Ivan, purely privately, was indifferent to the Faith, and was simply using it as a political weapon. That he meant to do so seems to be fully shown by his argumentation, but at the present

36. *Fennell* p. 162.
37. *Posl. Grozn.* p. 144.
38. *Fennell* p. 34, cf. *Migne gr.* t. LI, col. 429.
39. In epist. ad Rom. homilia XXIII, *Migne gr.* t. LX, col. 615.
40. Cf. *D. S. Lixačev* in *Posl. Grozn.* pp. 456, 467.

stage it is impossible to pronounce on his private faith—beyond the observation that he distinguished sharply between individual piety and the conditions of communal life, or, as it would now be put, between religion and politics. He was debarred, however, from carrying this point to its logical conclusion, and was compelled, instead, to carry on his political struggle with religious arguments, however difficult he might find it, consciously or unconsciously.

It can hardly be doubted that this dogmatic or axiomatic basis for Ivan's argumentation has had considerable influence on his thinking in concrete, political matters. He uses the description of Hellenistic heathendom from Gregory Nazianzen—according to which men made themselves gods in the images of their passions, so that sin was held to be not merely innocent but divine, since responsibility was attributed to the gods they worshipped—to show that Kurbskij praises the Czar's enemies in agreement with his own treason (41). Whether or not Groznyj was right in this judgement of Kurbskij, this is one of the rare cases in which a quotation is used efficiently, that is to say, as a parallel that explains and characterizes, and even with a certain pungency in the point. Kurbskij would have been justified, of course, in replying that the Czar himself acknowledged the Trinity as an image of his own absolute power. What is more important, however, is that the quotation probably seems so effective because it is a direct and genuine expression of a phenomenon in Groznyj's argumentation that lies at the centre of his method.

It must be seen as the result of Groznyj's axiomatic way of thinking, that his political polemics take to such a degree the form of *collective identification*. By this is meant that he condemns a person—particularly Kurbskij, of course—by identifying him, by means of a special type of argumentation, with a group that is *a priori* condemned.

In the case just mentioned, Groznyj could have confined himself to using the vituperative word "traitor" to Kurbskij, which would not have seemed unnatural after Kurbskij had gone over to a hostile country. It would rather have seemed so obvious that it would have fallen rather flat. His Majesty would thereby have betrayed that he was offended or upset by the defection of a single man, which would have been incompatible with the contempt a ruler must feel for an individual of such a calibre. When Groznyj uses words of abuse in a quite primitive way, it serves to emphasise his boundless and subjective contempt for the individual as such—as, for example, when in the middle of a formal explanation he spits out a "cur" or "wretch" at Kurbskij, or congratulates himself that he no longer sees his "Ethiopian face" (42). Kurbskij's individual act, his defection to King Zyg-

---

41. *Fennell* pp. 106–108 cf. *Migne gr.* t. XXXVI, col. 337 f.
42. *Fennell* pp. 30, 70, 84, 130, 142, cf. *Lur'je* p. 510.

munt, is not worth calling treason, it only shows that Kurbskij thereby "completed his devilish, currish betrayal" and that "in his devilish, currish desire" he has gone to a master who will let him live on in his arbitrary obstinacy, "self-will", *samovolstvo* (43). Therewith, Kurbskij is characterized as an individual.

When, on the other hand, it is a matter of primary importance, the invective is qualified, so to speak, by being raised to the plane of general principle, as with the quotation from Gregory. There crime and treason became a cosmic principle—like the Devil as against God—and thus the evil complement to the justice and order of the autocracy. And when the moral scope and consequences of the act are designated simply "treason", without adjectives, then it is a question of a collective phenomenon, a conspiracy of menacing extent, a wide-spread net of intrigue, the object of which is to persecute the Czar and all who support him, both clerical and lay—a conspiracy that can be traced back in history and in all the troubles and frustrations that Groznyj has ever experienced (44). Not until he has been "placed" in this conspiracy is Kurbskij properly characterized.

It is difficult to say to what extent Kurbskij, from an objective point of view, had qualified himself for this collective identification. The previous history of his defection is unknown, except from hints by the parties to the case, and we do not know, therefore, whether he evaded by his flight Groznyj's anger and punishment for some act of political opposition (45). All that can be said is that he lays himself open to Groznyj's condemnation by his general expression of sympathy with the Czar's victims and by including himself in their number. It is quite obvious, however, that this did not imply any declaration of political relations with or collaboration with these people. By virtue of his high birth, his membership of the Select Council (*izbrannaja rada*), and his position as an army leader, Kurbskij must of necessity have known and been more or less familiar with the Czar's victims, but his horror at their fate seems to have been primarily a humane, not a political, reaction. He is more interested in the fates of the individuals than in the collapse of the boyars' policy.

Groznyj seems to have felt this, and occasionally argues on this basis, especially by pointing out to Kurbskij that his peers at home in Russia, in spite of their manifestations against the Czar, are still living in complete freedom (*svoboda*) and increasing wealth. Here Ivan argues on the individual plane: when Kurbskij now prefers to go his own way rather than submit to the supremacy of the Czar, and his equals, however, continue to enjoy

---

43. *Ibid.* p. 154, cf. 102, 104, 192 (*samovolstvo*).
44. *Ibid.* pp. 128, 62–64, 68, 70, 78.
45. For Kurbskij's political attitude, see Chapter IV.

their freedom in their own country—why, then, does he not stop making a nuisance of himself? (46). Here, however, Kurbskij found no difficulty in replying. When Groznyj wrote again, thirteen years later, he was clearly suffering from pangs of conscience, and no longer mentions freedom (47). As early as 1567, he answered Zygmunt II August, who had accused him of violating the free nature of man, with a half-admission, that servitude prevailed everywhere, also in the realm of the Polish King himself (48). Kurbskij, on the other hand, spoke with renewed force of the victims of Groznyj's lawlessness (*bezzakonije*), of executions without law or justice (*bez suda i bez prava*), and said that Ivan had "shut up the kingdom of Russia, in other words, free human nature (*svobodnoje jestestvo čeloveče-skoje*) as in a fortress of hell", and that he killed everyone that tried to escape (49). This is to argue on behalf of the individual against the terror, against insecurity and lawlessness in the Czardom, but not for any political alternative to the autocracy.

If Kurbskij to a high degree polemizes on behalf of the individual and in defence of the rights of the individual, Groznyj speaks almost everywhere on behalf of the state, and sees his opponents as the state's opponents. It is typical that Groznyj goes far towards obvious insincerity when, as in the case just cited, he speaks of the position of the individual in the state. There are other cases where he directly contradicts himself in this connexion, as when he declares at one moment that he has not persecuted and exter-minated whole families, but in the next actually praise himself for not hav-ing made Sil'vestr's son pay for the sins of his father (50). Groznyj was not interested in the fate of the individual—as is shown even in his letter to his faithful servant, Vasilij Gr'asnoj, whom he would not ransom from the Tartars (51). He is uncertain in a discussion of this question, but all the more certain in his collective identification of the enemies of the state, of the traitors' interwoven and continuing net. What does interest him is to show the place of the individual mesh in the net.

This identification Ivan usually demonstrates by means of a type of argu-ment that might be called *implicative characterization*. By this is meant that, on the basis of a specific resemblance between a phenomenon and a particular category, he identifies the phenomenon with the general charac-

---

46. *Fennell* p. 102.
47. *Ibid.* p. 188.
48. *Posl. Grozn.* pp. 143 f.
49. *Fennell* pp. 228–30, 234, 214.
50. *Ibid.* p. 120, cf. p. 98. In the lists of those executed, including men, women and children, Groznyj has left confirmation, for that matter, of Kurbskij's accusations. Cf. below, p. 61.
51. *P. A. Sadikov: Očerki po istorii opričniny* (Moscow 1950) p. 531.

teristics of that category. It is consequently not a question of partial identification, as in applying the Aristotelean principle of subsumption.

Thus we already have an implication when Ivan counts Kurbskij among the traitors because he protests against Ivan's treatment of them, just as they themselves, of course, do (52). This example is not quite perfect, however, since in this connexion Ivan must have had in mind Kurbskij's defection to the King of Poland, even though he does not mention it. In many other cases, however, implication plays a predominant part, and especially where the conclusion follows from theological premisses.

The most peculiar case is the argument with which Ivan introduces his declaration that he must answer both for his own and his subjects' actions at the Day of Judgement (53). Here, he begins with an extremely ingenious double implication. Kurbskij's rhetorical question of whether the Czar believes himself to be immortal (54)—which clearly means that Groznyj would hardly act as he has done if he expected to be answerable in the other world —Ivan takes as his starting-point for the accusation that Kurbskij is postulating that Ivan does not acknowledge that he has a soul which must answer, after death, for the acts done in life on earth, and that therefore Ivan is guilty of a heresy like that of the Saducees, who, of course, denied that the soul survived death. In other words, Ivan implies that Kurbskij implies heresy is Ivan. After which Ivan goes on to the second implication, in that he answers Kurbskij's postulated accusation of heresy by the assertion that Kurbskij himself is a heretic. The Manichees maintain that Christ reigns in Heaven, man on earth, and the Devil in Hell. Kurbskij talks of the coming judgement in Heaven, but condemns God's punishment on earth—i. e. the punishment administered through the Czar by the grace of God—therefore he is a heretic, as well as a maker of false accusations of heresy.

In a similar manner, Kurbskij also becomes a disciple of the Cathars, because like Novatian he does not accept repentance, but requires that men shall rise above their human nature, which is implied in his reference to Judgement Day (55). In a single instance, Ivan kills two birds with one stone: what Kurbskij reproaches him for, says Ivan, is that he will not give himself up to destruction at the hands of his adversaries; but Kurbskij himself has broken his oath of allegiance because he feared death at Ivan's hands— this is at once Novatianism and Pharisaism, the first because Kurbskij demands that men shall be super-human, and the second because he does not himself act as he would have others act (56). Here, too, it is at bottom a

---

52. *Fennell* pp. 62, 68 supra, 150.
53. *Ibid.* pp. 122–124.
54. *Ibid.* p. 4.
55. *Ibid.* pp. 22–24.
56. *Ibid.* p. 28.

question of a double implication, since the actual demonstration of Novatianism and Pharisaism is done by implication, and the basis for the demonstration is likewise implied: Kurbskij's defence of the boyars who have become
Ivan's victims is taken as an accusation against Ivan for refusing to become
the boyars' victim.

Since Groznyj has adopted the Pauline theory of the state, it follows as
normal logical sequence of thought for him to declare that Kurbskij opposes
God in opposing the Czar, since the Czar's authority is of God. It is also
consistent, logical thinking when Ivan claims that Kurbskij's heresy is so
much the worse in view of the fact that Ivan succeeded to the throne without strife or bloodshed, and by inheritance, and consequently without any
circumstance whatever that could cast a shadow of doubt on the Czar's
authority (57). For Ivan, however, this is not enough. At the very beginning
of his message, he hints at an implication that is to show Kurbskij in even
darker colours—he, the former boyar, councillor and general for the autocracy and Orthodoxy, has now broken his oath of fealty, and has thereby
become a direct destroyer of Christendom by going over to the service of
the enemies of Christendom (58). This idea is extended a moment later.
When Kurbskij now goes to the wars with the enemies of the Czardom, he
will come to destroy churches, trample upon icons, murder Christians; the
soft limbs of Russian youths will be crushed and maimed by the hoofs of
the horses as the armies advance. And even though Kurbskij may perhaps
refrain from active participation in such things, he will still contrive this evil
work with the deadly poison of his thoughts (59). This is a line of thought
that has a much longer perspective than Kurbskij's particular case. Here it
is a matter of an implication that, when used by a ruler, is the most
portentous of all, that a person's thoughts can make him the accessory to
the acts of others and a sharer in the responsibility for them.

But the implication goes even further. The person's thoughts, in spite of
everything, belong to his characteristics as an individual, just like his actions,
and since they are under his control he is responsible for them, if not in a
legal, yet in an intellectual and moral sense. This might be the unexpressed
premiss for the implication just mentioned, even though it is scarcely probable. It is more difficult, on the other hand, to find such an immediately
explicable premiss for the implication by which Kurbskij is identified collectively with his forefathers, and consequently with the legal obligations
and crimes of his family. Here, the argument runs in two lines. On the one
hand, by breaking his oath of fealty and joining the enemies of Christendom, Kurbskij destroyed not only his own soul but those of his forefathers,

57. *Ibid.* p. 18.
58. *Ibid.* p. 14.
59. *Ibid.* p. 16.

since his forefathers had sworn, for themselves and their successors, fealty to Ivan's grandfather, Ivan Velikij and his successors. On the other hand, Kurbskij is described as a traitor because he comes of a race of traitors, as a spreader of poison because he is born of a generation of vipers. His grandfather intrigued against Ivan Velikij, his father against Groznyj's father, Grand Duke Vasilij, and the same tradition appears on the mother's side. From this point of view, Kurbskij has committed treason in the hope of regaining the ancestral land of the princely house of Kurbskij, Jaroslavl', which had been incorporated into the Grand Duchy of Moscow a hundred years before (60).

It is consequently a double taint that Kurbskij bears in consequence of his descent. By the breach of his oath, he has annulled the merits of his ancestors. And through his ancestors' crimes his own becomes the greater. It is conceivable, perhaps, that this reasoning reflects an ancient view of the solidarity of the family, transmitted in a vague and blurred form that approaches the popular belief of the kind that the apple does not fall far from the tree. The argument is more precise than it would have been had it been based merely on such a belief. This is shown not least by the reference to Jaroslavl'. But it shows, at the same time, a more primitive view of justice than Kurbskij's, who emphasises justice and judgement and free human nature as fundamental concepts. What probably decided Groznyj to use this argument, however, was that he found here yet another opportunity of classifying Kurbskij as an enemy of the Czardom. Both in thought and in act he shows himself to be a participant in the great treason plot, and by birth he is a member of the group that plots it, the boyars.

All these cases of implication have this in common, that they are deduced from religious premisses—the political oath of allegiance is, of course, a religious act, as was evidenced by the kiss on the cross (*krestnoje celovanije*)—and they lead to a judgement that is of a markedly political character. This seems to confirm yet again that Groznyj's primary interest lay in ensuring the vindication of his political principles with every means at his disposal, and apparently it is also the clearest revelation of the line along which Groznyj's thinking assumes its axiomatic character. The religious axiom is secularized, but retains its character as an axiom whence proofs can be deduced.

In the previous pages, an account has been given of Groznyj's conception of the autocracy by the grace of God, as an indivisible, religious-political whole, and of the just as indivisible, heretical-treasonable whole directed against the autocracy. Quite obviously, these ideas imply a highly axiomatic

---

60. *Ibid.* pp. 22, 62–64, cf. 14.

but loosely defined political programme, the concrete conditions and execution of which are not perceived or foreseen in detail. The question of whether Ivan Groznyj had a political programme is thereby answered with a simultaneous yes and no: yes, in the sense that there are clearly political intentions that are justified politically; no, in the sense of a later period's conception of a political programme as a fundamental charter issued by those exercising power, and conditioned by political empiricism. When, in what follows, the objectives, the justification of and the argumentation for this programme are confronted with the actual political realisation of Ivan's ideals, this will be done in the light of this ambivalence.

III

Guardian of Orthodoxy

In the previous pages, Groznyj's ideas and argumentation have been described formally, and considered *sui generis*. In general, the relations of his programme to a wider context have been ignored—partly to Groznyj's cultural data, his orientation with regard to the past and the present, and partly to his own personality and inner convictions. In other words, the question of the originality and sincerity of Groznyj's polemics has been disregarded, even though certain questions were formulated in this connexion, and left unanswered. The object now is to take up these questions on the basis of the description already given, and in the first place to discuss the religious basis of Groznyj's rule.

A first glance at Groznyj's programme at once shows a circumstance that is very conspicuous, the Czar's extreme dependence on Byzantine tradition (1). To him, Constantine the Great is the first Czar in piety. His historical world-picture is completely dominated by the history of the Eastern Empire as the background of Russian history. His reading was confined to Byzantine literature in Russian translation (2). His view of his responsibility to God as Czar for his subjects and for the Orthodox Church at once recalls "Caesaro-papism" as the time-honoured conception of the position of the Byzantine imperial government. There seems to be a beaten track from Byzantium to Moscow, unalterably running in the opposite direction from the westward road from Rome. We have seen that Groznyj appealed to St. John Chrysostom without thinking of his attempt to limit the Pauline theory of the state. And we must remember, on the other hand, that along the westward road runs a sharply drawn line from this very point, the distinction of St. John Chrysostom between the person and the institution, through Abélard's continuation of the idea in twelfth-century Paris and on to the sixteenth century's ideological clarifications in the West (3). Compared with this, the formation of ideas in Russia in the same period is still at a primitive, confused stage, as were Groznyj's also.

---

1. *I. Dujčev: Vizantija i vizantijskaja literatura v poslanijax Ivana Groznogo = TODRL* t. XV (1958) pp. 160–172.

2. *S. Belokurov: O biblioteke moskovskix gosudarej v XVI stoletii* (Moscow 1899) pp. 317ff.

3. *C. H. McIlwain: The Growth of Political Thought in the West* (New York 1932) pp. 152f., *J. W. Allen op. cit.* pp 312 ff.

On the other hand, however, it should not be forgotten that in Byzantium also there had been approaches to a more precise definition of religious authority and secular powers. With his Byzantine inheritance, Groznyj could well have taken over the distinction between person and institution from St. John Chrysostom, or the much later idea—probably originating from the Patriarch, Photios—of the co-ordinate responsibility of Emperor and Patriarch for the welfare of the subject, one for his physical and the other for his spiritual welfare, in *"Epanagogē"* (4). He could have adopted these ideas as his own, or he could have taken them as principles he was bound to argue against. "Caesaro-papism" was not something given in the sense that it was a ruling principle inherited from Byzantium by the young Moscow state. On the contrary, there was much uncertainty and hesitation, a tendency to provisional arrangements and changing generalizations, which inspired *Wilhelm Ensslin* to make the observation that a palace revolution to dethrone the Emperor was declared to be the result of the will of God if it succeeded, but a blasphemous usurpation if it failed—and to ask if there really was any justification for talk of "Caesaro-papism" while the Patriarch could excommunicate the Emperor (5). In the first Czar's Byzantine inheritance, he did not find any clear and definitive theory of the state (6).

Nor did he get it from the great transmitter of tradition, the Russian Church. It is striking, how ambiguous this transmission was, where it was a question of the relation between the spiritual and the temporal, church and state, Czar and God. There was nothing pre-determined about the result of the great controversy between Nil Sorskij and Iosif Volockij at the end of the fifteenth century, and thus nothing about what was to be the sign of true piety in the Orthodox Russian Czardom in the future. The world-rejecting hermits, "The Non-possessing" (*nest'ažateli*), whose ideal of piety originated in the Hesychasts' mystical-ecstatic confession, could hardly have opposed a political alternative to "The Possessing" (*st'ažateli*), whose victory was due, among other reasons, to their experience in the affairs of this world and their ability to polemize and manoeuvre in ever closer collaboration with the state. But neither did the victorious group have a consistent view of the position of the Czar. Such a view took form in step with the political developments. Even the leader of the group, Iosif Volockij, changed his attitude within a few years (7). It is true that what was called Iosifism became Groznyj's main source of inspiration, and looks, to posterity, like

---

4. *G. Ostrogorsky: Geschichte des byzantinischen Staates* (Handb. d. klass. Altertumswiss., Munich 1952) pp. 194f., *G. V. Vernadsky:* Vizantijskija učenija o vlasti car'a i patriarxa = *Receuil d'études dédiées à la mémoire de N. P. Kondakov* (Prague 1926) pp. 143 ff.

5. *N. H. Baynes* and *H. Moss: Byzantium* (Oxford 1948) pp. 271, 276.

6. *V. Valdenberg: Drevnerusskija učenija o predelax carskoj vlasti* (Pgr. 1916) pp. 48–58.

7. *Budovnic* pp. 92 f., 97 f., *Lur'je* p. 260.

the direct transmitter of his theory of the state also. The matter is not so simple, however.

The main reason for this is an important circumstance which contributes to its complication. The heretical movements, which, originating in Novgorod and Pskov, were threatening the Orthodox faith in Russia, were offshoots of the reform movement in Western Europe, and made new demands on the defenders of Orthodoxy. The Aristotelean tradition, which played so important a role for the western way, unlike the eastern, appeared here in the form of the heretics' interest in scientific knowledge and logical argument (8). *J. S. Lur'je* has shown how this current, a sort of reform movement, compelled Iosif and the Iosifists to take up—as a kind of Counter-Reformation movement—a new polemical form, in such a way that argumentation and counter-argumentation were forced into logical—one might add, at any rate quasi-logical—lines, instead of the simple method of proof by quotation from the Bible and the Fathers. This influence continued to work indirectly, long after the fires of the Inquisition had ended, in 1504, the heretical movements themselves, and a literary regimentation prevailed thereafter (9). The effect on Groznyj is also noticeable.

It is reported that Groznyj possessed and studied Iosif Volockij's anti-heretical pamphlet called *"Prosvetitel'"* (10). Directly, from this study, and indirectly from the then fashionable influence that marked both the Iosifists and their opponents in Groznyj's time, he has adopted characteristic traits of the new polemical form: the tendency to take up a particular argument and argue against it, while still continuing the traditional use of quotations; the use of invective and disparaging comparisons; regard for the effect of the argumentation on the public (11). Moreover, the form of argumentation that in previous pages was termed "implicative characterization" was a phenomenon that also appeared in the religious polemics between the Iosi-

---

8. *H. O. Taylor: Thought and Expression in the Sixteenth Century* (New York 1920) Vol. II, pp. 267 ff., 373 ff., *Budovnic* pp. 57, 64 f., *M. P. Aleksejev: Javlenija gumanizma v litera-ture i publicistike drevnej Rusi* (IV meždunar. s'jezd slavist., Moscow 1958) pp. 25 ff. cf. *Sbornik otvetov na voprosy po literaturovedeniju* (IV meždunar. s'jezd. slavist. Moscow 1958) pp. 55–59.

9. *Lur'je* pp. 74, 264 f., 283, 497, 501, *J. S. Lur'je: O sud'bax perevodnoj belletristike v Rossii i u zapadnyx slav'an v XV–XVI vv.* = Slav'anskije literatury, V meždunar. s'jezd slavistov (Moscow 1963) pp. 84 ff. For that matter, Bishop Gennadij of Novgorod pointed out a Western European example of a useful method of ensuring spiritual discipline, "how the Spanish King purged his kingdom", see *Akty AE* p. 482 A. Ironically enough, the Russian Counter-Reformation also had its foreign models—but *V. Žmakin* (*ČOIDR* (1881/I p. 59) is undoubtedly right in declaring this reference to foreign practice to be quite fortuitous. The Russian Inquisition had its own independent origin and forms.

10. *ČOIDR* 1881/II, *Andrej Popov* p. 64.

11. *Lur'je* pp. 504–510.

fists and their opponents (12)—which, for that matter, is not surprising, since it is common in polemical propaganda at all times and places.

As a new trait in Ivan Groznyj, in which he differed from the Iosifists and their opponents, *J. S. Lur'je* emphasises his tendency to irony and ridicule. The example that is used to illustrate this has already been cited (13) —his answer to Kurbskij's formal declaration that the Czar would never see his face again: Ivan expresses his relief at never having to look on Kurbskij's Ethiopian face again. This argument, *Lur'je* maintains, is, of course, not serious, but a sarcasm, and Groznyj chose it because he realised that an argument of this kind has more effect on the public than a boring, serious refutation (14). To this observation of the Czar's conscious use of a propaganda effect, however, may be added yet another explanation, that touches Ivan's relation to his religion. It seems fairly obvious that Groznyj was anxious to break away from the Iosifist style on this point, just because, as previously stated (15), he is strongly inclined towards a secularized, political argumentation. Groznyj could make use of the dogmatic solemnity and weight of religious controversy when he needed it, but he did not, like a prince of the church, feel obliged to maintain his dignity under all circumstances.

Thus it is quite clear where Groznyj's formal and stylistic roots were. They were deep in the Byzantine tradition as that had been transmitted through Iosifism, a tradition, that is, not unaffected by foreign influences. And at the same time, he himself was on the way to giving that tradition a new, more worldly tone. The question then arises, whether in the development of Groznyj's ideas and line of thought any similar tendency can be observed. To elucidate this question, it is natural to return to what, in principle, is the central point in Ivan's political doctrine, where he claims a religious mandate, which involves that the Czar is answerable not to his subjects, but to God, both for himself and his subjects (16).

As is apparent from the account already given, Groznyj's claim to his mandate falls into two parts, each with its idea. In the first, he claims that at the Day of Judgement he must answer for his own acts and for the sins of his subjects, if these sins have been committed owing to the Czar's remissness. And in the second place, he claims, in answer to Kurbskij's accusation of the use of torture on the people of Christendom, that on the contrary, he himself is not only ready to shed his blood but to lay down his life for this people in defending them against their enemies.

---

12. *Posl. Grozn.* p. 605.
13. See above p. 34.
14. *Lur'je* pp. 510 f., cf. *TODRL* t. XV (1958) p. 506.
15. See above pp. 27 ff.
16. See above p. 23.

The first of these the Czar seems to have advanced to some extent by chance. It is not an idea he returns to again and again, like e. g. the idea of the security of the realm under autocracy, or that of the Czar's right to punish and reward his subjects at his pleasure. Here, Groznyj seems to use the idea as an effective polemical antithesis: he has been accused of not being willing to answer for his acts on Judgement Day, and now he replies that he is willing not only to do so, but also to answer for the acts of his subjects—though with an important proviso.

However casually the idea may have presented itself at this point in the controversy, it is by no means an improvisation or an attempt by the Czar to go one better, but an apt echo of Iosif Volockij's final formulation after 1504 of his theory of the royal power, as given in the sixteenth chapter of his *"Prosvetitel'"*. Also according to this—after Iosif had had his way, and the heretics had been destroyed—the Czar is responsible to God for the maintenance of Orthodoxy and the spiritual and temporal welfare of his subjects (17). It is worth remembering, however, that Iosif had already, at an earlier period, formulated a religious basis for the right to resist, in declaring, in the seventh chapter, that a Czar who became guilty of sinful passions, hate, envy, falseness, pride, hubris or blasphemy was the servant of the Devil and not of God, a tyrant—*mučitel'*—and not a Czar (18). On the basis of this chapter of Iosif's programme, Kurbskij is a far more consistent Iosifist than Ivan Groznyj when he accuses the Czar of using torture (*mučitel'nyje sosudy*) on the people of Christendom and thereby displaying himself as a tyrant. But he was unlucky enough to be a "Iosifist" in a sense that in 1564 had long been old-fashioned, while Ivan used Iosifism's more topical and up to date formulations in the controversy. It was enough for Groznyj simply to make a casual reference to that formulation of the Czar's responsibility that in the meantime had become a high church dogma.

Hildegard Schaeder has emphasised that it was a historic achievement when Ivan Groznyj, as ruler, thus adopted the church doctrine of a Christian ruler, governing on the basis of a universal Christian tradition and with regard for universal Christian interests, and thereby gave it full acknowledgement as the official course of the Russian Czar (19). It is extremely difficult to accept this judgement, both formally, because this historic achievement seems to have come about rather accidentally, and really, be-

---

17. *Prosvetitel'* p. 602.
18. *Ibid.* pp. 324 f. Cf. *Lur'je* pp. 240 f., 260. It is true that also in his sixteenth chapter, Iosif foresees that a Czar may be a *mučitel'* (*Prosvetitel'* p. 604), but here in a much weaker formulation, in a parallel with the possibility that a bishop may prove to be more of a wolf than a shepherd.
19. *H. Schaeder: Moskau das Dritte Rom* = Osteur. Studien d. Hamb. Univ., Heft 1 (Hamburg 1929) p. 46 (= 2. Aufl. Darmstadt 1957, p. 64.).

cause the acknowledgement seems rather to have been in the opposite direction.

There was no historical disingenuousness in Ivan's appeal to a tradition from the time of St. Vladimir, of a Christian basis for the rules of the monarch. During the centuries since that time, the princes' loyalty to the Christian faith had been so self-evident that it would rather have been a historic achievement if Ivan had declared himself free of the obligation to such a loyalty. And there is the further point, that the formulation of this responsibility to God is so wide that neither Iosif Volockij nor any later ecclesiastical instance in Groznyj's reign had even the vaguest basis for a determination of the Czar's obligations. Provided that the Czar refrained from declaring himself a heretic or a free-thinker, and moreover refrained from challenging the economic and institutional interests of the Church, he had in reality full freedom of action in respect of his subjects as far as the church was concerned (20). It is consequently less a question of the Czar's acknowledgement of a Christian obligation than of an ecclesiastical acknowledgement of the Czar's freedom of action. It was this acknowledgement that Groznyj appealed to in his polemics.

This naturally gained further emphasis from the proviso Groznyj was careful to insert. He takes upon himself the responsibility for his subjects' sins only where these are due to the Czar's remissness. What ominous consequences of a political character follow from this proviso is quite obvious. Not a word is said of the criterion to be applied in distinguishing between piety and the opposite, between offence and righteousness. Nor is there any mention of the courts that might decide cases of doubt. The decision is quite simply laid in the hand of the Czar, and thus, with a reference to the need to ensure the salvation of his soul, he can act at his own discretion and arbitrary pleasure. In reality, he may commit all the sins in the calendar on the excuse of discipline, since he will not commit a sin of omission.

With this as his starting-point, Groznyj can also, in the second part of his claim, reject the accusation that he uses a tyrant's *mučitel'nyje sosudy*. Here, too, he replies with what looks like a higher bid: not only does he not torture the people of Christendom, but he is himself ready to suffer, to sacrifice his blood and his life for this people at the hands of their enemies. The logic of this argument is clear enough. In accordance with the principle above, the Czar has authority to decide what acts make the doer of

---

20. Against this political fact, it is of little importance that there were approaches to the formulation of a doctrine of an ecclesiastical supremacy over the royal power (See *V. Val'-denberg: Drevnerusskija učenija o predelax carskoj vlasti*, Pgr. 1916, pp. 230 ff. and the list of instances in *Moisejeva* pp. 89–92)—these attempts never gained any practical significance. Cf. *F. Dvornik: The Slavs in European History and Civilization* (New Brunswick 1962) pp. 370 f. and below pp. 57 f.

them an enemy of the people of Christendom. The Czar cannot deny that he punishes or tortures such people, but he can maintain that in doing so he is only performing the duties of his office on people who have put themselves beyond the pale of Christendom. And since it is he himself that determines the criteria for this act, he can never come to do such things to those who have remained within the fold. This category, defined by himself, he is ready to suffer for and to defend to the death against all enemies. Consequently, Kurbskij's accusation must fall to the ground, or rather, fall back on himself.

This line of thought has been interpreted by *I. U. Budovnic* as a quite new idea in Russian publicistics, the idea of a ruler's responsibility for his people, that his aim is his people's welfare (21). Here also, so categorical an interpretation must be met with reserve. It is typical that nowhere else does Groznyj use the same expression, but consistently refers to the indispensability of the autocracy for the unity and security of the realm. He talks here of his responsibility for the people of Christendom, *xristianskoj rod,* simply because Kurbskij uses the expression in his argumentation, and Groznyj wants to refute him with his own words. But neither of them is speaking of the welfare of the people. To Kurbskij, apparently, *xristianskoj rod* means that part of humanity above all that a Christian ruler should refrain from pursuing with torture and terror, i. e. the Christian part. Elsewhere, Kurbskij speaks more generally of Groznyj's violation of the free nature of man, *svobodnoje jestestvo čelovečeskoje,* but here he reinforces his accusation by defining the victims of Ivan's persecution as the noblest shoot of the human race, i. e. *xristianskoj rod,* and with this category, apparently, he is not thinking specially of Russians (22). To Groznyj, on the other hand, the expression means something quite different, the only true believers, the Russian people, who are under his sway and remain true to their Orthodox ruler.

Ivan does not recognize as Christians the neighbouring peoples of Roman Catholic or Protestant observance. Everywhere, he terms them "the ungodly" (23), and enemies of Russia. Russia and Orthodoxy are to him one and the same thing. And he himself, as Orthodoxy's Czar, has the task of securing the true faith against its inner enemies, which is performed by disciplinary means, and against outer enemies, which is performed by appropriate warlike measures. The first is a police matter. But the second may involve the Czar's dying for his country, or at any rate, coming to shed his blood in the fight. Ivan does not speak of Christian individuals, but of Christendom, and he speaks as the head of the only truly Christian state.

---

21. *Budovnic* pp. 293 f.
22. Cf. above p. 36, below p. 50.
23. *Fennell* pp. 14, 16, 26 cf. 154.

There is certainly no new idea in this. It says no more than that the Czar is ready to undergo a personal risk to preserve his realm intact, and that he considers it his duty to do so.

Rather than interpret Groznyj's line of thought as a new idea, it should be taken as a reminiscence of the idea that meant so much to Iosifism, the theory of Moscow as the Third Rome. It was the Iosifists who first put forward the idea in its most consistent form, especially in Filofej's message to Vasilij III from 1512. Ivan's emphasis on Russia as the fatherland of Orthodoxy, and on his own obligation to protect the interests of this fatherland, is undoubtedly inspired by the main idea of the theory of the Third Rome. Byzantium had been the heir after Rome, and Moscow was now to take over the inheritance as the guardian of Orthodoxy.

As to the political consequences of this theory, it has already appeared how vague was the tradition the Byzantine Empire had left to build on. Moreover, the Russian view of the obligation to take up the inheritance after Byzantium is not at all clear either. How widespread and how various this idea is may be seen from the fact that it existed in Tver' in 1455, only two years after the fall of Constantinople (24). Here, of course, it was Tver' and its Prince who were enjoined to take up the inheritance by a clerical ideologist, and characteristically enough, the heir was now designated by the same epithets that had been reserved hitherto for Byzantium, such as "The Promised Land", by which Jerusalem and Israel were meant. But the Iosifist Filofej's formulation of the theory had also been anticipated in 1492 by the opponent of Iosifism, the Metropolitan Zosima (25), who thus in a way came to furnish ammunition for the destruction of those who shared his opinions, since the theory was later realised in a much more concrete and practical manner than he had foreseen.

Originally, this theory had more to do with the politics of the church than of the state. Rome fell because of heresy, Byzantium fell to the Moslems because of heresy—it was God's punishment for union with Rome. Only Moscow was now left as the Third Rome, and no fourth will ever be granted (26). *George Vernadsky* calls the theory—also in Filofej's formulation—an eschatological warning to the Grand Prince of Moscow to realise his responsibility for the defence of the faith, since he is the last monarch left to undertake this task before the end of the world. It was not an earthly

---

24. *W. Philipp:* Ein Anonymus der Tverer Publizistik im 15. Jahrhundert = *Festschrift...* *Čyževskyj: Veröff. d. Abt. f. slav. Spr. u. Lit. des Osteur.-Inst. a. d. Freien Univ. Berlin,* Bd. 6 (Berlin 1954) p. 237.

25. *RIB* t. VI (2. izd. 1908) col. 799, cf. *Budovnic* p. 61.

26. *V. Malinin: Starec Jeleazarova monastyr'a Filofej i jego poslanija* (Kijev 1901) appendix pp. 55 A, 56 B. German translation in *H. Schaeder: Moskau das Dritte Rom* (2. Aufl., Darmstadt 1957) pp. 206–209.

kingdom that was announced by Filofej of Pskov (27). Even if this interpretation does not seem to be quite in harmony with Filofej's worldly,
ringing words about the only, great, Orthodox Russian Czar in the whole
world, it is clear, at all events, that Filofej gave the Prince the religious
mandate only with strong emphasis on his religious duties (28).

When Kurbskij and Groznyj exchanged their first letters, the idea of a
Russian succession to the Byzantine inheritance had been current in Russia
for a hundred years. It is therefore not surprising that Kurbskij alludes to
the theory—though, of course, in its then Iosifist form it must have been
repellent to him, bound up as it was with the high church support of the
Czarist power. When Kurbskij reproaches Groznyj with the way he has
treated the country's magnates, he begins with the rhetorical question, why
has Ivan destroyed "the strong in Israel" (29). He seems to allude, by this,
to the special responsibility resting on the ruler of the Orthodox realm, a
responsibility that obliges him to deal justly with his magnates and helpers
if he is to perform his task of carrying on the inheritance of piety. Perhaps
it is not quite by accident that Kurbskij speaks here of Israel and not of
Rome. The latter would necessarily have had a strongly Iosifist ring, and
in general there was, perhaps,—as maintained by *R. Stupperich* (30),—a
tendency to speak of Rome in a political connexion and of Jerusalem in a
religious one.

This view of the formation of Kurbskij's ideas seems to be further confirmed by his use of the concept of "Holy Russia" (*Sv'atoruskije zemli,
Sv'atoruskaja imperija, Sv'atoruskoje carstvo*) (31). The peculiar point, that
the expression is otherwise not used by the sixteenth century publicists,
A. Solovjev has sought to explain by the influence of ballads and hymns on
Kurbskij (32). That Kurbskij is the only one so influenced might well be
explained by the fact that he was in exile, isolated from the others, and
perhaps emotionally predisposed to popular patriotic expressions. On the
other hand, it needs further explanation, why this expression—though common enough on the lips of the people—never found its way to the pens of
the official, Czarist publicists, for whom it might have been expected to be
a find. Thus *Michael Cherniavsky* does not solve the problem by suggesting
that, as far as Kurbskij is concerned, the epithet may have appeared by
interpolation at the beginning of the seventeenth century, the period of the

27. *G. Vernadsky: Russia at the Dawn of the Modern Age = A History of Russia* Vol. IV
   (New Haven 1959) p. 169.
28. *V. Malinin op. cit.* appendix pp. 50 A, 51 B cf. 51 A, 51 B, 52 B. Cf. below p. 164.
29. *Fennell* p. 2.
30. *Zeitschrift f. slavische Philologie*, Bd. XII (1935) p. 352.
31. *Kurbskij* col. 56, 102, 107, 111, 145 (ll. 18 and 34), 146, 147, *Fennell* p. 214 supra.
32. *Festschr... Čyževskyj = Veröff. d. Abt. f. Slav. spr. u. Lit. d. Osteur.-Inst. a. d. Fr. Univ.
   Berlin*, Bd. 6 (1954) p. 285.

earliest manuscripts (33). More fruitful, undoubtedly, is this scholar's conjecture that the publicists of the sixteenth century felt the epithet to be out
of harmony with the line they were pursuing, the elevation and glorification
of the ruler, and even that it had a point directed against the autocracy,
or at any rate, against the political side of the Czarist ideology. In support
of this idea, it is emphasised that every time Kurbskij uses the expression,
it has the character of an antithesis of the Czardom, and that Kurbskij has
hereby taken the first steps towards the construction of a myth with a
national content as a counterpoise to the Czarist myth (34). It may be added
that the content of the myth was already suggested by Kurbskij's use of
the expression "the strong in Israel" in his first letter to Ivan (35). On
this interpretation, the epithet appears as a nationally defined parallel to
the concept of *xristianskoj rod* previously mentioned, whereby Kurbskij,
also antithetically, emphasised the degree of Ivan's offences against Christian humanity.

If the theory of Russia's Orthodox inheritance thus appears in Kurbskij
in a form defined in purely religious terms in speaking both of Christian
humanity and of the Russian nation, it is understandable that in Kurbskij
there is no purely politically defined alternative to Groznyj's theory of the
state. When Kurbskij talks of *Sv'atoruskoje carstvo,* and even, with his
classically influenced diction, of *imperija Sv'atoruskaja,* he is not opposing,
with traditional boyar concepts, the uniting of Russia under Moscow, but,
on behalf of the whole of Russia, the mishandling of the country by an ungodly Czar. On the other hand, it is quite evident that for Groznyj the theory
has had its last and decisive twist into state—or, if you will, imperial—
policy. Without the idea of the Third Rome, Groznyj could hardly have
claimed the role of ruler and protector of the only Orthodox realm with
such strength and conviction. At the same time, however, it is quite obvious
that Groznyj's version, even compared with the Iosifist formulation of the
theory, is highly secularized. He is not in the least interested in an imminent
end of the world, nor in Kurbskij's humanistically stamped religiosity, but
all the more in building up a strong, united, unconquerable realm here on
earth, where Russian Orthodoxy—as officially defined—can survive. The
only duty he acknowledges is the duty of working for that object. And because of this duty, he claims the unlimited right to dispose of the life and
fate of his subjects.

The sharp, worldly consistency in Groznyj's thinking has been mentioned
in connexion with his distinction between a life in piety and communal

33. *M. Cherniavsky: Tsar and People. Studies in Russian Myths* (New Haven 1961) p. 110.
34. *Ibid.* pp. 108 ff., cf. *H. Schraeder op. cit.* p. 85 (2. Aufl. Darmstadt 1957, p. 118).
35. It should be noted that in this connexion he also declared himself to be an out-
    cast from "God's Country" (*ot zemli Božii*), *Fennell* p. 4.

life (36). This implies a dualism, completely carried out, which presupposes the Czar's playing a double role as God's deputy and as man among men—and that he himself decides when he shall play one role and when the other. On the one hand, his double role serves to excuse the offences he may be led to commit in his anger at the traitors' disloyalty—for, since not even the Czar, but only God, is without sin, the Czar may very well err. On the other hand, it serves as a proof of the subject's duty to show humility and obedience to God's deputy on earth: even the ruler, clad in purple, gold and jewels, is at the same time only a mortal and invested with human weakness (37). How much more so his subjects!

In all this, there are clearly reminiscences of the popular and often used formulation in the sixteenth chapter of Iosif Volockij's *"Prosvetitel'"*, according to which the Czar must bear all the troubles of his subjects, just as the sun must shine on all creatures: the Czar, by virtue of his power, is equal to God on high, though by nature only a man (38). This agreed very well with the Byzantine inheritance. The actual formulation—together with many others—was taken directly from the deacon Agapetos, who, in Justinian's time, wrote his "Mirror of Princes", which became extremely popular in the sixteenth century (39).

There is thus a clear line from Byzantine literature, through *iosifl'anstvo*, and on to Ivan Groznyj, even in the formulation of what appears to be his boldest and most original idea in his message to Kurbskij, the distinction between religion and politics. But it is equally clear, and not least in this case that in adopting these ideas Groznyj changes them in relation to their original aim. *Ihor Ševčenko* explains Ivan's emphasis on his human weakness by his immediate, polemical need of a refutation of Kurbskij's accusation of apostasy (40). Here, however, Groznyj is evidently inspired by something else besides the immediate context. He is thinking and speaking as a politician and tactician. He will exploit his religious mandate to the utmost, but he will not undertake to play the part of a saint when it does not suit him. The question then arises, to what extent Groznyj found in Iosifism support for and prompting to this secularizing attitude.

At first glance, it may seem superfluous to seek for contacts with church

---

36. *Fennell* pp. 56–58, cf. above pp. 24, 34.
37. *Ibid.* pp. 26, 110
38. *Prosvetitel'* p. 602: »car' ubo podoben jest' vsem čelovekom, vlastiju že podoben vyžnemu Bogu«. *Posl. Volock.* p. 184.
39. *Migne gr.* t. LXXXVI, col 1172, *K. Krumbacher: Geschichte der byzantinischen Literatur* (Handb. d. klass. Altertumswiss. IX/1, 2. Aufl., Munich 1897) pp. 456 f., *Ihor Ševčenko: A Neglected Byzantine Source of Muscovite Political Ideology = Harvard Slavic Studies* Vol. II (Cambridge, Mass. 1954) pp. 146, 157, *Lur'je* p. 478.
40. *I. Ševčenko: op. cit.* p. 165.

circles on this question, since *a priori* it would naturally be probable that an earthly ruler, by virtue of his daily work and immediate tasks, would be inclined to place the main emphasis on worldly, political interpretations and applications of the ideology forming the basis of his exercise of power. This, in fact, is what Groznyj himself says, when he maintains that the power of the church is one thing, but that it is another thing to rule as Czar. And yet it is obvious that in this distinction—in its extreme consequence a quite revolutionary break with traditional theocratic ideas—the Czar had support in the Iosifist organization of monastic life. When Groznyj talked of communal life or life in common, he used the word *obščežitije*, which is precisely the term used by Iosif and the Iosifists for *koinobion*, with its rigid, disciplinary structure, in contrast to the anchorites' concentration on individual piety in full personal freedom (41). It was just by adopting the policy of a highly organized structure of monastic life, based as it was on extensive monastic estates, that Iosifism approached a worldly, administrative attitude, which Groznyj—and any other head of a state—could with advantage turn to account in his own administrative measures and methods. Groznyj's statement about the two tasks was consequently not nearly so challenging as it might seem. Not only had he support in Iosifism, it was clearly impulses from Iosifism that had turned him to secularization.

Part of the strict and disciplined organization of the Iosifist *koinobion* was an extreme limitation of all personal, independent, intellectual activity. Even before this, it was typical of the Russian development of Orthodoxy that there was no great interest in the intellectual aspect of religious matters. Theological, dogmatic, not to mention philosophic exercises did not appeal to the pillars of Russian piety (42). Heretics, however, as already stated, were another matter. But the influence of both Nil Sorskij's Hesychastic anchorite movement and of Iosif Volockij's disciplinary, coenobite wing militated directly against all tendencies to intellectual clarification and refinement of concepts. Iosif Volockij considered personal opinions an evil (43).

41. *Fennell* p. 58 cf. e.g. *Posl. Volock.* pp. 308 f. (*koinovije/obščežitije*). *I. I. Sreznevskij: Materialy dl'a slovar'a drevnerusskago jazyka* t. II (Spbg. 1895) col. 579.

42. *N. Zernov: Moscow the Third Rome* (London 1942) pp. 18, 52 f., *G. P. Fedotov: The Russian Religious Mind* (Cambridge, Mass. 1946) pp. 377 ff., *I. Ševčenko* (*op. cit.* p. 178) says, significantly, that Agapetos "not only affected political thinking in Muscovy, but often proved almost a substitute for such thinking". Against this, *J. S. Lur'je* urges that political thinking can also show originality by acceptance of and choosing among inherited ideas (*Posl. Volock.* pp. 91 f.)—which, however, must assume a clear consciousness of the consequences of the choice, and on this point Iosifism never got beyond the awkward stage.

43. An extremely sharp formula, traditionally ascribed to an anonymous pupil of Iosif: "*vsem strastem mati mnenije, mnenije vtoroje padenije*", see *ČOIDR* 1881/I = *V. Žmakin: Mitropolit Daniil i jego sočinenija*, p. 23. The result is the same, whether *mnneije* be taken as "opinion" or as "doubt"—in any event, it is the personal divergence that is the mother of the passions and the second Fall.

That he meant this seriously, appeared from the energetic campaign waged by him and those who shared his views to exterminate the heretics and *nest'ažateli* by means of the physical force of the temporal power. They were more dangerous than thieves and murderers, and should consequently be condemned to death like them, whether they repented or not (44).

The lack of intellectual conflict and clarification of ideas caused by the victory of Iosifism gave the movement a particularly sharp twist. It became disciplinarily, not to say, terroristically activated, whereas in Nil Sorskij's tradition it had had a merely passive character, with greater interest in mystical than in dogmatic piety. From the *nest'ažateli* the Czar could derive no impulse to set up a politically based discipline in the life of society or an ideologically based discipline in cultural life. But from Iosifism Groznyj got both impulses gathered into one strong tradition. And this he exploited to the full. Kurbskij has described this prompting in pointed, anecdotal form. He reports in his *"Istorija o Velikom Kn'aze Moskovskom"* that Groznyj, after his illness and the succession crisis of 1553, undertook a pilgrimage to a number of monasteries, with Kurbskij himself as one of his train. Old Maksim Grek, Kurbskij's teacher and ideal, the sworn enemy of Iosifism, strongly advised the young Czar against his plan of visiting the Iosifist Vassian Toporkov. Maksim went so far as to frighten Ivan with the prophecy that his son would die if he carried out his plan. In spite of this, Groznyj did do so. When, during the conversation, he asked Vassian what he should do to be a good Czar and keep his magnates in check, Toporkov answered by whispering in his ear that to be a real autocrat he should avoid having a single adviser who was wiser than himself, for then he would be the best of all and not need to listen to others. Groznyj thanked him for his advice by declaring that his father could not have given him better. But his son died soon after (45).

As Kurbskij gives it, his report has almost the stamp of an aetiological legend, a preparation for the shocking events described later in his account of the Czar's tyrannical period after 1560–64. It seems extremely probable, however, that Groznyj really did seek the advice of Vassian Toporkov, and also that Kurbskij accompanied him. In the first place, it was common practice for the monarch to seek the general advice of clerics, and in the second place, Kurbskij was at that time a distinguished member of Groznyj's train. Moreover, Kurbskij repeats his account of the conversation itself, though more briefly, in his fourth letter to Groznyj in 1579 (46). It seems improbable that he would wish to give this hint of a previous, common experience if the account were imaginary, and a proof that it was so

---

44. *Prosvetitel'* pp. 586–588, *Posl. Volock.* pp. 164, 176 f.
45. *Kurbskij* col. 50–52, 57.
46. *Fennell* p. 236.

would weaken the polemical force of the letter. The crucial point, however, lies elsewhere. Toporkov's advice, whether he really gave it, or whether Kurbskij invented it—is extremely typical of the Iosifist, anti-intellectual attitude. Groznyj expresses himself in a way that sounds like an echo of such promptings when he says that it is not fitting for a Czar to seek understanding from others (47).

Thus there is a kernel of truth in Kurbskij's anecdote, which gives it a surprising irony and subtlety. When Kurbskij, quite sincerely, calls Toporkov's advice "a Satanic syllogism" and his party "the over-cunning Iosifists", he betrays a peculiar naïvety, which lies in the fact that, in his own suspicion of intellectual sophistry, he ascribes to his opponents precisely this quality, which could scarcely be more unjust. And if the Iosifist, in his fear that cunning counsellors might ruin spiritual discipline and uniformity, warned the Czar against wise men, he thereby doomed himself and the rest of his party to become, sooner or later, passive tools in the hand of the Czar. If Toporkov did not do it, then Iosifism as a whole did it. It was a logical conclusion that Groznyj was not slow to draw. The irony lies in the fact that Groznyj got this impulse from the church, not from the twenty-third chapter of *"Il Principe"*.

Superficially, there may appear to be a contradiction between the conclusions of two acute cholars, when on the one hand *J. S. Lur'je* maintains that during Ivan Groznyj's reign, Iosif Volockij's position was almost that of the official Russian publicist, and that in that period his views could be attacked only abroad, as for example, by Kurbskij (48). And on the other hand, *A. A. Zimin* observes that Groznyj took over and exploited only certain aspects of Iosifism, i. e. those that could support the autocracy, and that in return, he cleared out all tendencies to claim for the church a role as a temporal power, an *ecclesia militans,* a *voinstvujuščaja cerkov'* (49). But what is really described is two aspects of the same thing. Groznyj had a use for Iosifism as a legitimation of his position as an absolute ruler, and was therefore interested in maintaining its unassailable validity against those who thought differently—but not until he himself had laid down an authoritative interpretation of the content of the ideology that corresponded with his political interests.

Of course, this formulation of Ivan Groznyj's attitude is only an interpretation, not an account of his version of his programme. But it is an interpretation that must appear to be the obvious and central conclusion from Ivan's political declarations in the first message to Kurbskij, and it is not weakened by any other statement by the Czar. On the contrary, it is given

---

47. *Ibid.* p. 154.
48. *Posl. Volock.* p. 96.
49. *TODRL* t. IX (1953) p. 177.

decided support by the observation of the concrete acts and decisions that together make up the political relations between the Czar and the church under Groznyj's rule. The main points are Groznyj's coronation as Czar on the initiative of the Metropolitan Makarij in 1547, whereby the monarch's absolute power was confirmed by the church's blessing, and Groznyj's removal of the Metropolitan Filip in 1568, whereby the church's role as a supervising instance was cut out of the play. In considering this pattern of action, it is no longer a question of seeking to make clear the ideological basis of Groznyj's religious foundation for his power, as in the previous pages, but of what were the interests and political objects that, in these situations, have been crucial for the acts of both the church and the Czar.

These questions are usually considered within the framework of a fixed and clear scheme, built upon the study of the religious movements in the period previous to Groznyj's reign. The heretical movements flourished in the middle classes, whose economic and social interests demanded a revision of the social order, which was founded on the traditional boyar system. To a certain extent, they had interests in common with the constantly more centralized Czardom, particularly in that both parties wished to oppose or limit the power of the boyars. Over against this came Iosifism as a high church movement, where the primary interest lay in the campaign against the heretics, using every means, spiritual and physical, and the maintenance of the material conditions of existence of the churches and the monasteries with their extensive estates. Support for these two objects Iosifism found in collaboration not with the temporal landowners but in the centralized power of the crown, which thus also found an ally against the boyar system in the st'ažateli. The crown, therefore, found itself in a dilemma, since in particular situations it was necessary to choose between two mutually antagonistic allies. The boyars, on the other hand, could find tactical support in the nest'ažateli movement, whose criticism of ecclesiastical estates and of the worldly engagement of Iosifism corresponded very well to the political and economic interests of the boyars. On the basis of this scheme, Iosifism is often described as a "progressive" movement, because it is regarded as a consistent and conscious champion of centralized government, directing its efforts against the "reactionary" power of the boyars (50).

A judicious reservation, however, on the usual view of Iosifism as consistently supporting a centralized government, has been made by *J. S. Lur'je* (51), and even more strongly by *A. A. Zimin,* who warns against overestimating the alliance between Iosifism and the crown, and correspondingly underestimating the crown's interest in collaboration with the forces

---

50. *Budovnic* p. 100 cf. *Lur'je* p. 35.
51. *Lur'je* pp. 209 ff.

behind the heretics (52). The explanation of the attitude and economic and political interests of Iosifism is also considerably weakened by the fact that originally the Iosifists—and especially Iosif Volockij himself—seem to have placed the main emphasis on the purely ideological interests and aspects, rather than on the material interests involved in the possession of estates. This last, as shown by *A. A. Zimin* (53), first appeared clearly and un-ambiguously in Iosif Volockij's argumentation when the question of the secularization of the estates of the church was raised by the opponents of Iosifism in 1503. Until then, it was the campaign against the heretics that dominated Volockij's polemics.

Thus comparatively clear permanent principles existed only in the sphere of dogma, while political interests and aims appeared in combinations de-pendent on circumstances. For the same reason, the conflict between the heretics and the Iosifists has a more consistent and permanent character than the alliance between the boyars and the *nest'ažateli* or between the crown and the *st'ažateli*. The enmities dominate the picture much more strongly than the friendships. It is thus impossible, without quite consider-able qualifications, to apply the usually accepted scheme in this context. Ivan Groznyj could by no means build upon a clearly conscious and clearly formulated agreement between the crown and the high church from the beginning of the century, yet he could use a theological tradition, of which the undefined relation to political questions permitted interpretation and shiftings as time went by.

There can hardly be any doubt that in this connexion it was of crucial importance that the relation between church and state for a number of years, during Ivan's minority—at any rate, from the death of Jelena Glinskaja in 1538 to the coup against Andrej Šujskij at the end of 1543—was stamped by the instability of the temporal power under the mutual rivalries of the boyar groups, and the ecclesiastical authorities' anxiety over the course of events. This is the period so drastically described in Groznyj's personal justification of his theory of state, and in the Czarist *"Carstvennaja Kni-ga"* (55), but in both, however, with such a wealth of detail that behind the tendentiousness it is possible to feel a basis of reality.

The state of the church, on the face of it, may seem to have been marked by no less uncertainty and vacillation than that that marked the temporal power during the changing groupings of the Glinskijs, the Belskijs and the Šujskijs. The Metropolitans followed one another in quick succes-sion, as those in power at the moment changed them,—Daniil for Joasaf in 1539, Ioasaf for Makarij in 1542 (56). Here, however, on the contrary,

---

52. *TODRL* t. IX (1953) p. 163.
53. *Posl. Volock.* pp. 370–74.
55. *PSRL* t. XIII pp. 420, 432, 439, etc.
56. *Ibid.* pp. 127, 142, 432, 440.

there are signs of an obstinate continuity, for if Daniil was removed because of his Iosifism, the boyars must have hoped that Ioasaf would prove to be more amenable, and that their hopes were disappointed appears from his replacement by Makarij, who, however, in a year proved more dangerous to the boyar regime than any of his predecessors. The boyar group was simply unable to find a Metropolitan who was at once worthy of the post and willing to be politically obedient or at any rate passive.

The leaders of the church were so disturbed by the uncertain position both of the crown and of themselves that they could not remain passive. And the boyars were so disturbed by the political activity of the church leaders that, in spite of the dangers involved, they could not avoid challenging them. And so the interests of the church became all the more strongly bound up with those of the centralized government. If at times this connexion had been weak or even non-existent under Ivan III and Vasilij III, when strong and determined Grand Princes often played their own game, even with the heretics, or considered secularizing the estates of the church in order to further the concentration of power in the crown (57), it was now strengthened and cemented by the lack of a strong and stable government that could follow a consistent policy.

A new generation had arrived, which, in spite of all the continuity in the church's ideological formulations, yet cast a veil over earlier difficulties with the crown—and did so the more easily as these difficulties had never found expression in an attempt to work out a consistent church attitude to the authority of the crown, its obligations, its rights and its responsibilities. Iosif Volockij and his contemporaries had somewhat superficially busied themselves with ideas of the ruler's responsibilities, after the problem had become topical in a time when a centralized government was about to become a fact (58). And certainly there were ideas of a *voinstvujuščaja cerkov'*, expressed most clearly in the anonymous *"Povest' o Belom Klobuke"* at about the turn of the century, which speaks critically of the monarch's exercise of power, and favourably of the primacy of the spiritual over the temporal authority (59). But it is characteristic of the vagueness and uncertainty of these tendencies that Volockij's adoption of the Byzantine comparison of the Emperor to the sun (60), was never contested by a clerical comparison of the temporal power to the moon, which must derive its light from the sun of the church authorities, as Innocent III had done long ago

---

57. *Očerki* pp. 103 f., 174, *J. L. I. Fennell: Ivan the Great of Moscow* (London 1961) pp. 332 f., *G. Vernadsky: Russia at the Dawn of the Modern Age* = *A History of Russia* Vol. IV (New Haven 1959) pp. 119 ff., 152.
58. Cf. *Lur'je* pp. 477 f., *D. S. Lixačev* in *Soč. Peresv.* pp. 40 f.
59. See *N. N. Rozen* in *TODRL* t. IX (1953) p. 213.
60. See above p. 51.

in the West (61). Makarij obviously had similar ideas (62), but he was primarily interested in the responsibility of the magnates to the monarch, for at that time there were strong tendencies to a decentralization of the royal power, and incalculable consequences were feared. He also gave up the attempt to define the church's view of the royal power, and instead, worked tactically to make good the lack of such a power.

Makarij acted more as a statesman than a leader of the church. With ideological zeal, he set himself to create the myth on which the Czarist power was to build. With his antecedents, he naturally chose the Iosifist tradition as the foundation. But Volockij's anti-reform fanaticism, which had the character of a defensive ecclesiastical campaign against forces that were new and foreign to Russian society, turned in the hands of Makarij into a political offensive for the consolidation of precisely this changed Russian society, which in the previous generations had begun to be conscious of its role as a great power, and had burst open the framework of the boyar system. Volockij wrested concessions and charters from the Grand Princes of Moscow, who needed his moral support. Makarij, on the contrary, built up the child Grand Prince Ivan to fill the role of Czar and autocrat of Russia. And he stopped at nothing that could promote his political object.

For young Ivan, these years were hectic, and his own part ambivalent. There can be no doubt that the Metropolitan was at the centre of the political events and intrigues—there is evidence, at all events, that he was the central figure of a scuffle during a heated dispute with the boyars. Both Groznyj and "Carstvennaja Kniga" report that his cloak was torn to shreds by a follower of the Šujskijs (63), only a year after he had become Metropolitan. So that it is no surprise to find the assailant among the banished when, a few months later, there was a purge after the leader of the boyar group, Andrej Šujskij, had been murdered by being thrown to the hounds by order of the thirteen-year old Grand Prince (64). Although Groznyj mentions the assault on Makarij in his personal justification, he does not, strangely enough, mention the removal of Andrej Šujskij, but merely says that in his fifteenth year "we began to put our kingdom in order" (65). It is conceivable that, twenty-one years after the event, it did not occur to him to think of himself—a child—as the originator of it, and *I. I. Smirnov* is probably correct in assuming that the real originator was Makarij (66).

61. *Migne lat.* t. CCXIV col. 377: "*sicut luna lumen suum a sole sortitur...sic regalis potestas ab auctoritate pontificali suae sortitur dignitatis splendorum.*".
62. See below pp. 120 f.
63. *Fennell* p. 78, *PRSL* t. XIII pp. 443 f.
64. *Ibid.* p. 444.
65. *Fennell* p. 80.
66. *Smirnov* p. 100. *Zimin Ref.* pp. 264–267 considers Makarij to have been originally a follower of the Šujskijs, but conjectures that he changed his attitude—suspending judgement on his possible share in the coup against Andrej Šujskij.

For Ivan, the situation during his minority was that ceremonially, and according to the admonitions of Makarij, he was the central figure and the master, but that in reality, he was the puppet of rival groups, and at best, a tool for Makarij's manoeuvres. In this milieu, among the magnates, and with this form of politics in mind, it is no wonder that the boy prince dealt with worthy people and dogs with the ruthless recklessness described by Kurbskij with such indignation (67). It was only a step from the iconostasis to the executioner's pit.

That Groznyj did not mention the coup against Andrej Šujskij in his account of his youth, may also be because the event did not seem so epoch-making to him as to posterity. The boyar regime was still not brought to an end. It is more surprising that he does not mention, either, an event so epoch-making in the eyes of posterity as his coronation as Czar. He jumps straight from his undefined action at fifteen to his account of the fire and the riot at Moscow in the summer after his coronation. And yet, according to the chronicle, it was in his sixteenth year that Ivan proclaimed his intention of marrying and having himself crowned as Czar (68), which politically and juridically, meant a leap out of the times the boyars and petty princes wished to preserve, and into the practical realization of the ideal type of state that hitherto had been confined to ideological dreams of Russia's future (69).

It is hardly conceivable that that solemn and pompous ceremony, or the obviously enervating negotiations and manoeuvres that prepared the way for it, could have faded in the Czar's memory eighteen years later, into merely an unimportant interlude. It seems rather that Groznyj was not interested in emphasising the formal introduction of the Czardom on 16 January 1547, partly because elsewhere he strongly emphasises the unbroken, but fictitious, continuity of the absolute autocracy right from the time of St. Vladimir (70), and partly because this ceremonial expression of his political position was not due to his initiative either, but was rather the crown of Makarij's labours and the fruit of the Metropolitan's political vision—and tactical manoeuvres (71). When once the vision had become reality, the Czar himself had no interest in emphasising its origin. The power of the Czar was absolute, and consequently without beginning or end, without debt, duty or responsibility except to God.

---

67. *Kurbskij* col. 6.
68. *PSRL* t. XIII p. 450.
69. *Smirnov* p. 118.
70. See above pp. 22, 25.
71. *Smirnov* pp. 115 f.; *Zimin Ref.* p. 274, would not ascribe the initiative to Makarij. It seems obvious, however, that the sources support the view that Makarij played the central part in the political preparations, cf. *N. Andreyev* in *The Slav. and East Eur. Review* Vol. XL No. 94 (1961) p. 259.

Makarij himself completed the formation of this myth on a Iosifist foundation. From his ideological orientation and his political interest in an orderly
kingdom, he made the monarch God's representative on earth. And when,
like his predecessor, he renounced the right to formulate conditions for the
monarch's heavenly mandate, he resigned the church's role as the monarch's
conscience. Iosif Volockij's original tendency to distinguish between the
divinity of the Czardom and the individual Czar's suitability—or unsuitability—measured by the church's ideals, finally took the form of Ivan Groznyj's
distinction between the absolute inviolability of the religion—i. e. the Orthodox Church—and the suitability or unsuitability of the individual Metropolitan according to the judgement and the interests of the Czar. The coronation as Czar ended the role of Iosifism as an ecclesiastical court in the affairs
of the kingdom. And the removal of the Metropolitan Filip confirmed that
the Czardom had taken over the full responsibility direct to God, not only
theoretically, but in brutal, political practice.

It is a trite observation, that the period between Makarij's triumph and
Filip's martyrdom coincides with the maturing of the Czar from disciple to
statesman, from walker-on to actor. Part of the explanation of the apparent
paradox, that the church's ideological victory led to its political defeat, must,
of course, be found in this development of Ivan's personality. But this is
not the whole explanation. There is no need to take it as an inevitable
necessity that the Czar's increasing independence must lead to the Church's
coming into a state of tutelage.

From what has gone before, we have seen that Ivan Groznyj's ideology
did not, at any crucial point, differ independently from the church tradition
that prevailed in the first half of the century. His concepts in politics, theory
of the state, religion and morals are simply taken over from this tradition.
With regard to ideological and dogmatic convictions, there is no trace of
any development towards a more independent, personal attitude to questions
of principle. Ivan's political attitude to the church is formulated in his first
message to Kurbskij, when he clearly declared that priests should not meddle
with politics. This was the view he maintained to Filip. His treatment of the
Metropolitan was brutal, humiliating, undoubtedly also revolting and fright-
ful in the eyes of other contemporaries besides those of Kurbskij (72). But
in principle, it was not new. And the Czar continued, all his life, to act as
the affectionate partisan and protector of the Orthodox Church. He threw
himself into such long and passionate discussions with representatives of
other confessions—as, for example, with the Papal Legate, Antonio Possevino (73)—that it is impossible to doubt his firm and sincere faith. When

---

72. *Kurbskij* col. 152 ff.
73. *Antonio Possevino: Moscovia. Eiusdem novissima descriptio* (Antverpiae 1587) pp. 134 ff.,
    cf. the Russian account: *Pam'atniki diplomatičeskix snošenij drevnej Rosii s deržavami*

all comes to all, it was, of course, his divine mandate—or, if you will, the ideological axiom—that functioned as the foundation and justification of Ivan Groznyj's actions. And here it may be justifiable to bring in a psychological postulate, that such passionate acts could hardly have been performed with such passionate ruthlessness without a passionate belief in their absolute justification.

Only at one point, hitherto, has there been reason to speak of an independent and original tendency in Ivan Groznyj, and that is in connexion with his tendency to secularize concepts and lines of thought (74). When it is a question of the relation of the monarch to the church, this point, on the other hand, is naturally of quite cardinal importance, assuming that the church takes up a consistently spiritual position. Had this been the case in Groznyj's Russia, the church's ideological victory would not necessarily have led to its political defeat, nor the independence of the Czar to its tutelage. It could have represented a clearly formulated and defined attitude to the temporal power, struggling against it or collaborating with it, victorious over it or in subjection to it, but in any case, unchanged and unshaken in its principles. The Iosifist-dominated church did not take up this role, but itself turned, at important points, to secularization, especially with its own commitment to worldly possessions and forms of organization, and with its hostility to all forms of intellectual mobility and clarification of dogma.

A church movement that, to such a degree as the Iosifist, pursued its aims with the most extreme worldly means must necessarily have inspired and urged its disciple on an earthly throne to use these means with complete ruthlessness also. Iosif Volockij's urge to see heretics at the stake, and Makarij's fight against his political opponent by getting the boy prince to order him to be thrown to the hounds, does not differ in principle, in morals or in ethics from Groznyj's acts against Filip, in having him accused of sorcery and immorality or—as it is reported—in having him killed in his monastery cell by one of his henchmen (75). Nor, therefore, is it a sign of a psychological mystery—though certainly of extraordinary religious consistency and zeal—that Ivan sent to the monasteries lists of the victims of his executions, with the necessary money enclosed, so that prayers might be said for the dead, and added that God in His omniscience would certainly be able to fill out the lists himself, where they were incomplete (76).

---

inostrannymi, t. X (Spbg. 1871) col. 298 ff. On the political aspect of these conservations, see below pp. 162 f.

74. See above, pp. 27 ff., 51 f.

75. *Kurbskij* col. 156; *Karamzin* t. IX p. 143 gives an account of Filip's *Vita*, extant in two unpublished manuscripts, cf. G. P. Fedotov: *Sv'atoj Filipp, Metropolit Moskovskij* (Paris 1928) pp. 164 f., and the account in *Žitija Sv'atyx rossijskoj cerkvi. Janvar'* (Spbg. 1857) pp. 128 f.

76. *ČOIDR* 1859/III *smes'* pp. 89–100. See e.g. p. 93: "*Vasilija s ženoju, da s trema synov'-jami: imena ix Ty Sam, Gospodi, vesi; pom'ani ix v carstvii svojem!*«

Those executed were sacrificed on earth so that they might be saved for eternal life. This was the legitimation of the terror. To Iosifism, all means were good that served Orthodoxy. And Ivan Groznyj was fully conscious of his role as Orthodoxy's Czar.

What Filip's basic attitude was, on the other hand, is far from clear. He allowed himself to be elected Metropolitan in 1566, a critical moment, when the Czar—just like the boyars in 1539 and 1542—was having difficulty in finding a Metropolitan who was both worthy of the post and willing to remain politically passive. German, who had just been appointed, had been removed by the Czar immediately before, after having given expression to his critical attitude to the Czar's policy. Possibly Filip hoped to be able to exert a moderating, moral influence during the terror, without, in principle, criticising Groznyj's government. He must have been conscious of the physical danger and the moral risks of such a role, and he probably made his decision after weighing all the personal and church interests involved—rather than, as others have conjectured, letting himself be chosen with the intention of seeking martyrdom (77).

But if he had any illusions about the possibility of exercising his influence in the normal manner, he obviously lost them in the course of the first year he was in office, as it became clear that he got no result by exercising his traditional right to intercede with the monarch on behalf of the condemned. He could not, by accepting Groznyj's system, save the victims of that system. The system and the terror were one, and could not be divided. Filip then brought his period of office to a heroic close by a public demonstration against Groznyj. When the Czar with his train came to Mass at the Church of the Ascension in the Kremlin, one Sunday in 1568, the Metropolitan refused to give him his blessing, and when he was urged to do so, declared that he did not recognize the Czar in the shape of Ivan. He referred to Groznyj's shedding of innocent Christian blood. He declared him to be a blind victim of flatterers. And he reminded the Czar that he too was of earthly dust, and needed forgiveness for his sins (78).

With these last words, Filip repeated what Kurbskij had written in his letter of renunciation to the Czar four years before—which had given Groznyj occasion to make one of his important declarations of principle, that he would answer at the Day of Judgement for both his own acts and those of his subjects. The similarity may be accidental. What is more important, Filip's formulation—as shown by *Ihor Ševčenko*—was taken from Agapetos. Kurbskij's question, whether Groznyj thought himself immortal, does

---

77. *N. Zernov: The Russians and their Church* (London 1945) p. 62, cf. also *Karamzin* t. IX pp. 89–93, *Kurbskij* col. 150 f., 157 f., *G. P. Fedotov op. cit.* pp. 104 ff. *Žitija sv'atyx* etc. pp. 95 f.

78. *V. Malinin op. cit.* p. 763. *G. P. Fedotov op. cit.* pp. 146 ff., *Žitija sv'atyx* etc. pp. 107, 112.

not much resemble the words of Agapetos. But Filip's talk of earthly dust is obviously an echo of the Byzantine (79). Ševčenko has precisely on this point, been able to show the probability that Filip really did keep so close to the Iosifists' Byzantine classic in his speeches to Groznyj, and that it is not merely an invention in the legend of the saint (80). Whether this lack of originality on Filip's part was tactical, cannot, of course, be known. But it may well have had its effect, that the Metropolitan denounced the Czar in the very same terms as had been used for two generations in Iosifism's religious support of the Czarist power. The crucial point, however, is that Filip, even with this tactical intention, yet confined himself to carrying on the discussion on the existing ideological basis, and thereby debarred himself from setting up a clear church alternative to Groznyj's system. He formulated no theory of a *rex iniustus* and a religious foundation for a right of resistance, which he could very well have done on the basis of Iosif Volockij's definition of a *car' mučitel* in the seventh chapter of *"Prosvetitel'"* (81). By this remaining within the limits instead of breaking out of them, he gave Groznyj a free hand.

This was a fateful choice, which, at bottom, was taken on an ideological basis. It was characteristic, that when, a hundred years later, Nikon attempted to set up a church alternative—a *sacerdotium* against the *regnum*—he had to make a break with the traditional Iosifist ideology by declaring himself a Greek in religion, just as he was a Russian in a national sense (82). Thereby he set up a supra-national alternative to the state, and he gained for himself as Patriarch the operative advantage of being able to appear in two roles, a spiritual and a temporal. An end was put to this attempt by Peter the Great, who thus in a sense carried on the line from Ivan Groznyj (83). What was demonstrated by the developments from Makarij to Filip was that the leader of the church represented no alternative to the state, but was simply the administrative head of a religious organization, the task and objects of which were nationally defined. Makarij saluted Ivan as a new Constantine, a new Aleksander Nevskij or Dmitrij Donskoj, after the conquest of Kazan' (84), and thereby bound his church to a national goal and mission.

---

79. *I. Ševčenko op. cit.* p. 172, *Migne gr.* t. LXXXVI col. 1172: *"ei eikoni theikē tetimētai, alla kai konei khoikē sympeplektai"*.
80. *I. Ševčenko op. cit.* pp. 173 f.
81. See above p. 45.
82. *P. Mil'ukov: Očerki po istorii russkoj kul'tury, č.* II (4. izd. Spbg. 1905) pp. 42 f. See also *V. Val'denberg: Drevnerusskija učenija o predelax carskoj vlasti* (Pgr. 1916) pp. 373 ff. and *William K. Medlin: Moscow and East Rome* == Études d'histoire économique, politique et sociale, I (Geneva 1952) pp. 174 ff.
83. *N. Zernow: Moscow the Third Rome* (London 1942) pp. 70, 87 ff.
84. *PSRL* t. XIII p. 226.

To the extent that the church was nationally committed, the Czar had correspondingly a free hand. For his part, he could exploit the operative advantage of being able to appear in two roles, a divine one and an earthly one. He exploited the advantages of a theocracy, which permitted him to exercise earthly power by a kind of *translatio imperii* from God—but he did not undertake the burden of being himself a living, personified theodice (85). Filip condemned Ivan Groznyj for his lack of Christian mercy, but Groznyj could reply that only he himself was responsible to God for his merciless persecution of the enemies of the Orthodox Czar. Every reproach of the Metropolitan turned automatically into an untimely meddling with politics, and the Czar could neutralize him by a reference to his religious mandate.

Ivan's ideological background made it easy for him to play his double role as *imperator* and *pontifex maximus*. He speaks of it in such a matter of fact way as shows that he saw no insoluble problem of conscience or untenable paradox in his union of political terror and religious piety. His personal relation to God and his state function were—as he said himself—two different things. The question then arises, what determined Groznyj's political views and acts apart from the religious ideology—which was determinant only in that it bound him to feel that he had freedom of action.

---

85. *V. O. Kl'učevskij* (*Sočinenija* t. II, Moscow 1957, p. 196) talks of a political self-deification in Groznyj, but without documentation for this assertion taken in a literal sense. Taken metaphorically, the observation of "self-deification" in Groznyj means nothing, since it could be applied to the majority of autocrats in the history of the world. *S. A. Korff* (*Zeitschr. f. osteur. Gesch.*, Bd. IV, Berlin 1914, pp. 336 f.) soberly points out that Ivan did not regard himself as divine, without thereby having excluded all talk of theocracy. Perhaps it is most correct to speak of "indirect theocracy" where Groznyj is concerned.

IV

The Wise Counseller

If, as Lord Acton maintained, power corrupts and absolute power corrupts absolutely—and where is the evidence that tells against this?—then the influence of Iosifism on the Russian Czardom was catastrophic. It gave the ruler an ideologically determined conviction that he had absolute liberty of action. This in itself is perhaps a dangerous conviction, since it may cause a Herod to out-Herod himself. But in politics, primarily, it is an illusion, since all exercise of power sooner or later, in one connexion or another, meets with resistance, conflict, demand for consideration. And the more powerfully this appears, the more compulsive is this conviction of liberty of action, which starts an endless causal chain of self-assertion by terror.

In a sense, this is what Kurbskij pointed out to Groznyj in his letters to him and in his historical review of his reign. When Kurbskij attacked Iosifism, he did so with the emphasis on its unfortunate moral effect on Ivan, as, for example, in the account of Vassian Toporkov's advice. Kurbskij's attitude seems to be dictated by a conviction of human weakness, when confronted by tasks requiring the exercise of power: the individual cannot, alone, rejecting all assistance, act so as to interfere in people's lives without these actions taking on the character of oppression and tyranny. The Czar is as weak as all other mortals, and in his weakness he has no right to attack *svobodnoje jestestvo čelovečeskoje.*

Kurbskij's words convey a repulsion, as on meeting a dangerous perversion, when he reproaches Ivan for at one moment humiliating himself exceedingly, and the next, raising himself up without limit and beyond measure (1). Kurbskij thus makes no distinction between the Czar with a divine mandate and a human being under God's guidance. He recognizes no divine-human double role. In his third letter to Groznyj, Kurbskij quotes from Cicero. It is typical, that in the quotation, which otherwise he translates correctly, he deviates from the original at one place—whether deliberately or accidentally—whereby the Stoic's self-sufficiency, as expressed by Cicero—*"nemo potest non beatissimus esse qui est totus aptus ex sese quique in se uno sua ponit omnia"*—is changed to Kurbskij's Christian

---

1. *Fennell* p. 200

humility—*"nikto že možet preblagoslovennejše byti, kotoryj jest' vsesover-šen v sebe, i jaže v sebe jedinom vs'a svoja polagajet"* (2).

Hitherto, it has been maintained, provisionally and in order to elucidate Ivan Groznyj's way of thinking, that Kurbskij polemises on behalf of the individual and from a religiously defined view of humanity, but not as an advocate for a politically defined alternative to Groznyj's government and view of the state (3). Since the next to be discussed is what determined Groznyj's political attitude and actions—either by limiting or by prompting them—besides the religious ideology, it will be natural first of all to consider more closely how Kurbskij was placed among the Czar's opponents and in the political currents of the period. This is done not only to make the connexion with the previous discussion, but also to make a start for what follows with the fullest and most clearly articulate criticism of Groznyj, which, of course, was Kurbskij's.

When it is considered that we have, as a basis for evaluating Kurbskij's standpoint, five letters to Groznyj over a period of fifteen years, his detailed *"Istorija o Velikom Kn'aze Moskovskom"* from about 1575, and other smaller treatises, it is significant that from all this material it is not possible to deduce any clearly defined political view, beyond the critical attitude to Groznyj. On this basis, it is probably reasonable to go so far as to say that there is cause to doubt whether Kurbskij had actual, concrete, political objectives, conceived as an alternative to the Czarist system as shaped by Groznyj. Naturally, this does not lead directly to the conclusion that Kurbskij only concentrated on arguing individualistically from a religious view of humanity. Against this view, at any rate, it may be urged that Kurbskij's polemics in one particular respect were clearly political, i. e. to the extent that it meant a challenge to Groznyj's political views. We have already seen how Groznyj implied Kurbskij's participation in a plot against the Orthodox Czardom—and this simply meant that Kurbskij, by taking up an attitude that was perhaps individualistic, yet automatically—whether deliberately or not—committed a crime of far-reaching political character. It was Groznyj who decided what was criminal or permissible. But the obscurity justifies asking whether Kurbskij's reasons and intentions were unpolitical or boyar-

---

2. *Paradoxa stoicorum* 17, cf. *Fennell* p. 218. *Stählin* p. 116 and *Fennell* p. 219 insert the negation in accordance with the basic text, but without the authority of any Russian manuscript. *H. Schaeder: Moskau das Dritte Rom* (Hamburg 1928) p. 88 (= 2. Aufl., Darmstadt 1957, p. 123) takes the omission of the secondary negative particle as a neat equivalent to Cicero's emphatic affirmation, which, however, must require in the first place, that the translation of the superlative form is to be taken as the comparative, and in the second place, is weakened by Kurbskij's frequent omission of the secondary negative particle, see e.g. *Fennell* p. 218: *"tomu ničeso že byti možet izvestnogo"*, p. 4: *"nikojego...bezčestija privedox"*, *"nikogda polkov tvojix...obratix"*.

3. See above p. 50.

political, whether he represented only himself or a group, whether he was an apostate or a rebel.

It is maintained clearly and unambiguously by *I. U. Budovnic,* that Kurbskij carried on propaganda for a system of government based on the boyars (4). This interpretation closely coincides with the scheme previously described, according to which "reactionary" forces oppose the centralized Czarist power, which in consequence of objective laws replaced the boyar system, and "progressive" forces, on the other hand, opposed the supporters of the boyar system and were on the side of the new order. From this point of view, the Iosifists become "progressive". And Kurbskij becomes a "reactionary" whose actions, moreover, stamp him as a morally reprehensible individual, since by his defection he commits treason both against true progress and against his fatherland. Kurbskij is thereby implicitly regarded as a representative of boyar policy, the object of which was to combat the Czarist power. There are no grounds, however, for this view of Kurbskij.

The criteria for Kurbskij's appearance as advocate for the boyar system would be

that he maintained the traditional, feudal forms of contract between the magnates and the monarch,

that he showed a preference for the maintenance of the division of Russia in petty principalities,

that he emphasised the Czar's obligations towards the institutional representation of the boyar group, and finally,

that he maintained the rights and interests of the boyars in discussing political reforms and measures that contributed to limit the prerogatives and power of the boyars.

If only one of these criteria could be seen to be met, it would be possible to speak of an intimate connexion between Kurbskij and boyar policy. But it will be seen that none of these four conditions can be met.

With regard to the feudal contract relation, it must certainly be admitted, that there are reminiscences of this in Kurbskij. When, earlier in these pages, Kurbskij's first letter to Groznyj is spoken of as a letter of renunciation of allegiance, this is due to the impression of these reminscences. It seems obvious that Kurbskij found it more natural than Groznyj did that he should renounce his obligation of loyalty—not only because the act was to his advantage and to Groznyj's disadvantage, but also because he was not so steeped in the way of thinking of the centralized government as was the Czar. Clearly, Kurbskij feel no pangs of conscience in referring to his new loyalty to Zygmunt August, but merely emphasises that he is a pleasanter lord than Groznyj had been (5)—an assertion that undeniably could

4. *Budovnic* p. 282.
5. *Fennell* p. 8.

be disproved only by Groznyj undertaking to disprove it. On the other hand, however, it is extremely difficult to find any statement that can be read as a definite reference to a right to depart. There was plenty of opportunity to appeal to such principles in his controversy with Groznyj, but characteristically enough, the traditional Russian expression for "departure", *ot'-jezd,* does not appear in Kurbskij's writings (6).

Certain of Kurbskij's words, however, have been interpreted as allusions to the right of departure. His reference to the words of the Evangelist, that if they persecute you in one city, flee into the next, and his maintenance of the right of the individual to go to a foreign country by virtue of free human nature, are taken by *Karl Stählin* as references, admittedly not very direct, to *ot'jezd* (7). Similar remarks, such as that men are shut in like pigs in a stye and prevented from going over the border into a foreign country, are to be found in Kurbskij's preface to the Chrysostom anthology *"Novyj Margarit",* probably written a few years before the third letter to Ivan— the one in which the remarks mentioned above appear, written in 1578 (8). In other words, these remarks come rather late in relation to Kurbskij's defection in 1564. If he intended to refer to an actual right of departure, it might have been expected to come in immediate connexion with Kurbskij's action, in his first letter, for example, which could then justifiably be called a letter of renunciation of allegiance. It is striking, too, that all these remarks are in extremely abstract terms, and that in their context they are closely connected with general religious and humanistic principles, which were certainly not at all characteristic of traditional boyar thinking. On this basis, it seems safest to accept the interpretation proposed by *Ferdinand Liewehr,* that here, Kurbskij is not thinking of the right to depart but of the free man's right to seek education and spiritual enrichment abroad (9). It may be added, that perhaps he is thinking primarily of a man's fundamental right to preserve his life.

Nor in other connexions does Kurbskij seem to be more bound by traditional feudal thinking about a contract relation than does Groznyj himself. In his first message to Kurbskij, Groznyj speaks of the defection of the traitors and their alliances with the Czar's enemies in terms that have a markedly traditional ring—they "seceded", *otstupili,* from the Czar, and

6. On *ot'jezd* see *S. A. Korff* in *Zeitschr. f. osteur. Gesch.,* Bd. IV (Berlin 1914) pp. 328 f., *J. L. I. Fennell: Ivan the Great of Moscow* (London 1961) pp. 214, 296 f. on restrictive measures in the fifteenth century. During Groznyj's minority, *ot'jezd* was not only of limited validity, but carried a taint of revolt and treason, cf. *Zimin Ref.* pp. 194 f., 228– 230, *Smirnov* p. 54, *PSRL* t. XIII pp. 77–79.

7. *Stählin* pp. 168, 171, cf. *Fennell* pp. 206, 214; *Matth.* X, 13.

8. *F. Liewehr: Kurbskijs "Novyj Margarit"* = Veröff. d. slav. Arbeitsgem. d. Deutsch. Univ. in Prag, Rh. II, Heft 2 (Prag 1928) p. 55 cf. p. 14.

9. *F. Liewehr loc. cit.* cf. *H. Schaeder op. cit.* p. 86 (2. Aufl. p. 120).

"adhered to", *priložilis'a,* his uncle (10). This is even clearer in connexion with the oath of fealty, the traditional sealing of the relation of loyalty to the monarch by kissing the cross (*krestnoje celovanije*). This act plays an extremely important part in Groznyj's polemics. He returns again and again to this binding expression of loyalty, which, with its religious significance, naturally leads to his general religious basis for the Czardom as the protector of Orthodoxy (11). One of Groznyj's most crushing invectives—which, characteristically enough, can stand alone, without supplementary adjectives—is the term for "one who breaks the oath on the cross", a *krestoprestupnik* (12). The clearest example of the weight that Groznyj attached to the oath of fealty is his reaction in the succession crisis during his illness in 1553, when the boyar group refused to swear allegiance to Ivan's son Dmitrij by kissing the cross (13).

It is conceivable that the oath assumes a somewhat ambivalent transitional position in Groznyj's consciousness. On the one hand, he must have ascribed to it a primitive binding power, since without it he had no hope of solving the succession problem simply by an oath taken by persons whose hostile attitude to his dynasty was well known to him. On the other hand, even under his predecessors the oath was of diminishing importance as a form of guarantee that was acceptable (14), and Ivan himself seems in his polemics to attach less importance to the actual legal consequence of the oath than to its religious symbolism. A *krestoprestupnik* is not so much a contract-breaker in a legal sense as a morally corrupt traitor and heretic.

To Kurbskij, on the other hand, the oath is a minor matter—not only for the obvious reason that he had broken the oath and therefore it was to his interest to minimize its importance, but also because in his eyes it had been degraded to a dishonouring and meaningless ceremony of subjection, which Ivan's subjects submitted to only under compulsion and the threat of death if they refused (15). What was basic for Kurbskij was clearly a view of God and man that was just as far removed from the traditional concepts of the boyar system as from the Czardom's new ideology. The crux of the matter to him was the free human nature created by God, *svobodnoje*

---

10. *Fennell* p. 70.
11. *Ibid.* pp. 14 f., 22, 28, 40, 60, 78, 94, 100.
12. *Ibid.* pp. 14 cf. 60.
13. *Ibid.* pp. 94, 62.
14. *H. Fleischhacker: Die staats- und völkerrechtlichen Grundlagen der moskauischen Aussenpolitik* = Jahrb. f. Gesch. Osteur., Beiheft 1 (Breslau 1938) pp. 33 f. During Ivan Groznyj's minority, the minute recording the act (*celoval'naja zapis'*) had the legal force of a form of contract, cf. *Smirnov* pp. 53–55.
15. *Fennell* p. 206. Even in 1534, it was possible to speak of the taking of an oath under compulsion, "*nevol'noje celovanije*", see *PSRL* t. XIII p. 78 B, though in the context this cannot be taken as a proof of Kurbskij's dependence on the boyar tradition.

jestestvo čeloveceskoje, that no earthly authority had the right' to oppress. Kurbskij never speaks of concrete, codified rights of the magnates against the Czar, but only in a more abstract manner of Groznyj's arbitrary dealings with human lives: his "lawlessness", *bezzakonije,* and his extermination of whole families "without law or judgement", *bez suda i bez prava* (16), whereby in his lack of self-control he breaks his natural obligations: to judge according to law, and to protect his subjects (*pravednyj sud i oborona*) (17). He is obviously thinking of some form of contractual relation between ruler and subject—but neither implicitly nor explicitly is it a matter of the original forms of contract of the boyar system.

The second criterion—the question of Kurbskij's attitude to the disappearance of the petty principalities and the union of Russia under Moscow—gives even less a basis for describing Kurbskij as the advocate of the boyar system. It is true that Groznyj in his message hints that Kurbskij cherished the ambition of becoming the lord of Jaroslavl', and thus to re-establish his family's original principality (18). In this accusation, however, it is difficult to see anything but a variation of Groznyj's general description of Kurbskij as an adherent of the boyar system and the sworn enemy of the Czar's government. Nowhere does Kurbskij express himself in a manner that can be interpreted as a criticism of the union of the kingdom or a desire to see the petty principalities re-established. He signs himself, at the end of his third letter to Groznyj, as "Prince of Kovel'", but this, however, can be taken only as a reference to the honours he is enjoying under his new lord, and not as the expression of any political ambitions, as far as the Polish-Lithuanian state was concerned (19).

Whenever the area under Groznyj is mentioned, it is consistently described as the object of the ruler's tyranny and caprice, but this abnormal situation does not cover the Czardom as such. It has been said that it is typical of Kurbskij's boyar attitude that he refuses to call Groznyj Czar, and writes his *"Istorija o Velikom Kn'aze Moskovskom"* using throughout the traditional title used right up to Groznyj's coronation as Czar in 1547 (20). This, however, is not a convincing argument, since in their correspondence Kurbskij addresses Groznyj perfectly correctly, and in his historical account speaks of Ivan as the Czar, and moreover describes the first period of the

16. *Fennell* p. 228, 234.
17. *Ibid.* pp. 238, 236, cf. the accusation *Kurbskij* col. 106: "*sud bez očevistnago veščanija*".
18. *Fennell* p. 14.
19. *Ibid.* p. 216. Elsewhere, Kurbskij states that he enjoys his rights at Kovel' in return for his service under Zygmunt August in the latter's capacity of Grand Duke of Lithuania. See *Skazanija kn'az'a Kurbskago,* izd., vtoroje N. Ustr'alova (Spbg. 1848) pp. 441, 443.
20. *Budovnic* pp. 282 f., cf. *Bol'šaja Sovetskaja Enciklopedija,* 2. izd., t. XXIV (Moscow 1953) p. 83, where it is actually asserted that Kurbskij consistently refuses to call Ivan Czar.

Czardom up to Groznyj's alleged change as a happy period (21). It was Ivan's later development into a tyrant, a *mučiteľ*, that caused Kurbskij to lament the condition of his country and to flee from it.

It seems to be quite natural for him to speak of the Russian realm as a unity, also at moments when he is most feelingly repudiating Groznyj's terrorist regime. He speaks of *Sv'atoruskaja imperija* twice, of *Sv'atoruskoje carstvo* once, of *Sv'atoruskaja zemľa* once, and five times of *Sv'atoruskije zemli* (22). The fact that he thus, in most cases, speaks of the realm as a plurality cannot support a conjecture that he did not accept the uniting of the Russian realm under Moscow. In four cases out of nine he does speak of the realm as a unity, and further, by the same token, a similar attitude should be ascribed to Groznyj, since in his intitulation he lists all the Russian principalities—Moscow, Tver', Vladimir, R'azan', Rostov, Jaroslavl', and so on—separately.

It might be maintained that Kurbskij, on purely psychological grounds, speaks of Russia as a unity because, after years in exile, he thinks primarily of that territory that is defined by its being under Ivan's lawless rule. But in that case, it is most improbable that Kurbskij would use words like *imperija* and *carstvo,* which designate an acknowledged constitutional unit, or that he would express his love of the Russian nation as a whole, *ko jedinoplem'anoj Rosii* (23). Thus there are no convincing indications that Kurbskij was an opponent of the unification of the Russian realm as such, nor is there any fundamental statement to this effect in his writings. Considering the prevalent development in the previous generations, it would have been an astonishing anachronism if Kurbskij had had plans of making himself master of Jaroslavl', which had been subjected to Moscow a hundred years before his defection.

It would be more probable, if—in reply to the third criterion—it was possible to find a basis for the supposed tendency in Kurbskij to maintain, at any rate, the Czar's obligation to the boyars as participants in the government of the country, which in practice means an obligation to govern jointly with the Boyar Council, *bojarskaja duma.* This view would be a contemporary form, so to speak, of advocacy for boyar policy. It would also be in complete agreement with Kurbskij's general maintenance of the position of the magnates in the community almost as something determined by a law of nature: since they are given to the Czar by God (24), the logical con-

---

21. *Fennell* pp. 2, 4, 6, 8, 10, 180, 184, 198, 202, 204, 206, 208 *(carica),* 210 *(carica),* 214 *(carstvo),* 216 *(carskaja vysota),* 228, 236 *(san carskij),* 242 *(sluxi carskije),* 246 *(blaženne carstvoval jesi* – sic!), cf. further *Kurbskij* col. 8, 10 *et passim,* where Ivan after 1547 is quite consistently spoken of as the Czar.
22. See above pp. 49.
23. *RIB* t. XXXI col. 418.
24. Cf. above p. 21.

sequence must be that the Czar's responsibility to God includes consideration for the boyars, both human and political. Kurbskij's writings make it
abundantly clear that he maintains the first part of this view, fully and
consistently, that is, that the Czar has humane obligations to his magnates,
and that he cannot permit himself to persecute them arbitrarily and without
ceremony. But in Kurbskij's account of the matter, the Czar's political responsibility to the boyars is much more complicated.

His general political views are most clearly expressed in *"Istorija o Velikom Kn'aze Moskovskom"*. No reference, however, can be found to the
Boyar Council, *bojarskaja duma,* as an organ to which the Czar is morally
or actually legally obligated. This is not at all due to Kurbskij's refusal to
acknowledge the unification of the realm under Moscow's Grand Duke, and
thereby the status of the boyar families as the Czar's assistants, since in
that case he would not, of course, have described the first part of Ivan's
reign up to 1560 as a happy and fortunate period for the country, as he in
fact does. What is striking is that Kurbskij brushes aside *bojarskaja duma*
and instead calls attention to another organ, "the Select Council" (*izbrannaja rada*), to which he ascribes the fortunate period of the reign (25). Kurbskij thus weakens every conceivable argument in favour of the traditional
instrument of boyar power, since the fortunate results of the first period
of Ivan's reign, both in home and in foreign policy, were ostensibly due to
collaboration between the Czar and this quite untraditional and never before
heard of organ, which thus acquires the character of a radical innovation
in the Muscovite government, a manifest replacement of the boyar government of the previous years during Ivan's minority.

The natural consequence of this is that Kurbskij cannot be described as
an advocate of the traditional boyar government, since he actually as a
programme presents a political and administrative break with the boyar
tradition as the pattern according to which Groznyj ought to govern. The
matter becomes more complicated, however, when it is considered that the
expression *izbrannaja rada,* which otherwise is unknown—and which, as
far as the second word is concerned, is a Polonism like the many other reflections of Kurbskij's new life to be found in his diction (26)—designates
a construction which covers a phenomenon already well known, the small,
executive organ within *bojarskaja duma,* normally called "the Privy Council", *bližn'aja duma.* Thus we get the peculiar—and from a historical point
of view extremely misleading—situation, that on the one hand, Kurbskij
invents a special organ, that is to have both the responsibility and the credit
for the fortunate period of the reign, and that on the other hand, Groznyj
declared that he was a minor and a passive instrument in the hands of the

25. *Kurbskij* col. 12.
26. Cf. however *Fennell* p. 204: *"izbrannyj sovet"*.

political leaders during this same period, and thus renounced all part in both the responsibility and the credit, which seems further to confirm Kurbskij's invention (27).

Nor is there from this point of view any basis for describing Kurbskij as an advocate of the traditional boyar system, but it is evident that the interpretation requires particular consideration in connexion with the fourth and last of the criteria mentioned above, whether Kurbskij maintained the interests of the boyars in discussing political tendencies to limit their prerogatives and their power.

A priori, it must appear quite evident that Kurbskij does not maintain the interests of the boyars when he speaks of the reform period as a happy and ideal epoch in Groznyj's reign. The special mark of that period was the attempt to reach a compromise between the political and economic interests of the boyars and the objectives of the centralized government. The policy of compromise naturally meant limitations of the powers the boyars had hitherto possessed, and Kurbskij could not have avoided knowing and being conscious of this, even though he praised this same policy by reference to *izbrannaja rada*. The question is, however, whether he tried— as *I. I. Smirnov* claims (28)—to give the credit for the reform period to *izbrannaja rada* so as to give the men in that organ the prestige accruing from that glorious period. Kurbskij certainly ignores completely the part played by the bureaucracy, the growing class of civil servants recruited mainly from the middle class, in the reform period and the subsequent years. It must be taken as certain that Kurbskij's *izbrannaja rada* was identical with the boyars' *bližn'aja duma*. And the result of these assumptions must necessarily be that Kurbskij is trying, one-sidedly, to ascribe to at any rate a section of the boyar group all the credit for the reform policy, at the expense of the Czar, the church, the bureaucracy—called *d'jačestvo*—and other forces in the community.

This, then, is the utmost that can be said in confirmation of the criteria mentioned above for determining Kurbskij's attitude, to boyar policy. On the one hand, it is too slender a foundation to support the allegation of Kurbskij's traditional, political attitude, or, if you will, of his "reactionary" advocacy. But on the other hand, it is probably an adequate basis for the conjecture that Kurbskij wanted to point out the boyars' part in that glorious period so as to show how politically unjustifiable it was to persecute the boyars with terror. It is tempting to put it in this way, by saying that at most, Kurbskij shows a "reactionary" attitude by ascribing to a section of the boyars a "progressive" attitude. This formulation, however, is not only

27. *Smirnov* pp. 157–165, *Zimin Ref.* pp. 323 ff.
28. *Smirnov* p. 157.

anachronistic, but is also undoubtedly formed as a reply to a question that is wrongly put.

It is extremely likely that Kurbskij himself would have been unable to answer the question of whether he supported the boyar system or the autocracy. He shows no sense of perceiving dividing lines in questions of political principle, and it may well be that he would have dismissed the question on the ground that whether the country had one type of government or another, was of less importance than that, whatever the government, it should be minded to live and act in accordance with divine and human laws. If Kurbskij is to be labelled, it is perhaps most correct to call him a representative of a sort of "aristocratic neutrality". He never says how the government ought to be carried on, whether wars should be fought or not, or whether they should be fought against this or that enemy; whether the nobles or the clerics, the citizens or the peasants should be first considered. His programme, constantly repeated, is simply that the country must be governed with the help of good advisers, and that certain intellectual and moral qualifications must be assumed in the ruler.

The aristocrat shows in Kurbskij when he declares that it is not seemly that a gross and uneducated, perhaps even irascible, man should be ruler or general or assume the role of judge over more refined spirits, praising some and censuring others (29). There can be no doubt of whom he is thinking here—he speaks elsewhere of Groznyj's savagery, *l'utost'*, both in style and in act (30). But in this connexion it must be remembered that Kurbskij's demand for an aristocratic style by no means brings him into line with the boyar policy as such. Kurbskij's ideas of what is fitting for knights— *muži rycerskije* (31)—were quite foreign to the boors who had created the atmosphere round Ivan in his boyhood and who had inspired him with hate. Kurbskij's attitude is consequently based more on the aristocracy of intellect than on that of birth. Of course he could throw up his long array of ancestors to Groznyj (32), but for him the crux of the matter was quite obviously that Groznyj did not correspond to his idea of a noble and worthy ruler, purely personally. As to ancestors, Groznyj's descent was not worse than Kurbskij's.

There is a certain connexion between Kurbskij's requirements in the well qualified ruler and his requirement that this ruler should govern with the help of good advisers. One of the worst disqualifications that Kurbskij can throw at Groznyj is the assertion that he surrounds himself with flatterers and sychophants—*laskateli*—whose attitude to the Czar, for they have

29. *Skazanija kn'az'a Kurbskago*, izd. vtoroje *N. Ustr'alova* Spbg. 1848) p. 253.
30. *Fennell* pp. 180, 134, 234, cf. *Kurbskij* col 8, 109, 191 f.
31. *Fennell* p. 184.
32. *Ibid.* pp. 182, 210.

neither principle nor conscience, brings him to lead an immoral life, both as a ruler and as a man (33). To Kurbskij, this may probably be considered less the result of the unfortunate effect of the milieu on the individual, but all the more as the consequence of this morally weak and vain individual under conditions that do not support the urging and controlling function of conscience (34).

Thus in two ways the ruler ought to be limited and restrained in the instinctive, primitive and vulgar self-assertion of the individual: partly by refinement by intellectual exercise and experience, and partly by the influence of elevating and inspiring surroundings. Viewed in a concrete, political context, this is naturally a perfectly neutral view, and characteristically enough, Kurbskij's form of demonstration of the justice of his view is more religious than political. In the preface to *"Novyj Margarit"* he shows how the flatterers' proposals and advice causes the Czar to commit acts for which sooner or later God must punish him, for example, by allowing enemies to enter the country. The fact that the Tartars of the Crimea could burn down Moscow itself in 1571 then becomes Kurbskij's principal proof in his argumentation (35). The enemies are God's instrument of punishment, just as the fall of Constantinople was regarded as divine punishment because the Byzantines wavered in the true faith.

This is not Kurbskij's own, original line of thought, nor is it typical of the boyar group. It will be remembered that Ivan Groznyj himself uses the idea on several occasions, sometimes as proof of how badly things go when the Czar does not govern efficiently, and sometimes as proof of how much God appreciates the autocracy (36). Certainly, it must be added that Groznyj, to a much greater extent than is usual, connects this proof with a quite concrete assertion of causal connexion. The decline and fall of the Byzantine empire in his historical review is explained not only as a sin that brought God's punishment, but above all as due to political division and relaxation of discipline, which through weakness led to destruction. Groznyj has in fact taken the final step from a religious to a political causal explanation, although—as we have seen—without abandoning religious argumentation at very important points. Groznyj's last and decisive argument against Kurbskij, when he wants to justify his acts, was precisely the long-term claim that God showed His grace and satisfaction by permitting the Czardom to flourish and the Russian armies to conquer. Even in 1577, Groznyj could write triumphantly to Kurbskij that God drowned all the Czar's transgressions in

33. *Ibid.* pp. 8, 204, 230, 234, 236, 240, 242, *Kurbskij* col. 109, moreover 6, 99, 102, 103, 104 105, 107, 110, 119.
34. *Fennell* p. 128 infra, *Kurbskij* col. 102.
35. *F. Liewehr op. cit.* p. 56, cf. *Fennell* pp. 204–206, 228.
36. *Fennell* pp. 56, 71, 84, 188.

the depths of his mercy, and all the enemy towns fell before his armies on all fronts, powerless before the life-giving cross, *životvor'aščij krest,* and before God's will—also the town of Wolmar, whence Kurbskij had written his first letter to the Czar (37). Here his secularized, political thinking gives way to a religiously based belief in his good fortune—which, of course, from a polemical point of view leaves Groznyj extremely vulnerable to corresponding arguments advancing failure of his military fortune as the expression of divine displeasure.

Kurbskij was not slow to exploit these polemical chances when the fortunes of war turned against Groznyj. With ill-concealed malice, he writes from the newly conquered Polock of the sad consequences of Groznyj's bad government. Polock had once been taken for Groznyj by his good men and generals, including Kurbskij, but now he can see the result of Toporkov's advice to avoid wise counsellors. He has had to surrender Polock, and he has had many other military reverses, and the only thing he can do is to quarrel like a drunken servant-girl (38). Here we recognize the motif from *"Novyj Margarit":* the Czar's moral decay under the influence of evil counsellors and flatterers is answered by failing fortune in war. The repitition is not identical, however. In the letter to Ivan, it is not said explicitly that his adverse fortune in war is God's punishment for Ivan's sins, but only that it is a consequence of Ivan's replacement of good advisers by bad ones, which approaches an explanation that is secularizing and political, like Groznyj's.

This difference is worth noting, because Kurbskij's use of the formula in *"Novyj Margarit"* is quite obviously the most conventional at that time. It is known from the anonymous *"Povest' nekojego Bogol'ubiva muža",* which is usually taken to have come from the ranks of the service nobility, like Peresvetov's writings (39). This is an account of a Czar, whose predominant traits were orthodoxy and love of law and justice (*sud i pravda*). He shone over the world like the sun—this, of course, was also Iosif Volockij's expression, borrowed from Agapetos (40)—and his enemies feared him, since God was his helper (41). But one of his favourite advisers— called a *sinklit,* from the Greek *sygklētos,* and thus a member of a council— enters the service of the Devil, and practises "sorcery", *čarodejstvo,* on the Czar, so that both ruler and people come to suffer many misfortunes thereby (42). As the Czar gradually becomes confused as the consequences of

---

37. *Fennell* pp. 188, 194–196.
38. *Ibid.* pp. 234–236, cf. 240, 244.
39. *N. K. Gudzij: Istorija drevnej russkoj literatury* (5. izd., Moscow 1953) p. 322.
40. *Migne gr.* t. LXXXVI col. 1180 (kefal. 51), *Prosvetitel'* p. 602 cf. *Posl. Volock.* p. 184.
41. *F. Buslajev: Istoričeskaja xristomatija cerkovnoslav'anskago i drevne-russkago jazykov* (Moscow 1861) col. 877.
42. *Ibid.* col. 878.

his "lawlessness", *bezzakonije,* appear, one of his evil counsellors prompts him to gather his armies and march against the menacing enemies, which brings the Czar to suffer an overwhelming defeat (43). The Czar now appeals to God for Help. The reply is that he does not deserve help, since he has put his trust not in God but in evil counsellors in the service of the Devil. God tells him, however, that his sins are forgiven and that he must again march against the enemy. This time the Czar wins a great victory and can return home in triumph (44). The evil *sinklit* and his fellow conspirators are then executed at the instance of the Czar and the bishop, and all sorcery is formally forbidden (45).

It seems impossible to determine when this pamphlet was written. *P. A. Sadikov* ascribes it to the circle of writers round the Metropolitan Makarij, and considers it an attack on the group that Kurbskij calls *izbrannaja rada* (46). *I. U. Budovnic,* on the same basis, thinks that he can show that Sil'vestr was the target for the unknown writer's polemics, and emphasises that, because of the date of composition, it cannot be taken as an attack on Groznyj's advisers in the terrorist period (47). *A. A. Zimin* conjectures, on the other hand, that it was written in the second half of the sixteenth, or rather in the seventeenth century, and that it is directed partly against the boyars in general, and partly, perhaps, against some of Groznyj's assistants in *opričnina* (48).

This last view is less surprising than it might seem at first glance. It is, of course, not improbable that a publicist has felt that the most extreme representatives of both the boyar system and the autocracy must be repudiated. Thus it seems probable that Kurbskij—with his outlook and cultural orientation, described in the previous pages—must have been repelled by the traditional boyar policy, carried out by "proud lords" (*gordyje pany, pregordyje sinklitove*) in the period before the break with Groznyj, in the same way that he was revolted by the autocracy's use of force (49). That it is possible to draw from his writings only the negative conclusion that at any rate he does not express adherence to the boyar policy, the explanation may well be that he did not begin to write until after the break with Groznyj, when the autocracy had become the supreme problem in his eyes, while the boyar policy belonged to the past. Kurbskij's polemics are

---

43. *Ibid.* col. 879.
44. *Ibid.* col. 880 f.
45. *Ibid.* col. 882.
46. *P. A. Sadikov: Očerki po istorii opričniny* (Moscow-Leningrad 1950) pp. 11 f. See also *Smirnov* p. 202.
47. *Budovnic* pp. 220 f.
48. *Zimin Per.* p. 430, cf. *R. P. Dmitrijeva* in *TODRL XIV* (1958) pp. 278 ff.
49. *Kurbskij* col. 5: *gordyje pany,* cf. col. 6 on the rivalry between *pregordyje sinklitove* round about 1547. The "proud lords" and "inordinately proud Councillors" do not correspond to Kurbskij's ideal, which will be defined below.

always topical. It must be assumed that the author of *"Povest' nekojego Bogol'ubiva muža"*, too, had a topical object. Unlike Kurbskij's publicistics, however, this tale is told in such abstract terms that nothing definite can be said about its polemical aim.

If it is assumed that the tale was written very late, that is at all events during or after the *opričnina*-period, perhaps even as late as in the *smuta*-period, it seems most improbable that the author's aim should have been so objective as to be directed at both the most brutal assistants of the autocracy and its most out and out opponents. The polemiser must be expected to train his guns against one particular side, and only one. Moreover, it would seem probable that the author—if he wrote his tale during the terrorist period—would turn against those perpetrating the terror and not against its victims. On this view, it seems strange that also *A. A. Zimin* assumes summarily that the tale is mainly for Czarism and against the boyars, as is generally taken for granted. If the tale was written at a relatively late period, it must be supposed that the talk of sorcery would refer to Groznyj's court, of which Kurbskij mentions rumours that foreign wizards and magicians had been brought in to point out lucky days and to read omens (50).

If now the other possibility be taken, that the tale was written at an early period, that is, while Makarij was active, and in any case, before *opričnina*, it is easier to accept the view that it is directed against the boyars alone. For several reasons, this seems to be the most probable. The argumentation is so simple that it is difficult to imagine that it was composed later than the correspondence between Kurbskij and Groznyj or than Kurbskij's *"Novyj Margarit"*, with which, as stated, it has some traits in common. *A. A. Zimin* emphasises that on the one hand, the tale has a quite primitive character, operating exclusively with extremely tangible religious reasons and even with magic as a decisive factor, and that, on the other hand, the tale has certain obvious likenesses to Peresvetov's secularizing, political writings (51). But that these two traits appear together is better explained if an early date is assumed for the tale, closer to Peresvetov's active publicist work, than if it is taken as having been produced so late that there would seem to be little probability of the coincidence of these two traits, which in themselves are incommensurable.

There is other evidence pointing in the same direction. It seems to fit best into Makarij's ostentatious period that here we meet the classical picture of the Czar as the radiant sun. In Kurbskij's mention of the warnings given to Groznyj against Sil'vestr, which included accusations of sorcery (52), there may perhaps be an allusion to the ideas that permeate the tale. Finally,

50. *Fennell* p. 242.
51. *Zimin Per.* pp. 430, 431.
52. *Kurbskij* col. 101.

there is the remarkable point, that the Czar in the tale is not directly, personally, to blame for the misfortunes that occur, for these derive from the sorcery of the evil counsellors, of which the Czar himself is also a victim. The guilt is that of the evil counsellors alone. This conception is very close to the mediaeval Russian description of a *nepravednyj kn'az'*, who, according to *V. Val'denberg* sins by choosing ill advisers instead of good ones, and though on their advice brings misfortune to his people, yet has no responsibility for the evil doings—a conception that differs from the Western European description of a *rex iniustus* or *rex tyrannus,* who takes part in the criminal acts himself and is responsible for them (53). This primitiveness seems more in keeping with the tale's origin in the time before the terrorist period than after it.

These observations are not meant to point to a particular time as that of the composition of the tale. The lack of clear internal evidence either of style or of content compels resignation on this point. But the observations that can be made undoubtedly serve to set Kurbskij's position in a clearer light. The anonymous author, Kurbskij and Groznyj are at one in regarding good fortune in war as a sign of divine grace. This author and Kurbskij show a striking likeness in the way they use central concepts: both speak of the Czar's *bezzakonije,* one in consideration of *sud i pravo,* the other of *sud i pravda,* and both—and Groznyj too, for that matter—use the foreign word *sinklit* for councillors, instead of the more usual word *sovetnik* (54). On the other hand, there are conspicuous differences between the three parties: compared with the anonymous author, whose ideas are purely religious, Kurbskij—in the correspondence, at any rate—adopts a more concrete, political attitude, which finds expression in his tendency to explain ill fortune in war by political causes; but compared to Groznyj, Kurbskij is clearly less inclined to think on secularizing, political lines. Then there are the differences in intention. The anonymous author was probably directing his attack against the boyars, possibly against the leaders of the policy of compromise such as Sil'vestr, possibly against certain representatives of the *opričnina* system. Kurbskij turns against the Czar and his terrorist system, but not on behalf of the boyar system. The Czar argues for the system of which he wields the power.

If it is to be assumed that the resemblances between Kurbskij and the anonymous author are due to direct influence of one upon the other, then the conclusion must be that it was Kurbskij who was the borrower. As a political publicist, he is far more advanced than the anonymous author. Next, it must be concluded that Kurbskij—who of course is generally re-

---

53. *V. Val'denberg: Drevnerusskija učenija o predelax carskoj vlasti* (Pgr. 1916) pp. 111 f.
54. *Kurbskij* col. 6, 51, 53, 118, 137 etc., cf. *Fennell* pp. 8, 32, 40, 50, 56, 88, 94, 134, 156, 204, 216 cf. 236 (*sovetnik*).

garded as a representative of boyar policy—had taken over certain central concepts and motives from an author whose attitude is generally interpreted as decidedly hostile to the boyars. If, conversely, it is to be assumed that the anonymous author was the borrower, then in the nature of the case, it must be assumed that Kurbskij's far more concrete and differentiated criticism of Groznyj's system had been changed into a comparatively naive and primitive political tract, the object of which is so undefined that it is impossible to decide with any certainty whether it is Czarism or the boyar policy that is the object of its criticism. Moreover, when it is remembered that the very chief motif, of the fortune of war, is also shared by Groznyj, it is evident that such conclusions are untenable.

On the other hand, it seems obvious that great caution must be observed towards the prevailing tendency to interpret the attitudes of Kurbskij and the unknown author as respectively friendly and hostile to the boyars. Likewise, it must be concluded that the resemblances between the three polemisers is due less to direct influence of one another, than to common dependence on ideas, concepts and motives that were in the air at that time, and which were used with varying intentions and degrees of political precision during the growth of an independent political literature. That Kurbskij so strongly emphasises the role and the importance of evil counsellors, must be regarded as the result of a common line of thought, and not as advocacy of a clearly defined political line. He adopts a traditional formula so as to be able to express his political thought. And his thinking is occupied more with the fundamental conditions for political activity than with the attitude to be adopted to concrete, political alternatives.

To Kurbskij, the fundamental point is the acknowledgement of the fact that the individual is weak, and therefore dangerous when exercising power. He willingly admits that Sil'vestr was by no means a pattern for humanity—he was cunning and an intriguer. But at any rate he intrigued for good ends, that is to say, he treated the Czar's soul as a physician treats the body of a sick person: he cuts away the bad flesh with sharp knives so that the healthy flesh may remain undamaged and the body finally be healed (55). If therefore, the individual is weak and needs medical care to avoid dangerous diseases, it will be disastrous both for the individual himself and for those on whom he exercises power if those round him, by flattery and sychophancy, disguise the diseases or actually make virtues of them. Kurbskij thinks more rationally than the traditional dogma on evil counsellors who alone bear the responsibility for the misfortunes. To Kurbskij, the misfortunes are the result of evil deeds, and the evil deeds are the result of the individual's weakness when this is allowed to develop without restraint. The weak individual who is the Czar has yet been given a con-

---

55. *Fennell* p. 202, cf. *Kurbskij* col. 9.

science by God, and must therefore himself take the responsibility for his actions, if only before God on the Day of Judgement—a point, for that matter, on which Kurbskij and Groznyj are in touching agreement (56). But that this innate weakness can come to develop particularly powerfully if sychophants—*laskateli*—exercise a bad influence on him, naturally throws a responsibility on them also.

This is where Kurbskij's cultural ideal comes in. The Czar's opportunist and intriguing sychophants, who offer an immoral "cunning" or "craftiness", *lukavstvo*, instead of wisdom, and who bring only misfortune, represent a type most frequently called a *laskatel'*, but in some cases also a *man'jak*—from the Greek *maniakos*—thereby to indicate their vulgar lack of restraint (57). The aristocratic Kurbskij betrays no little contempt for these uncultured upstarts, who willingly serve Groznyj in maintaining the terror—they are bastards, vagabonds, parasites, good-for-nothings (58). There is no evidence, however, for believing that Kurbskij would have allowed himself to be led away by this contempt had it not been a matter of just those who were the agents of the terror. He directs his indignation also against the well-born Bogdan Jakovlevič Belskij, who was Ivan's favourite for many years, and maintains on the other hand that good advice may also come from "the common man", from *vsenarodnyj čelovek* (59).

If one must use an anachronistic term, then "reactionary" is not the most obvious term for Kurbskij. For this would bring one into the peculiar situation, that it would then be necessary to call the author of *"Povest' nekojego Bogol'ubiva muža"* a "progressive", because of the prevailing interpretation of his intention. Rather—if it must be so—call Kurbskij a sworn enemy of the dangerous and disastrous "personality cult", which in his opinion surrounds the Czar and is evoked by him. The crux of the matter, however, is that underlying this line of thought there is a cultural ideal of Christian and humanistic character, based on a dualist tension between sin and salvation, evil and good, weakness and strength of character. To Kurbskij's negative portrait of the evil counsellor, whom the ruler ought to avoid, there is therefore, quite logically, a corresponding idea of a positive contrast, "the wise counsellor", *mudryj sovetnik,* whose help the ruler ought to seek (60).

---

56. *Fennell* p. 228, cf. above pp. 23, 45 ff.
57. *Fennell* pp. 184, 202, 204, 230, 236, 242, *Kurbskij* col. 110.
58. *Fennell* pp. 8–10, 212–214, 242, 234.
59. *Ibid.* p. 242, *Kurbskij* col. 54 f., cf. *V. Val'denberg op. cit.* pp. 317 f., where he denies that Kurbskij is thinking of actual political representation of *vsenarodnyje čeloveki* as a counterpoise to *bojarskaja duma,* but admits that he is at any rate inconsistent, from a boyar point of view.
60. *Kurbskij* col. 51.

This opposite to a *laskatel'* and *man'jak* is sketched in clear and simple outlines here and there in Kurbskij's writings, with diligent use of standard epithets. The ideal distinguishes himself by piety and devoutness, wisdom and self-control, strength and courage, by culture acquired by the study of the Scriptures and classical literature, by experience in war and government (61). He is "distinguished"—*naročityj*—in manly virtues and in discipline, which may be seen from the many scars he has acquired during his devoted service of his country, and recognized in his temperate authority and equable speech—and that his manner is *razumnyj i tixij,* "understanding and moderate" (62). In other words, he is at once the devoted servant of a worthy cause and a worthy master, and a person whose integrity forbids that he should be treated arbitrarily. Harmonious balance is his distinguishing characteristic: he is *presvetlyj v telese i v razume,* "brilliant in respect of both physical and mental qualities" (63)—the Hellenic *kalokagathia* at once comes to mind—and thereby he has earned the right to be called a *rycerskij muž* and to play the part of the ruler's help and support.

Men who can meet such requirements in qualities and abilities are not, of course, common. Kurbskij undoubtedly considers that it is very important for the formation of this noble type that there should be favourable conditions of good birth and the upbringing that corresponds to this. He sometimes applies the epithet *blagorodnyj* or *velikorodnyj* to his ideal, which denote good birth (64). This closes the ring of required qualities, and it seems to be simply the definition of "the strong in Israel", without whom the realm cannot be governed—more or less corresponding to the older Western European concept of *meliores regni.* There is no doubt, however, that with Kurbskij much greater importance must be attached to the nobility of the spirit than to that of birth or possessions. On the one hand, it must be remembered that in the overwhelming majority of cases, his ideal portraits appear in Kurbskij's catalogues of Ivan's victims, and thus have the character of epitaphs over the martyrs to the terror, reckoning up every conceivable virtue of these unfortunates, in order to emphasise all the more strongly the senselessness and cruelty of the terror. And on the other hand, Kurbskij himself declares, as previously mentioned, that wisdom and other virtues do not necessarily go with high birth and external greatness—a man may be born to be Czar without being born with the qualities desirable in a Czar. Similarly, a man may be humbly born and yet have received the most distinguished qualities from God (65). In other words, noble birth may

---

61. *Ibid.* col. 11, 120 f., *Fennell* p. 2.
62. *Fennell* p. 230, *Kurbskij* col. 7, 136 f.
63. *Fennell* p. 234.
64. *Ibid.* pp. 210, 234, *Kurbskij* col. 7.
65. *Kurbskij* col. 54 f.

be an advantage, but is not a necessary condition for the good counsellor. It can lead to the ideal, but it is not itself the ideal.

Kurbskij's picture of the wise counsellor is undoubtedly very much an echo of former times. He himself points out that it has origin in the Middle Ages (66), and viewed in the light of his period it may well seem to contain much of the romance of chivalry. It is not always quite easy to recognize the persons behind Kurbskij's epitaphs when one meets them in other sources—he seems, like another Pindar, to use the occasion to write of noble qualities that are indispensable to him, by embodying them in heroes who in reality were boors. Groznyj himself, and not without a certain effect, contributes to reduce the temperature of the all too enthusiastic reader of Kurbskij, when he describes his childhood's experiences and the intrigues round his person (67). It is also striking, how much Kurbskij's ideal portrait resembles his self-portrait—which may seem to connect the last flattering trait with a not altogether becoming lack of modesty. Though of course a sinner, says Kurbskij of himself, he is, however, nobly born. He has undergone suffering and privation in the service of the Czar and carries the resulting scars as proof of his past as a faithful servant. He also carries the good counsellor's stamp of nobility: he is self-controlled and equable—which he emphasises with malicious irony to the Czar—and in spite of original sin, he has an understanding heart (*oči serdečnyje*) and a not untrained tongue (68). Trait for trait the reader himself recognizes the high ideal of a good counsellor, expressed in concrete, autobiographical form. What was reality, and what was imagination?

It has already been indicated that Kurbskij's descriptions of the victims of the terror are scarcely to be taken as realistic portraits, but rather as symbols of the contrast between the goodness of the martyrs and the wickedness of the tyrant. The whole of *"Istorija o Velikom Kn'aze Moskovskom"* —where these epitaphs specially appear—is built up on the contrast between the good and the evil in the person of the Czar and thereby in the community, a fight that is fought out between the good and the evil counsellors, roughly as between angels and devils (69). The devilishness of the terror is proved by the angelic character of the victims. Compared with this, Kurbskij's letters to Groznyj are quite otherwise realistic, and his self-portrait should undoubtedly be viewed in this context. In his historical account, he sketches the fight between principles, but in the correspondence, he is fighting a personal battle against the Czar. For the contrast he needs here to Groznyj's destructive and immoral savagery, his own achievements in

---

66. *Ibid.* col. 11.
67. *Fennell* p. 90.
68. *Ibid.* pp. 210, 6, 236, 198, 204, 216, 80–182.
69. See e.g. *Kurbskij* col. 120: *angelom podobnyje.*

the service of his country must be the example. And this example will show what the country loses because of the autocrat's madness. It is not surprising that he places himself in the most favourable light, since this is a weapon in his duel with Groznyj, just as Groznyj also places himself in the most favourable light in order to emphasise the darkness of the shadow of treason that lies upon Kurbskij.

There are thus two factors that must modify any consideration of Kurbskij's efforts as a political publicist and controversialist.

In the first place, it is clear that his style and his concepts are extremely reminiscent of traditional, not to say bygone ideals and standards. This is not surprising, for the same is true, in many ways, of contemporary Russian publicists, including Ivan Groznyj. Like everyone else, Kurbskij needed accepted forms of expression in which to clothe his thoughts, and he has taken those that lay nearest to his own position—but not without giving them a new content which was not directly compatible with the old. Kurbskij expresses himself in old-fashioned terms, but he is no boyar politician. Kurbskij professes Orthodoxy, but not without being strongly influenced by a humanistic outlook.

In the second place, it is evident that Kurbskij has a tactical controversial aim in his picture of the good counsellors. His historical account of Ivan's reign, covering the good and the evil periods, is the expression of a philosophy of history with a topical message. And his letters to Ivan are weapons in the campaign to spread this message. They are propaganda. The content of the message is just as simple as Groznyj's doctrine. If Groznyj's theory of the state could be roughly expressed by the formulation in the Epistle to the Romans, Kurbskij's could be said to be the requirement of the limitation of power by an earthly responsibility. When Vassian Toporkov whispered his warning against wise advisers in the Czar's ear, he sowed a seed that germinated and grew in Groznyj, and finally caused him to throw off all earthly responsibility (70). Had good seed, however, been sown in the mind of the ruler, he would have learnt to love his wise advisers like his own limbs, whose help is indispensable to the Czar, who is in the position of the head (71). For human reasons, the autocracy is impossible, both because man is weak by nature, and because there is no guarantee that he who is to exercise power is particularly suited to do so (72). Briefly, what Kurbskij wants is the limitation or distribution of power by a definition of the Czar's responsibility to his subjects.

Kurbskij was not alone in turning his thoughts to the responsibility laid on the Czar. D. S. Lixačev has emphasised that the idea of the Czar's re-

---

70. *Ibid.* col. 81.
71. *Ibid.* col. 51.
72. *Ibid.* col. 55.

sponsibility was prevalent at the time, and in this connexion maintains that in general it is not justifiable to identify this with a desire for the re-establishment of the boyar system of government, since that would not imply a limitation of the power of the Czar, and also that with Kurbskij this is joined with a demand for a limitation of the power of the Czar, and that only in this case does it take the form of an object of boyar policy (73). But Kurbskij has nowhere even so much as hinted that the definition of the ruler's responsibility should correspond with the boyar line. He has not done so for the simple reason that he himself has not contributed to the formation of a definition anything but his highly abstract ideas of the wise advisers. And as we have seen, this ideal cannot be identified with the political line of the boyar system. It will be remembered that the Iosifists also, and particularly Iosif Volockij himself, busied themselves with the idea of responsibility, in continuation of the tendencies in Agapetos (74). This was done, however, in a still more abstract form then Kurbskij's, and this line of thought, in itself imprecise and vague, had to yield to the later acceptance of the unlimited autocracy, in other words, of the limitation of responsibility to a relation between God and the Czar. Kurbskij's original contribution to a development of really political thinking in the Czardom was his persistent demand for an earthly responsibility, and his approach, at any rate, to a definition of it. Since it is difficult to imagine a political responsibility without implying a limitation of power, this general requirement cannot justify the assertion of any specific intention in line with boyar policy.

It was because of his Christian and humanistic outlook that Kurbskij opposed the autocracy and condemned the terrorism used to maintain it. He does not appear to have interested himself in the question of what would be the political alternatives if the autocracy were to be replaced by some form of limited exercise of power. When it was a matter of human rights of an individual, Kurbskij's campaign was positive, but in a political sense his campaign was negative. The immediate object of his *"Istorija o Velikom Kn'aze Moskovskom"* was perhaps just the negative one of warning the West Russian Magnates and other groups in the Polish-Lithuanian *Rzeczpospolita* against supporting Groznyj's candidature to the throne of the Jagiellons and thereby contributing to the extension of the Muscovite autocracy (75). And with this intention, he had quite naturally to remain neutral with regard to Russian domestic problems.

Here, perhaps, lies the explanation of Kurbskij's peculiarly isolated position in political history. As a publicist, he is head and shoulders above his contemporaries, and occupies a unique position in his period. But he made

---

73. *Soč. Peresv.* pp. 41 f.
74. Cf. above p. 45.
75. *Budovnic* p. 282, *Zimin Ref.* p. 8, cf. below pp. 163 f.

no contribution to the solution of the great and pressing problems that marked Russian society of his day. He did not understand where they came in. He did not perceive the forces that were at work. Above all, he did not realise that it might be a question of a just as dangerous, just as destructive and unlimited exercise of power by an oligarchy of magnates and boyars as by the autocrat and his men. But it was precisely this that was the main problem. Therefore Kurbskij did not help to prepare the way for political decisions and settlements, but left that task to others.

V

Oligarchy or Autocracy

When two irreconcilable adversaries both seem to be right, it is highly probable that neither is right. Groznyj was undoubtedly right in maintaining that he could not exercise his power as ruler without offending against his ideals of piety as an individual. And Kurbskij was just as right in asserting that the maintenance of the system by terrorism cost hundreds of innocent lives, which brought guilt on the system. One was right when he talked of the interests of the system. The other was right when he talked of those of the individual. But both were wrong, because they talked of only one of two things that are inseparably connected.

By "wrong" in this context, we mean something not very exact, a feeling that not only do the two parties not understand each other, but that they are talking in empty space. It is true of both Groznyj and Kurbskij, that if a picture of the Muscovite-Russian community were to be made based on the writings of either of them—which would not be unreasonable, for they busied themselves with the fate of that community and expressed themselves at great length—then the picture would be extremely unsubstantial and unreal. Both Kurbskij's epitaphs and Groznyj's implications leave behind them an impression of emptiness, which is the reaction to all propaganda.

Groznyj's programme was based on a view of the autocracy that was theocratic in the sense that the exercise of power denied every form of temporal control and every restraining influence of spiritual standards and definitions, but stood in a direct relation to God. On the basis of this axiom, the Czar acted as though all opposition were the work of the Devil, to be rooted out by him on behalf of the Lord and to the glory of God. He talked as though his hands were free, though they were of course bound to the sceptre and the orb, to the community whose forces and potentialities must condition his decisions and choices. Through the eyes of Groznyj we see a heavenly, not an earthly kingdom. And through those of Kurbskij we see the courtyard of Hell where good advisers should have been helping a just ruler to create an earthly abode for the free nature of man. Kurbskij, too, set up an axiom, an abstract model of a community, without considering the conditions in the community that actually existed. His postulate was that if only the Czar and his evil counsellors were denied a free hand to oppress and lead astray, then the community would come into a state of bliss of itself, automatically. Which of the two of them was the more utopian it is difficult to decide. The difference between them was primarily that the ruler both could act and had to act, while the exile could only think and polemise.

It can hardly be doubted that this difference between the situations of Kurbskij and Groznyj has had considerable influence on their thinking, wherever this can be followed, that is to say, in their writings in the period after 1564. The question is, how great was the distance between them in the period up to that decisive break.

We have seen that Kurbskij completely approves of Groznyj's government up to about 1560. He himself occupied an increasingly responsible position in the government and administration of the country; even in the years—critical and stamped by terror as they were—from the fall of Adašev and Sil'vestr to his own flight, he played, according to his own statement and that of Heinrich Staden (1), his part as the Czar's faithful servant and helper without reserve. Kurbskij was morally part-responsible for the Czar's government until his flight, and in what he wrote afterwards he did not repudiate his responsibility, except as far as the last four years were concerned. Until then, he gives the Czar, with his *blaženne carstvoval jesi,* "you, who ruled well-pleasing to the Lord" (2), a certificate of good behaviour, and a clear declaration of loyalty to what, until that moment, had been the essence of the government's policy, i. e. the reform policy, which was directed against the traditional boyar system.

We have also seen that Groznyj repudiated all responsibility for the reform period, with the tactical aim of getting Adašev, Sil'vestr and their sympathisers stamped as disloyal, self-assertive and self-appointed oligarchs. It is obvious that this claim has no greater weight than Groznyj's insinuation that Kurbskij aimed at re-establishing his family's long since abolished petty principality in Jaroslavl'. Even taking into account the point that the sources naturally ascribe to the Czar generally all the honour of acts done by others in his name, it seems improbable that from the time of his coronation Groznyj should not have had an increasing and increasingly more important share in policy and administration. Kurbskij would hardly have been interested in emphasising Groznyj's part in the happy reform period if it would not have been an obvious perversion of the truth had he denied it. Moreover, there is the fact that in the course of the reform period's decade—from 1549 to 1559—Groznyj underwent the development from the youth

---

1. *Epstein* pp. 23 f.
2. *Fennell* p. 246.

of the nineteen-year old ruler to the state of maturity that is not very far from what Kurbskij considered to be old age (3). There is nothing to indicate that Groznyj developed and matured late. On the contrary, even from his thirteenth year he was drawn to take part in violent and decisive events, which culminated in his coronation as Czar at seventeen. Consequently, it is difficult to accept the idea that, as at the waving of a wand, he should be changed into the determined and masterful ruler who appears after 1560, from the hitherto passive tool of a self-willed *camarilla*. There is no doubt that Groznyj played a central part in the policy of reform, not merely formally but also really. That later on he wrote off that policy cannot serve as a proof that he never had any share in it.

Even when allowance is made for a certain difference in interests and in character, also before 1560, it seems reasonable to assume that until the period of discord, Groznyj and Kurbskij had certain ideas in common and were united in the same main effort. The peculiar thing is that neither in Groznyj nor in Kurbskij is there anything even approaching a clear description of what is implied by this effort.

Only incidentally does Groznyj mention one of the practical results of the policy of reform in the sphere of imperial policy, the extension of the kingdom by the conquest of Kazan' (4). Kurbskij offers the reader something similar, adding merely a quite abstract description of the period as the expression of a fortunate and beneficial conduct of the government, whereby he wants to set up the radiant contrast to the shadows of the subsequent period of terrorism (5). But what were the motives behind the reform policy and what was its actual content is to be learnt only from other sources, such as the writings of Ivan Peresvetov or the monuments left by the reforms, such as *"Sudebnik"* and *"Stoglav"*. Because of this lack of clarity, it is impossible to find in Groznyj any substantial declaration of points in the policy of reform from which he might dissent. He simply declared that the whole period was dominated by an oligarchy, and that this had to be brought to an end so that the autocracy could be fully realised. Nor is it possible to find in Kurbskij any concrete reason why he commemorates with panegyric epitaphs the same magnates whom, with evident repulsion, he calls *pre-gordyje sinklitove*. The most probable explanation is that the oligarchy he had helped to remove, now, in retrospect, seemed to him the lesser evil in comparison with the terrorism of the autocracy.

It is naturally this attitude of Kurbskij's that has given rise to the persistent view of him as the typical representative of *bojarstvo*, the boyar system and the boyar class. The argument of the previous pages has aimed

---

3. In his 36th year, Kurbskij spoke of himself as having arrived at old age, *Fennell* p. 182.

4. *Ibid.* p. 92.

5. *Ibid.* p. 204 cf. *Kurbskij* col. 12 ff.

at showing that this view is fundamentally wrong, and that in reality Kurbskij did not represent any political alternative to the course of the autocracy and Groznyj. That, none the less, an attitude quite obviously not his has been attributed to him for centuries, is beyond doubt primarily due to the complete lack of a clearly formulated boyar policy in that period. Groznyj's polemical implications cannot serve as a source for elucidating the views and intentions of the boyar group, but only for clarifying the Czar's interpretations or tactics. Nor, in the light of these observations, can Kurbskij be accepted as a source. And there are no other voices. It is precisely this lack of a formulation of boyar policy that has led to the vacuum being filled out with Kurbskij's manifestos. There were no statements from any other source that could correct the error.

A more realistic conclusion of the lack of a formulated boyar policy has not been drawn until recently, by *A. A. Zimin,* who maintains that the boyars in Groznyj's time did not aim at a return to the feudal division and disruption of the past, but, on the contrary, had recognized that centralized government had come to stay—and consequently now sought to exploit this form of government for their own advantage, above all, their financial advantage (6). In the presentation of this view, the occasion is not taken, strangely enough, to revise, at the same time, the traditional view of Kurbskij as the typical representative of the boyars, though on the basis of the new evaluation, this description of him is less tenable than ever.

This picture of the boyars as opportunists and tacticians, who exploit the system of government for their own advantage and gain, but do not set up any political alternative to the Czardom, corresponds very well indeed with the evidence from all sides. The chronicles relate one story after another to illustrate the arrogant and scheming self-assertion of the boyars. In his polemics against the boyars, Groznyj could bring many direct and convincing accusations of greed and egoism, but no proofs of a really political opposition. Kurbskij does not hide his misgivings with regard to the self-assertive, proud magnates, *gordyje pany,* and actively helped to strengthen the Czar's government against them. Were there any possibility of talking of a boyar policy or of boyar opinion within the framework given here, there is at any rate no possibility at all of putting Kurbskij into this category. The boyars are primarily characterized by their opposition to reforms and measures that for them would mean loss and not gain. But Kurbskij is characterized politically by the fact that he helped to carry through these measures, and ever since declared that this was a happy epoch in Groznyj's reign.

We have here spoken of the boyars in contradistinction to Kurbskij, al-

6. *Zimin Ref.* p. 224 dissociating himself from *Smirnov* pp. 3, 27.

though Kurbskij also was a boyar. The two parties cannot be spoken of as an identity, because they belonged together only socially, not politically. In his implicative characterization of Kurbskij, Groznyj was guilty of an untenable generalization, so far as his person was concerned. But it must be added that it is quite extraordinarily difficult to generalize about the boyars as a group when the traits just mentioned are taken into consideration. Kurbskij was not the only member of this social group who differentiated himself from them politically. *A. A. Zimin* emphasises the obvious fact that other members of the boyar nobility had realised that there must be a break with traditional concepts and institutions, in other words, that there must be reforms in the centralized Russian state (7)—reforms that, directly or indirectly, meant a limitation of the prerogatives of the boyars. For this reason alone it is difficult to operate with the term *bojarstvo* as an unambiguous political concept.

It is not surprising that it should be so. By the unification of the old petty principalities under Moscow, and the incorporation of the Muscovite boyars into the court of the Grand Prince, the foundations of a new structure of society had long ago been laid, a structure that faced the boyars with new conditions and tasks, and consequently with a variety of choice. And therefore the variation in the choices actually made ranges from support of the Czar by Kurbskij and other reformist boyars, to Adašev's administration, through cases of hesitation and double-dealing—as during the succession crisis of 1533—to opposition to the policy of reform. This spectrum of possibilities of choice and reaction makes the traditional scheme of interpretation—according to which the central government of the Czar met with compact opposition from the conservatism of the boyars—both illusory and unsatisfactory. It is only by assuming the presence of an extremely various and often highly improvised political activity, in which there was both subtlety and stupidity, traditionalism and reformism, cupidity and self-sacrifice, that it is possible to attempt to understand the widely different roles assumed by the boyars under Groznyj's rule.

Such an extremely varied pattern gives rise to extremely varied judgements and interpretations, corresponding to the outlook of the rest of the cast or of the historical observer. It has already been mentioned that two such distinguished historical observers as *I. I. Smirnov* and *A. A. Zimin* make, at an essential point, what are formally incompatible judgements, in that the first maintains that as a political group the boyars were characterized by the desire to return to the feudal state of division, while the latter maintains that, on the contrary, they wanted to promote their financial and political interests by exploiting the existing, centralized apparatus of

---

7. *Zimin Ref.* p. 311, *Očerki* p. 293.

government. Neither of these interpretations is supported by explicit, formulated manifestos from *bojarstvo* or sections of them. The study of the boyars' political practice tends as a whole to support the second interpretation. But there seems to be no doubt that both these main attitudes were represented—rarely in clear, undiluted form, usually in various combinations—during the boyars' fight for their interests. Neither interpretation can be taken as final.

Something similar is undoubtedly true of the other point, where *I. I. Smirnov* and *A. A. Zimin,* starting from the same sources, also go their own, individual ways, and that is, on the question of the political role of the Metropolitan Makarij in relation to the boyars (8). When, on the one hand, it is assumed that Makarij, as one of the most prominent and consistent of the Iosifists of the period—and as a distinguished political tactician— took Czarism forward to victory, it is clear, at the same time, that he had to carry on his tactics in conjunction with the boyars, and even that the given forum for his manoeuvres was *bojarskaja duma* itself (9). And when, on the other hand, it is asserted that Makarij attained his key position by the support of the Šujskijs, and that in the first part of his tenure of the office of Metropolitan, at any rate, he acted in the interests of that group, then it is equally clear that Iosifism, in its patently political form and its consistent support of Czarism, was not presumptively incompatible with the interests of a powerful and leading boyar group. And here the sharp dividing lines fade into ambiguous confusion.

These observations are not intended as a contribution to a fuller description of *bojarstvo* as a political group, but only to show the need for such a broad investigation. Nor are the previous observations on Andrej Kurbskij claimed to be exhaustive, but are meant as operative means for the formulation of clearer definitions. Even though the need for more extensive and intensive research has occasionally been acknowledged, on the conditions determining Kurbskij's writing (10), for example, there has been remarkably little interest in historiography and in literary research in these phenomena, compared with the thorough and pioneering work done on the other social and political groups of the period, especially on the publicistics of the Iosifists, the heretics and the reformists. In spite of the perspicacity and thoroughness that, especially in recent decades, have been devoted to the study of the politics and publicistics of the sixteenth century, students have been content with the traditional conception of *bojarstvo* as a united, anti-Czar and anti-reform group with Andrej Kurbskij as their spokesman—

8. See above pp. 58 note 66, 59 note 71.
9. See above p. 59, note 68.
10. *Moisejeva* p. 4. *M. P. Aleksejev: Javlenija gumanizma v literature i publicistike drevnej Rusi* (IV meždunar. s'jezd slavist. Moscow 1958) p. 34.

which admittedly is a clear definition, but a definition in conflict with the facts. The road to clear conceptions and formulations must be carried round this traditional judgement and straight through acknowledgement of the caprices of the confusion.

It is not surprising that in that period, too, unjustifiable generalizations were made. Groznyj's condemnation of the boyars *en bloc* as one great conspiracy against the Czar's government was such a generalization. And so was, as mentioned above, his characterization of Kurbskij as one of the conspirators and as claimant to the sovereignty of Jaroslavl'. This was Groznyj's judgement in 1564 and later. It is scarcely possible to determine whether he was himself fully convinced of the correctness of this judgement, or whether it served merely as a weapon in his propaganda war and a justification of his terrorism. On the other hand, it can be stated that his judgement was not in accordance with reality.

Not only was his characteristic of Kurbskij fundamentally wrong, but his condemnation of the boyars in general was in disregard of the fact that a number of boyars served him and his system with consistent loyalty, both in the period up to the decisive break and in the years after 1564 (11). Moreover, Groznyj included in his condemnation persons who did not belong to the traditional boyar group, Adašev and Sil'vestr. These leading figures in the reform policy were accused, after the change of system, of having conspired with the boyars and promoted their interests, so that they were full participants in the great conspiracy against the Czar. In reality, this means that the boyar concept as a designation for a social group is broken up, leaving behind a term for a political group, which is characterized by its inclusion of all forms of treason against the Czarist government. And the concept of treason against the Czarist government is again defined as including every form of opposition to the will of the Czar (12).

The only concept that is not defined within the framework of Groznyj's argumentation is his own will. It has previously been stated that it is inconceivable that the policy of reform could have been contrary to the will of the Czar in the reform period itself, but that Groznyj later maintained that it was carried through against his will. In considering Groznyj's own statements and actions, it must be asked whether it is possible to describe his intentions as anything but the arbitrary exercise of power—and whether his judgements of his opponents, whether real or imaginary, express anything other than arbitrary interpretations.

On the basis of what has been advanced hitherto, it seems that the answer

---

11. Kurbskij himself is an example of the first. Examples after 1564: Afanasij V'azemskij, Mal'uta Skutarev-Belskij, Vasilij Gr'asnoj, Aleksej and Fedor Basmanov, cf. *Epstein* p. 28, *P. A. Sadikov: Očerki po istorii opričniny* (Moscow-Leningrad 1950) p. 48 f.
12. See above p. 23 with references.

must be in the negative. In the first place, Groznyj's own theory of the state bound him only to look after the interests of the realm and of the faith, and to nothing else, both obligations to be understood in a sense defined by himself, and fullfilled by whatever means he might at the given moment find appropriate. In the second place, the religious ideology by which he justified his own exercise of power did not represent a supra-state check, that could limit his liberty of action on moral criteria. In the third place, his great adversary in political propaganda, Kurbskij, set up no political alternative to his system, nor did he represent any active opposition group within the frontiers of Russia. And in the fourth place, the boyar class was so heterogeneous a group, considered as a political factor, that the Czar could utilize sections of it as his tools and yet at the same time condemn it as a whole on the basis of an arbitrary, collective characterization.

The picture that thus emerges does not, consequently, show a struggle for power between the Czar's centralized government on one side and on the other, a united boyar group's well defined attempt to resurrect the de-centralized division of power. It shows rather a struggle between autocracy and oligarchy on the basis of the centralized governmental system—a struggle between the Czar's increasing demand for an individual, arbitrary exercise of power and the magnates' just as individually inspired and ar-bitrarily realised wishes to share in the government and obtain a share in the privileges of power. It would be premature, however, to assume that the question is answered by these considerations. The question of the exercise of power was not decided by a duel between the Czar and the boyars, nor was the reform policy the result of their rivalry. The course of the reform period is often, and with justice, described as a policy of com-promise (13), since both Czar and boyars had to act on the basis of the common condition which was that other forces in Russian society made themselves felt with decisive effect.

Six months after Ivan's coronation as Czar, the great fire at Moscow set some of these forces off in an explosion. There had been warnings of such an eventuality. The chronicle reports unrest among the unprivileged ele-ments of the population of the capital, the *černyje l'udi,* as early as ten years before (14). And the catastrophic fire on Tuesday 21 June 1547 has evidently evoked the dangerous and uncontrollable connexion between dis-content and panic. Both Kurbskij and Groznyj, in a more restrained man-ner, express their horror at the catastrophe, the extent of which must have seemed to have a transcendental significance. Both interpreted it as a divine judgement (15). But to the common people, whose wooden huts had become

---

13. *Očerki* p. 301, *Zimin Ref.* p. 311.
14. *PSRL* t. XIII p. 118: *"mnogije l'udi Moskov'skyje pokolebalis'a byli",* cf. *Zimin Ref.* p. 289 f.
15. *Kurbskij* col. 8, *Fennell* p. 80.

bonfires and whose thoughts ran on the crooked paths of superstition, it was obvious that the explanation must be sought in dark deeds done on the spot. According to Groznyj and the chronicler, a group of boyars made use of the panic to excite the population against the Glinskijs, accusing the Czar's grandmother, Anna Glinskaja, and her children of having taken out human hearts and steeped them in water, with which they thereafter sprinkled the streets of Moscow and so caused the fire (16). What the learned called the admonition of the Lord from on high, the people thought had been done by Satan's helpers on earth. And the tumult was directed against the sinners pointed out to the people.

It should be remembered that the distance between the learned and the common people was hardly so great as might at first sight have been expected. It is typical, that it is only Kurbskij who passes over the tale of Anna Glinskaja's magic in complete silence. He notes simply that the riot arose after the fire, and that it was directed against the Glinskijs, of whom Prince Mixail Glinskij was "the leader in the evil deeds", *vsemu zlomu načal'-nik* (17). This must undoubtedly be understood purely politically, as a reference to Mixail Glinskij's part in the Czar's exercise of power (18), and not as an indication of his being a party to arson by magic. Kurbskij remains neutral between the Czar's accusation of the boyar group for raising the populace, and the boyar group's accusation of the Czar's family of causing the fire by sorcery. To him, magic was only nonsense. Groznyj, however, accepts the idea to some extent, for in his reply he asks why his own familiy should wish to destroy his inheritance from his forefathers, or how it would be possible to sprinkle a high church tower with the magical water from below in the streets (19). This reply is only half-rational. Had it been wholly so, Groznyj might have asked why anyone should take the trouble to use human hearts to start a fire, let alone water, when a well placed torch would have been the most effective means of achieving the desired result.

Rational arguments had but little value in this context. It is true that Groznyj declares that it was "people of the utmost simplicity", *narod xudo-žajšix umov,* whom the boyars stirred up with their story. It was at that time, however, not only the poorest in spirit to whom fire and water were mystic elements, and not merely physical phenomena, and to whom a decoction of human viscera for magical sprinkling or burnt sacrifices were realities. Conditions in Russia did not differ from those in Western Europe, where the records of the courts reflect the seriousness of the belief in

---

16. *Fennell* p. 80, *PSRL* t. XIII p. 456.
17. *Kurbskij* col. 8 f.
18. Thus *Zimin Ref.* p. 299.
19. *Fennell* p. 82.

magic (20). Consequently, it is by no means improbable that certain of the boyars really did explain the catastrophe as due to magic worked by their opponents, and that their explanation won widespread acceptance. The very fact that the boyars lacked clear political ideas and formulated programmes made it natural to turn to the traditional, mystical forms of expression, just as Groznyj felt it quite natural to call his opponents servants of the Devil, or to accuse his enemies of trying to murder him by means of *čarodejstvo*, sorcery (21).

It cannot be taken for granted, however, that with this explanation the boyars simply exploited the superstition of the populace, deliberately and with cynical cunning—or, if you will, with tactical genius—with the object of turning popular anger against the subject of their own hostility. Perhaps they themselves were fully convinced that Anna Glinskaja was a witch, and that here lay the explanation of all problems. Perhaps, too, there was panic in the highest circles also, that had to find an outlet in mystifications. It seems convincing when *I. I. Smirnov,* in his penetrating interpretation of the sources for the history of the crisis, comes to the conclusion that the accusation against the Glinskijs was made at the highest level as early as Thursday 23 June, three days before the disturbances, and that at that moment Ivan Groznyj had had to agree to a serious discussion of the accusation and to order an inquiry, and even that the Metropolitan Makarij himself seems to have had a hand in the game (22). The accusation of witchcraft was thus probably something other and more than a demagogic trick played on the ignorant mob. It was the expression of a struggle for power round the person of the Czar, fought out in his entourage. It was his own family on his mother's side, and thereby the leading magnates of the last

---

20. *Wallace Notestein: A History of Witchcraft in England from 1558 to 1718* (Washington 1911) pp. 8 f. on accusations of sorcery in political intrigues, *ibid.* pp. 282 f. on accusations of arson. *Margaret Murray: The Witch-Cult in Western Europe* (Oxford 1921) p. 158 on decoctions of viscera for use in magic. On sorcery in popular Russian superstition, see *Dmitrij Zelenin: Russische (Ostslavische) Volkskunde* (Berlin-Leipzig 1927) pp. 395 f., *D. Ušakov:* Materialy po narodnym verovanijam velikorussov = *Etnografičeskoje Obozrenije* t. XXIX–XXX, 1896/1–3 (Moscow 1897) pp. 165 ff. It is remarkable that everywhere fire and water have a double, magical function in the service of both the good and the evil. The witches were purged of the evil in them by burning, and in certain cases the presence of evil was proved by using water, see *W. Notestein op. cit.* p. 99. In Russian Orthodox religiosity, the water of baptism played a magical, not merely a symbolic part, see *Ad. Stender-Petersen: Russian Studies* (Copenhagen 1956) pp. 56 f., *E. E. Golubinskij: Istorija russkoj cerkvi. Period vtoroj, Moskovskij,* t. II/2 Moscow 1917) pp. 514 ff., cf. modern Protestant criticism of the Eastern Church as inclined to sorcery, so *Ernst Benz: Die Ostkirche im Lichte der protestantischen Geschichtsschreibung* (Munich 1952) pp. 245 f., 258 f.
21. *Pozl. Grozn.* p. 178. See also above p. 78.
22. *Smirnov* pp. 125 f.

four years, after the fall of Andrej Šujskij, who were now the target. And the action against them was undertaken by an alliance, the leaders of which came partly from the Czar's wife's family, the Zaxar'ins, partly from the Iosifists with the prelate Fedor Barmin, who may have had Makarij behind him, and partly from the Šujskij group, led by Fedor Skopin-Šujskij and Jurij Temkin (23).

When the partners in this alliance are considered separately, it is not difficult to explain their hostility to the Glinskijs. The Šujskijs had a four-year old account to settle with them. The Zaxar'ins could well have reason to be jealous of their power. In both cases, a purely political explanation is in itself adequate, but an alliance between the two parties, however, is surprising. The Šujskijs were hostile, the Zaxar'ins friendly to the Czar (24). As for Makarij and the Iosifists, the matter is more complicated. Politically, the high church movement consistently supported the Czar, and may have been anxious at the influence of the Glinskijs as a power group, just as Makarij, four years before, had found it necessary to neutralize the Šujskijs. But for that very reason, an alliance with this last group must have been rather improbable. It is natural here, to include religious motives in the explanation. The high church must have felt that it was vital to fight every kind of superstition, witchcraft and magic—*volxvovanije, čarodejanije, koldunstvo*—that lay outside the dogmas of the church and threatened its integrity (25). Makarij or prelates under him can hardly be thought of as agreeing to a tactical exploitation of the superstition of the populace for purely political motives, however much they were themselves affected by them. Such a proceeding would be tantamount to encouraging the belief in witchcraft. If, on the other hand, they had any reason to suppose that the accused really practised magic arts, it then becomes extremely probable that they would support an action against the accused, even though they had no particular sympathy with the political motives of the other accusers. The most likely solution is that Makarij, from both political and religious motives, was deeply concerned by the situation and what might develop from it.

In considering this alliance, it is natural to assume that this heterogeneous bloc was formed by external pressure. It is a fact, at all events, that such a pressure existed, and that it came from the open discontent with the government among the *černyje l'udi*. From Novgorod, the chronicler reports quite frankly that the misrule, *nepravda*, of the magnates flourished primarily in Moscow, and thence spread over the country, and that they broke the

---

23. *PSRL* t. XIII p. 456 cf. *Smirnov loc. cit.*
24. For the Zaxar'ins, see *Smirnov* pp. 202 ff.
25. See the traditional, canonical provisions against *koldunstvo* in *RIB* t. VI (2. izd., 1908) col. 919, cf. 4 and appendix 332.

peace, gave arbitrary judgements (*nepravo*) and levied heavy taxes (26). When now this situation—in itself intolerable—became strained to break-ing-point in Moscow in consequence of the catastrophic fire, those at the head of affairs naturally considered the possibility of bringing it under con-trol by making certain sacrifices. It was precisely at this moment that the Glinskijs were at the height of their power and were the most exposed, the most envied, the most feared, the most tainted with the arrogance of power, and also, perhaps, seriously suspected of seeking the support of supernatural forces. It was therefore they it was easiest to agree to sacrifice before it was too late.

Three days later, on Sunday 26 June, it was clear that the sacrifice must be made, but that even so it was too late to get the situation under control. Ivan Groznyj's uncle, Jurij Glinskij, who had apparently come to the Krem-lin to take part in the inquiry into the cause of the fire, was chased by the excited mob into the Uspenskij Cathedral, where he was murdered before the Metropolitan's throne (27). Apparently the authorities made no effort to save Jurij Glinskij, which would also have been both risky and undesir-able in the given situation. The excited populace was not calmed even by the sight of the body of Jurij Glinskij in the carrion pit. After three more days, on Wednesday 29 June, the mob marched out to Vorob'jevo, outside the capital, where the Czar was staying, with the object of forcing the Czar to deliver up old Anna Glinskaja and her son Mixail Glinskij. This involved the Czar personally in the dangerous situation, with consequences nobody could have foreseen.

According to the officially inspired "*Carstvennaja Kniga*", the Wednes-day passed without any great trouble, from the Czar's point of view. It was a casual crowd that came to Vorob'jevo with its demands, and the Czar disposed of the matter by ordering the leaders to be arrested and executed. Many of the participants fled, according to this account, repentant of their foolish doings, to other towns (28). Thus the crisis is said to have been re-solved by a display of force, and the rising fanfare of revolution faded out in a *cadenza d'inganno*.

Seventeen years after these events, Groznyj gave a similar account, but added, however, that the mob intended to kill him also, besides the Glin-skijs (29). This addition may be understood in two ways. It may be a tactical strengthening of the accusation against the boyars: according to Groznyj, not only had they stirred up the populace against the Glinskijs, but also

26. *PSRL* t. IV (1929) p. 620, cf. *Smirnov* p. 122.
27. *Smirnov* pp. 126–130 with references. *Istoričeskij Arxiv*, t. VII (Moscow 1951) pp. 220, 272.
28. *PSRL* t. XIII p. 457.
29. *Fennell* p. 82.

against the Czar himself in order to get him out of the way. But the addition may also be taken as a hint that the situation at Vorob'jevo was far more dangerous and unpredictable than the officially inspired chronicle makes it. The Novgorod chronicle also says that the Czar was taken by surprise and was panic-stricken, that he *udivis'a i užases'a* (30), on seeing the crowd from Moscow. Further, *I. I. Smirnov* adduces strong arguments to show that the mass demonstration was in reality a levy of train-bands, in fact, a regular military formation, ordered out by the decision of the Muscovites' town assembly, *veče*, and that it succeeded in forcing the Czar to make certain concessions, for example, to allow his quarters to be searched (31). On this interpretation, Ivan was himself in the situation that in order to save himself he had to persuade the force from Moscow that the Glinskijs were not, in fact, with him, with the prospect that—if the Glinskijs had been there—he would have had to surrender to the Muscovites and hand over his grandmother for execution in order to save his life and his crown.

Whatever the truth of the matter, one result of the crisis, at all events, was that the role of the Glinskijs as a power group was played out. The policy of compromise and reform did not follow immediately after (32), but in the long view it was a reply to the challenge made manifest so clearly by the crisis. These long-range political effects of the crisis are probably a complete proof that the social tension, visible long before the great fire, were the main reason for the development and that the catastrophe itself and the subsequent accusations of witchcraft were only secondary causes. It was a question of a permanent problem, needing fundamental measures for its solution, and not a casual crisis, the expression of which could be supressed by administrative measures.

That *"Carstvennaja Kniga"* presents the affair within the framework of this last mentioned view is obviously to allow the Czar to figure in the most flattering role and to hide his problematic situation. That there is no hint, from the boyars' side either, of a realistic, political evaluation must be due to the fact that the disturbances in Moscow were primarily directed against the magnates' exercise of power, and that they themselves were primarily occupied with defending their interests. If the general object of the boyars was to gain a share in the centralized government, and thus obtain the greatest possible share in the privileges of power, this object, individualistically inspired and high-handedly realized, is difficult to reconcile with the realization of a permanent problem, the fundamental solution of which must be wholly or partly at their expense. This does not, however, apply

30. *PSRL* t. IV (1929) p. 621, cf. *Smirnov* p. 134.
31. *Smirnov* pp. 132–135 with references.
32. *Zimin Ref.* pp. 311 f. against *Smirnov* p. 136.

to Moscow's *černyje ľudi,* whose position made them vitally interested in emphasising the permanent character of the problem and in extorting fundamental solutions. But although their political interests and motives were the exact opposite of those of the boyars, it is clear from all the sources that the rising in Moscow was never at any time accompanied by a manifesto going beyond the very narrow, short-term and therefore quite inadequate object, that of killing off the Glinskijs.

The lack of the formation of political ideas naturally helps to explain this. Considering that political phenomena were regarded, also in the narrow circle of power, as aspects of religious concepts and described in religious terms, it is not surprising that among the common people similar conditions prevailed. There were not the means for perceiving and reasoning politically, nor for formulating political standpoints. Unknown forces were in action. These forces were taken to be something other than they were. Since political concepts did not exist, concrete problems had to be viewed in the light of non-political generalizations and abstractions. And so action was taken, an action conditioned either by intrigue or by superstition, and which never at any time served a clear strategy. Thus the action was ambiguous and confusing.

If the Muscovite populace—as maintained by Groznyj, seventeen years later—allowed itself to be stirred up by a boyar group to murder the Czar's family and the Czar himself, this meant that Ivan could rely neither on *bojarstvo* nor on *černyje ľudi.* As we have seen, however, the situation was more complicated. Against the Glinskijs acted also another branch of the Czar's family, the Zaxar'ins, and the Iosifist prelates, in other words, two of the Czar's buttresses. And they acted in alliance with traditional enemies of the Czardom, especially the Šujskijs. What Ivan experienced, six months after he had been crowned as Czar, was that he found himself in a situation without clear and certain front lines. The Czar's family was divided against itself. The Glinskijs had been the support of the Czardom against the other boyar families from a very early stage, but were now, in the eyes of the people, compromised as the very quintessence of the magnates' system, of the oligarchy of the boyars. In their reaction against the oligarchy, the people had threatened the Czar himself—in a sense they had identified him with the oligarchy. According to one source, he replied with terrorism, according to another, with panic. Neither of these heralded political collaboration. And the church, the Czar's traditional, ideological supporter, including perhaps Makarij too, Ivan's guide and champion for many years, had helped to force on this ambivalent situation. In reality, the seventeen-year old Czar found himself in the midst of a *bellum omnium in omnes.* Formally, he was the autocrat, whose word all must obey.

It must be emphasised

that belief in witchcraft was not confined to the most primitive of the common people, and that irrational, uncontrollable forces formed part of the considerations and ways of thinking of those in power,

that none of the forces or groups discussed so far represented clear political objectives or plans, but that such were required in the intolerable situation of things, and finally,

that the Czar, not only as ruler but also as a person, had been drawn into a dangerous and obscure situation. On this basis, the question of Ivan Groznyj's political arbitrariness, as far as his intentions and interpretations are concerned, must be answered in another way than seemed natural at first glance. If the view is to be taken that Groznyj's intentions were only the arbitrary exercise of power, the rejoinder must be that his acts were his reply to arbitrariness. And if it seems obvious that Groznyj's judgements of real or imaginary adversaries consisted of arbitrary interpretations, the reply must be that his surroundings afforded no grounds for interpretation other than precisely arbitrariness.

Attention must now be directed to ideological and political forces which, unlike those discussed hitherto, represented tangible political intentions, and to a great extent also a rational political way of thinking and formation of ideas. These forces may be roughly grouped in two social categories, the civil servants, *d'jačestvo,* and the service nobility, *dvor'anstvo.* Both categories were closely bound to the Czarist government, since they were in its service and dependent on its grace, and at the same time they were the indispensable pillars of this government and could consequently exercise great influence on its dispositions. They had grown up, so to speak, with the centralised royal government and could not be divided from it.

Kurbskij maintained that the Czar should value the wise advisers, *mudryje sovetniki,* as the head values the limbs of the body (33). It is typical of Kurbskij's lack of political realism that with this metaphor he is not thinking at all of the Czar's *d'jaki,* although these had occupied a position in the growing administration of the kingdom that was constantly increasing in importance, especially in diplomacy and finance (34). They had grown from simple chancery clerks into politically influential chancellors, while the class was still to a large extent recruited from the common people. There was thus a double reason for antagonism between the boyar nobility and this class. The privileged felt contempt for these upstarts in the government of the country, corresponding to the arrogance of the nobility of later times

33. See above p. 84.
34. *G. Vernadsky: Russia at the Dawn of the Modern Age = A History of Russia,* Vol. IV (New Haven 1959) pp. 4, 118, cf. *N. P. Lixačev: Razr'adnyje d'jaki XVI veka* (Spbg. 1888).

towards the bureaucrats, *krapivnoje sem'a* (35). And the nobles were irritated by their role in the apparatus of the centralized government—an irritation that could explode in hate and murder. When Kurbskij talks of the "Russian clerks" who enjoy the Czar's confidence though he draws them neither from the nobility nor any other well-born source, but from *prostoje vsenarodstvo,* and whom he uses against the magnates—this is undoubtedly an echo of the boyars' ordinary hostility, and also, of course, a sign of the position of the hated clerks in relation to the Czar's government, as emphasised by *I. I. Smirnov* (36).

Here, too, however, there is reason to shake the traditional, undifferentiated identification of Kurbskij with the boyar standpoint. It will be remembered that in another context he emphasises the priority of personal qualities over inherited position, even going so far as to enjoin the Czar to seek counsel not only from noble counsellors but also from the common man, *vsenarodnyj čelovek* (37), provided they have understanding. Thus he by no means maintains, unconditionally and consistently, the monopoly of political influence of born aristocrats. Moreover, his approval of the political course from 1549 to 1559 shows that for that period, at all events, he cannot have identified himself with the boyars' hostility to the *d'jačestvo* and the role of this group in the new administration. It seems probable, however, that he found these civil servants unworthy to be called *mudryje sovetniki* for the quite particular reason that they did not—as his ideal required (38) —unite loyalty to the sovereign with dignity and integrity, which the Czar could not outrage without formality. In Kurbskij's eyes, the lack of this last quality must have stamped many of them as *laskateli,* time-servers and yes-men.

The position of civil servant could be unenviable. Great influence was often bought with great risk, and in many cases was paid for with great misfortune. At the beginning of the century, under Vasilij III, the distinguished diplomat Vasilij Dalmatov was thrown into prison when he declined a mission, and the property left by another *d'jak* was confiscated without ceremony by the Czar (39). During the boyar regime after Vasilij's death, Fedor Mišurin was murdered by agents of the Šujskijs (40), and under Groznyj, Ivan Viskovatyj rose to great power and influence, and finally, after many years of service, was executed (41). Cases like these

35. *R. Pipes: Karamzin's Memoir on Ancient and Modern Russia* (Cambridge, Mass. 1959) pp. 16 f.
36. *Smirnov* p. 261.
37. *Kurbskij* col. 61.
38. *Kurbskij* col. 54, cf. above pp. 81 f.
39. *G. Vernadsky op. cit.* p. 140.
40. *Materialy* pp. 38, 49, *Fennell* p. 74.
41. *Materialy* p. 79, *Epstein* p. 40.

were not foreseen in Kurbskij's ideal picture. He imagined a harmonious state of society, where wise advisers were rewarded and respected for their services without being exposed to arbitrary treatment. His lack of political realism is shown, in the first place, by the fact that such conditions could be achieved neither under the oligarchy of the boyars nor under the autocracy of the Czar, and that consequently his ideal could not be realised, and in the second place, that the *d'jaki,* in spite of their unprivileged position in society and their unstable conditions as individuals, could yet exercise great influence in spite of other pressures in the community.

In Groznyj's growing administrative apparatus, *d'jačestvo* represented administrative continuity through all changes and fluctuations. It is difficult to trace their influence from case to case, but it is indicated by their appointments, participation in negotiations, and diplomatic missions, involvement in conflicts and intrigues. Behind these outer manifestations, there was, as indicated by Kurbskij, a tangible and practical activity which laid no ideological or other restraint of principle on the Czar, but which yet bound him to concrete decisions in particular cases on the basis of administrative judgements and deliberations. If *iosifl'anstvo* with the religious basis for the Czardom was Groznyj's reflection as God's representative on earth, then *d'jačestvo* was the mirror in which he saw himself as the administrator of the kingdom, responsible for the appropriate handling of business and its effective accomplishment.

It can by no means be taken for granted that the spiritual and the temporal mirrors gave the Czar the same answer. On the contrary, in many cases there was open rivalry between church and administration. In the critical years round the turn of the century, when the *st'ažateli* fought for the ecclesiastical estates and Ivan III leaned towards the heretics, his *d'jak,* Fedor Kuricyn was clearly in favour of an extensive secularization, both economically and politically, for in the administration he showed himself to be an adherent of the liquidation of the ecclesiastical estates, and in his writings as a spokesman for intellectual freedom in relation to the church's spiritual discipline (42). Kuricyn thus linked the financial interests of the state with heretical free-thinking in a common front, the decisive strength of which was to come from the royal power itself. In *"Skazanije o Drakule Vojevode"*, which must undoubtedly be ascribed to Kuricyn (43), a prince is described who certainly had a number of evil passions, envy, pride, even heresy, and thus corresponds almost word for word to Iosif Volockij's sketch of *car' mučitel',* a tyrant and a servant of the Devil (44), but who, with his harshness and ruthlessness towards all alike, high and low, rich and poor,

---

42. *Posl. Volock.* p. 370.
43. *J. S. Lur'je: Povest' o Drakule* (Moscow–Leningrad 1964) pp. 8 ff., 42 ff.
44. Cf. above p. 45.

yet at the same time fought against injustice in his kingdom. Although he paid no attention to traditional religious requirements and ideals, he was a good ruler because he was *groznyj* towards every sign of *nepravda* (45).

This was an extreme formulation of ideas that were widespread among the intellectual officials, and in varying forms came to have their effect during Ivan Groznyj's reign. In the course of the decades, these ideas gained further strength by the adhesion of the spokesmen for *dvor'anstvo*, the service nobility, at the same time as this group's importance and influence as the Czar's instrument increased.

In Ivan Peresvetov, as spokesman for the service nobility, the same motifs appear in clearer ideological form. Against *nepravda* he sets up *pravda*, as cosmos against chaos. One principle is the ideal of society and the object of all good government, and the sign of it is that uniform legal rules and laws prevail, and that judgement is impartial and without respect of persons (*pravyj sud, suditi pr'amo*). The other principle is expressed in arbitrariness and high-handedness, in the oppression of the weak by the strong, and thereby also in disorganization and divisions in the kingdom. Good government is achieved by the ruler exercising his power over all his subjects with ruthless authority, *groza*, while the evil system is maintained by the unrestrained display of their *krotost'* by the magnates, their effeminacy or lack of principle. Thus the Czar and autocracy stand for cosmos. For chaos, stands the oligarchy of the magnates. And between the two principles no compromise is possible (46).

It must have been in the years round the beginning of the reform period that Peresvetov laid his thoughts before Groznyj (47), and the ideologically related, anonymous tract *"Beseda valaamskix čudotvorcev Sergija i Germana"* appeared about the same time, probably in the spring of 1551 (48). Its kinship with Peresvetov's writings classifies it as an expression of the opinion in the *dvor'anstvo*, while its quite fundamental differences from Peresvetov shows the breadth and differentiation in that opinion.

Here, also, the ideal is *pravda*, realised by means of the Czar's *groza* (49). The Czar must be strong enough to rule alone and absolutely—if he is not, he had better abdicate. He must, of course, have helpers, but they must have no power over the Czar himself (50). The ruler does not deserve the title of Czar if he allows the slackness and high-handedness of his subjects to undermine discipline and thereby doom the kingdom to destruction (51)

45. *J. S. Lur'je op. cit.* pp. 117–122.
46. *Soč. Peresv.* pp. 153 ff., 167.
47. *Zimin Per.* pp. 268–271.
48. *Moisejeva* p. 87.
49. *Ibid.* pp. 166, 170 f., 174, 192.
50. *Ibid.* p. 163.
51. *Ibid.* pp. 175, 164.

—a warning that corresponds to Peresvetov's emphasis on the danger in the ruler's remissness towards the magnates' *krotost'*, whereby the kingdom collapses and breaks up, as happened with Byzantium and with Israel (52). Both authors, however, consider it proper for the Czar to rely on his paid troops, *dvor'anstvo,* who are his faithful and obedient helpers in the securing and the maintenance of the kingdom (53).

This line of thought, which in the main was a continuation of the principles in Fedor Kuricyn's writings, was directed against both the boyars and the church. Peresvetov and the anonymous author have this in common, that they move forward with greater tactical caution than Kuricyn had done a generation earlier. It was probably only his political influence and his evident prestige with Ivan Velikij that saved him from being condemned as a heretic (54). His successors both sought cover, each in his own way, and therewith their ways in forming this line of thought more concretely came to diverge. Peresvetov directed his attack primarily against the boyars, and presented more or less detailed proposals for the reform of the system of justice, the army, and financial administration (55). With respect to the church, however, he was strikingly neutral. The anonymous author, on the other hand, is primarily interested in liquidating the ecclesiastical estates and in resisting every form of church influence in politics, but at the same time betrays a much more strongly marked interest in spiritual discipline than Peresvetov.

According to Peresvetov's theory, the autocracy, by exercising *groza,* is to secure a state of society that is marked by *pravda.* This state is characterized by an efficient and uniform organization, appropriate to ensure a united and independent kingdom, a *volnoje carstvo* (56). The ultimate aim, in other words, is purely worldly. But Peresvetov does not maintain a worldly basis for his argumentation. The efficient organization of society "is a heartfelt joy to God" (*pravda Bogu serdečnaja radost'*), he claims as the decisive argument—nothing is more strongly asserted in the Scriptures than this, he continues, even that to God, *pravda* is dearer than *vera,* the "faith" (57). The fate of the Byzantine empire is the best proof of this assertion: the Moslem Mohammed won God's favour by introducing *pravda* into the empire, inspired by what he had read about it in the Christian literature; on the other hand, it roused God's anger that Christian Byzantium, maintain-

52. *Soč. Peresv.* pp. 152, 182, 183.
53. *Ibid.* pp. 174 f., 178 f., *Moisejeva* p. 166.
54. *J. L. I. Fennell: Ivan the Great of Moscow* (London 1961) p. 331, *E. E. Golubinskij: Istorija russkoj cerkvi. Period vtoroj, Moskovskij,* t. II/1 Moscow 1900) p. 590, *J. S. Lur'je op. cit.* p. 58.
55. For a full account and discussion, see *Zimin Per.* pp. 339–392.
56. *Soč. Peresv.* pp. 161, 177, 182.
57. *Ibid.* pp. 153, 177, 181 f.

ing in externals the true faith, yet fell into weakness and division because of the offences of the magnates (58). All this is maintained by Peresvetov, with unambiguous reference to the contemporary state of Russia. He warns the Czar against the dangerous heresy (*jeres'*) of the magnates, their sorcery (*čarodejstvo*) (59), thereby himself assuming the position of the faithful champion of Orthodoxy.

This, however, was quite obviously a purely tactical position. Peresvetov operates with the accepted concepts, but he means by them something quite other than the official meaning. What he calls heresy and sorcery are simply the characteristic results of the traditional boyar position, especially their use of the right of departure, *ot'jezd*, and their exercise of local administration, *kormlenije*. Thus he gives some examples of the most passionately held religious concepts a purely worldly, political definition. It is also quite evident that he measures God's approval and joy in a particular form of government by a purely tangible and worldly yardstick, that form of government's ability to survive all political trials and tribulations. Good fortune in war is here taken as proof of God's grace (60).

It must be assumed that Peresvetov, by this mode of proceeding, hoped for two advantages. First, he wanted to underline the absolute priority of his political ideals by connecting them with the most absolute form of legitimation of the period. Secondly, he wanted, as a precautionary measure, to pay his tribute to the officially accepted dogmas, which it was dangerous to oppose. Considering Peresvetov's sudden disappearance from the scene in the fifties, however, it is doubtful if he succeeded in veiling his challenge to the prevailing dogmas (61). His heresy was scarcely less evident to his contemporaries than it is to posterity (62).

It is evident that *"Beseda valaamskix Čudotvorcev"* also goes very far in the direction of a secularized way of thinking. As with Peresvetov, God's grace is measured here by the strength and prosperity of the state under the rule of the autocrat, *samoderžec* and his soldiers (63). It leads only to misfortune, however, if a kingdom is governed by clerics and according to the rules of the cloister. Priests must not meddle in worldly affairs. The church must look after its own, spiritual matters, and the Czar and his helpers must strengthen and secure the kingdom (64). Consequently, the Czar is not answerable to any church authority. He is also over the church in the sense that he is answerable direct to the Highest Judge for all who are

---

58. *Ibid.* pp. 152 f., 157, 160, 177.
59. *Ibid.* pp. 173, 176, 178, 183.
60. *Ibid.* pp. 137, 169.
61. *Ibid.* pp. 355–358.
62. *Ibid.* p. 392, *Lur'je* pp. 499, 507 f.
63. *Moisejeva* pp. 173, 163.
64. *Ibid.* pp. 172, 173, 174, 175.

under his jurisdiction (65). In this sharp distinction between spiritual and temporal comes also the anonymous author's open criticism of the role of the church as a landowner, and his call to make over the land to those who by military or other worldly service have earned it (66), in other words, the *dvor'anstvo*.

And so with complete consistency, the author turns on vital political and financial interests of the church. It has been emphasised previously that the financial interests survived a royal attempt to change these conditions, but that the political ones, on the other hand, the church had completely written off (67). But what remained of the desire to assert an *ecclesia militans*, especially Makarij's evident partiality for the idea of such a *voinstvujuščaja cerkov'* (68), was here faced with an open challenge. It is noteworthy, however, that both financially and politically this challenge corresponds closely to a tendency in the crown right from the time of Ivan Velikij. Apart from these clearly defined objectives, the author has nothing to criticize in spiritual matters. He strongly attacks the heretical movements, and openly breaks with Fedor Kuricyn's assertion of the individual's intellectual freedom. Man cannot be *samovlastnyj* "his own master" or *samovolnyj*, "doing what he likes", he cannot have liberty of action when he must live under a *samoderžec* (69). The two principles cannot be combined.

By this the author put a distance between himself and Peresvetov, who though he maintained the necessity of discipline, yet asserted that God created man to be *samovlastnyj*, to be master and not slave (70). Here, Peresvetov and Kurbskij stand near each other, on a common, humanistic basis—Peresvetov's formulation closely corresponds to Kurbskij's *svobodnoje jestestvo čelovečeskoje* (71). But the anonymous author, contrary to all humanistic principles, maintains the men should keep within the framework of spiritual discipline: certainly, the individual cannot prevent himself from thinking, but he must not lose himself in doing so (72). *G. N. Moisejeva* is undoubtedly right in maintaining that the author's intention with this is to break the common front between heresy and free thought on the one side and the campaign to secularize the ecclesiastical estates on the other. The tactical advantage in this was that it prevented the church from identifying the two things and fighting them together, as in Kuricyn's time (73).

---

65. *Ibid.* p. 162.
66. *Ibid.* p. 173.
67. Cf. Chapter III.
68. Cf. below p. 121.
69. *Moisejeva* p. 174.
70. *Soč. Peresv.* p. 347.
71. Cf. above pp. 65, 70.
72. *Moisejeva* p. 171. Cf. the Iosifist attitude to personal opinions, above p. 52.
73. *Ibid.* p. 113.

With Ivan Groznyj's manifesto of 1564 and his later writings in mind, it is clear how much he had in common with the ideological opinion originating in *d'jačestvo* and *dvor'anstvo*. The points of agreement may be listed as follows:

1) Groznyj's religious justification for the Czardom leads logically to the position that he is answerable to God for the acts of his subjects as for his own. This closely corresponds to the declaration in *"Beseda"*, that the ruler must take the responsibility for all (*ko otvetu za vsex*) to the Highest Judge. The resemblance to this formulation is greater than with the place in *"Prosvetitel'"* mentioned earlier (74).

2) Groznyj's historical justification, with references to Byzantium and Israel, corresponds in principle to Peresvetov's historical justification, but represents an extremely secularized interpretation of the church thesis of Moscow as the Third Rome (75).

3) Groznyj's political justification, that the autocracy is necessary for the security of the kingdom, corresponds to Peresvetov's conditions for a *volnoje carstvo,* and to the emphasis in *"Beseda"* on the security of the kingdom under an autocrat (76).

4) Groznyj's appeal to political and military good fortune, including the fortunes of war motif, as proof of God's grace, corresponds to the ideas on this in *"Beseda"* (77).

5) Groznyj's declaration that the Czar must rule, but not be ruled by others in the kingdom, is anticipated in *"Beseda"*. He agrees with the rejection in this tract of individual freedom (*samovlastnyj* or *samovolnyj čelovek)* and clearly repudiates Peresvetov's humanistic ideal, since he condemns the individual's *samovolstvo* and partly also the concept of *svoboda* (78).

6) Groznyj declares clearly and unambiguously that priests, and thereby the church, must not meddle in politics, which is the basic idea of *"Beseda"* (79).

7) Corresponding to Peresvetov's rejection of the concept of *krotost',* which has a religious ring, Groznyj declares that it cannot be right for a ruler to turn the other cheek in accordance with the biblical precept (80).

8) The distinction consistently made by Groznyj between a life in piety and life in the state, as two different aspects, is presented in *"Beseda"* as a basic idea (81).

---

74. *Fennell* p. 124, *Moisejeva* p. 162, above p. 45.
75. Cf. above p. 50, *Soč. Peresv.* pp. 152, 157, 160, 177.
76. Cf. above pp. 26 ff., *Soč. Peresv.* pp. 161, 177, 182, *Moisejeva* pp. 163, 173.
77. Cf. above p. 76, *Moisejeva* p. 173.
78. Cf. above pp. 23, 35 f., *Soč. Peresv.* p. 347, *Moisejeva* p. 174.
79. Cf. above p. 24, *Fennell* p. 26, *Moisejeva* p. 175.
80. Cf. above p. 26, *Soč. Peresv.* pp. 152, 182, 183.
81. Cf. above pp. 24, 52 f., *Moisejeva* pp. 172–175.

9) Like Peresvetov, Groznyj characterizes *ot'jezd* as a violation of *kresto-celovanije* and thereby a sacrilegious act similar to heresy (82).

Whether it is preferred to explain these points of agreement as the result of direct influence of these writings on Groznyj, or as the expression of a more indirect spreading of ideas then in the air, it must at all events be clear that Groznyj's manifesto on the Czardom and especially his tendency to a secularizing way of thinking have their origin as far back as in the years round the beginning of the reform period. At a time when the traditional forces in the kingdom—the boyars, the church, and also the Czar's own family—presented a confusing and capricious play of circumstance and intrigue, Groznyj met a far more consistent, purposeful and well defined line of thought emanating from the new forces in the society, from the men in the administration and from the service nobility. These circles presented arbitrariness, intrigue and high-handedness as sin that would lead to the destruction of the kingdom. And the way to fight this arbitrariness, they claimed, was the resolute abolition of the oligarchy and the introduction of the Czar's autocracy. A *volnoje carstvo* was conditional on a *volnoj car'*, a ruler whose will could not be curbed (83).

On this basis, it cannot have surprised Ivan that Peresvetov makes his mouthpiece in one of his tracts burst into tears at the thought that *pravda* had not yet been brought into the Russian realm (84). It was, of course, Groznyj himself who was to do this. And the justification for his existence as ruler depended on his doing it—if not, he was told, he had better abdicate (85). The only question was, with what means and by what decisions this aim was to be achieved. And with this, we have come to the crucial criterion for the evaluation of Groznyj's relation to the reform period and the question of his political arbitrariness.

---

82. Cf. above pp. 39, 68 f., *Soč. Peresv.* pp. 173, 175 f.
83. *Soč. Peresv.* p. 177.
84. *Soč. Peresv.* pp. 176, 344 f.
85. *Moisejeva* p. 163.

VI

The Gordian Knot

We must now turn our attention for a while from the word to the image.

In the Tret'jakov Gallery's collection of icons there is one of the most peculiar and most fascinating of the monuments of the reform period, known as *"Cerkov' Voinstvujuščaja"* (1). Under the pressure of a new doctrine the traditional forms were broken. The traditional, vertical form, which compels the eye to concentrate on the relation between the heavenly and the earthly, is here replaced by the horizontal, epic breadth in a *makimono*. Most of the horizontal field of vision is occupied by three compact columns, the riding and marching warriors of which are given with many realistic details and differentiating shades of colour, but taken as a whole appear as the heavily advancing, collective and anonymous instrument of worldly power. The army is moving away from the right, where, at the extreme edge, and enclosed in a circle, there is a glimpse of a burning town, and towards the left. Here the upper part is occupied by a circle or halo, which surrounds a sort of *kreml'*, the holiness of which is emphasised by the presence of the Mother of God. Under this holy city, there runs a river through a landscape, flowing out of a large pool and thence running further through one of two smaller pools, while the other is empty and dry. From the left, angels are flying towards the army, with palm branches in their hands.

While this and similar icons were being made, Pieter Bruegel, in another corner of Europe, was painting in a manner that permits posterity to enjoy the direct, aesthetic viewing and to become immersed in deciphering the ingenious symbols and allegories of the pictures. To a Western eye, there is nothing surprising in finding that an icon like *"Cerkov' Voinstvujuščaja"* unites supple composition and refined artistic expression and a symbolism, the presence of which is obvious, but the meaning of which is hidden for the uninstructed observer. To the Russian of the time, however, it was by no means to be taken for granted that the language of symbol should go

---

1. Reproduced in *I. E. Grabar': Istorija russkogo iskusstva*, t. III (Moscow 1955) pp. 568 f., 571. Height, 1·42 metres; breadth, 4·26 metres, cf. *Demetrius Ainalov: Geschichte der russischen Monumentalkunst zur Zeit des Grossfürstentums Moskau* (Berlin-Leipzig 1933) p. 104.

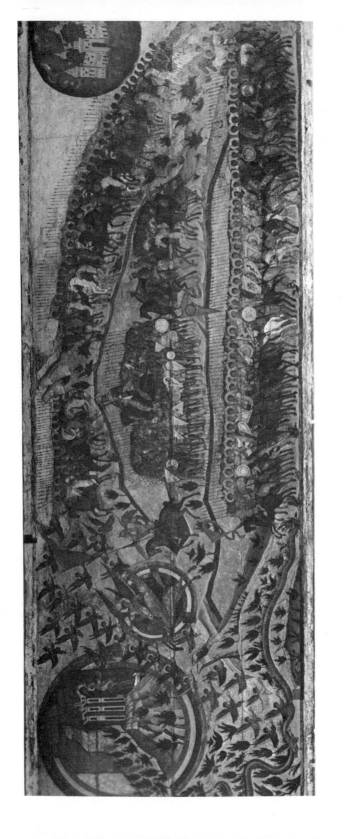

Plate 1 : The icon *Cerkov' Voinstvujuščaja* (Gosudarstvennaja Tret'jakovskaja Gallereja, Moscow).

Plate 2: Detail of plate 1. Left part of the icon.

Plate 3: Detail of plate 1. Central part of the icon.

Plate 4: Detail of plate 1. Right part of the icon.

outside the traditional formulae for the expression of piety. This was a disruption and a complication of the symbolism hitherto in use.

The meaning of *"Cerkov' Voinstvujuščaja"* in its main features is clear enough (2). It is possible to discuss whether the holy city represents the heavenly Jerusalem described by St. Paul (3), or whether it symbolizes Moscow itself. But such discussion is probably a waste of time, when it is remembered that the boundary between the heavenly and the earthly were vague in the notions of Moscow as the Third Rome or the New Jerusalem (4). The river flowing from the landscape round the holy city is, of course, a symbol of the faith that gives life, which fills one pool—but, be it noted, only the Orthodox faith—while the other remains ·empty like the heretical movements and the erroneous forms of Christendom, not to speak of heathendom. The burning town is undoubtedly heathen Kazan' after Groznyj's capture of that town in 1552. The returning forces are led on by the Archangel Michael (5), St. Vladimir, Dmitrij Donskoj and Aleksander Nevskij (6), probably also by Constantine the Great—but first and foremost by a central figure that must certainly be identified as Ivan Groznyj (7). The philosophy of this picture thus consists in a stressing of the historical continuity of the Czardom as the worldly instrument of Orthodoxy.

The art of painting is thus taken up as a means of expression by the publicistics of the period. It is no longer only a form in which to manifest piety, but now, also part in a discussion and a struggle. *"Cerkov' Voinstvujuščaja"* is one of the clearest examples of this, but in its time it was only one of many. It is known that a whole series of frescoes with the same motifs decorated the Gold Salon, *Zolotaja Palata,* in the Moscow Kremlin from the beginning of the fifties until it was destroyed in a fire (8). In the Church of the Ascension in the Svijazsk Monastery, there are still frescoes a good ten years younger, and as donors Groznyj and Makarij are represented side by side (9). On the face of it, it would seem natural to draw a parallel between this publicistic tendency in painting and the general tendency to engage the church in worldly matters and in the life of the nation. It is obvious, however, that these tendencies cannot be identified with the Czardom's utilization of the support of the church and of a religious

2. Cf. *N. E. Mneva* in *I. E. Grabar' op. cit.* pp. 574–576.
3. *Hebr.* XII,22.
4. Cf. above pp. 48 ff.
5. Cf. *Fennell* p. 110.
6. Cf. *ibid.* p. 12.
7. For another, but less probable interpretation, see *D. Ainalov op. cit.* p. 104.
8. *I. E. Grabar' op. cit.* pp. 565 f. with references.
9. *Ibid.* pp. 557, 559, 560, *D. V. Ainalov:* Freskovaja rospis' xrama Uspenija Bogorodicy v Svijažskom mužskom Bogorodickom monastyre = *Drevnosti. Trudy Imper. Moskovskago Arxeologičeskago Obščestva,* t. XXI, vyp. 1 (Moscow 1906) pp. 3 f.

mandate—and not at all with that view of the tasks and position of the church in the community held by Groznyj himself, and to be found, for example, in *"Beseda valaamskix Čudotvorcev"*.

It is true that there is, as already mentioned, an obvious tendency to secularization in *"Cerkov' Voinstvujuščaja"*, both in form and in content. The vertical form with its worldly breadth, and the massive body of troops on the way back from the burning town imply a breaking up of the traditional horizon of piety and a drastic extension of the radius of action of Orthodoxy—but an extension, not a curtailment. The whole structure and symbolism of the icon serves to glorify the church. The parade of worldly power is in the service of the faith and the church, and because of this role, is saluted by the holy city and its angels. It is the apotheosis of the church and the spiritual authorities that is seen here, not that of the Czar and the worldly authorities. It recalls the fifty years older emphasis on the supremacy of the church over the crown in *"Provest' o Belom Klobuke"* (10). Here we are the nearest that period came to Bernard's and Boniface VIII's doctrine of the subjection of the worldly sword to the spiritual. What appears to be a secularization is in reality a spiritualization: the church makes capital out of the temporal power, and not vice versa.

As we have already seen, Ivan Groznyj, on the contrary, made capital out of the church, when, at a later period, he formulated his political principles. There is a crucial difference between the use made of the same motifs by Groznyj and by the icon. Groznyj's invoking the Archangel Michael as his patron saint, his reference to the Emperor Constantine's victory by virtue of the life-giving Cross, *životvor'aščij krest*—characteristically, the icon shows Constantine with the cross in his hand—and his recalling St. Vladimir, Dmitrij Donskoj and Aleksander Nevskij as his predecessors, is all for the purpose of legitimizing his worldly power with historical and religious bases. The history and the religion serve his purposes and interests as ruler. Judging by these manifestations, Groznyj can hardly have been content with, let alone have taken the initiative to the new tendency in painting, where, though it is true he has a prominent position, he is shown as the servant of the church among other such servants.

And yet the initiative came from Groznyj's own entourage. This is shown by the fact that both the frescoes in the Gold Salon and originally also *"Cerkov' Voinstvujuščaja"* were made for the court apartments in the Kremlin. And the conflict over these pictures shows quite definitely that it was Sil'vestr and Makarij who were behind them.

The discussion of the art of painting in the beginning of the fifties was a result of the catastrophic fire of 1547. The destruction in Moscow resulted

---

10. Cf. above p. 57.

in a great need for rebuilding and therewith also for redecoration. For this purpose, icon painters were called in, under the auspices of the state, from the West Russian towns, particularly Novgorod and Pskov, whence not only had the dangerous heretical movements spread in the previous decades, but also an untraditional, unorthodox view of art had now reached the capital, a view not uninfluenced by western painting (11). So that in these very years, when so much was uncertain and so much was at stake, an extremely important and richly traditional aspect of Orthodox piety—which again was the ideological foundation of the Muscovite community—was exposed to a movement that might well be called a renewal, but that from the establishment's point of view must be called a tendency to dissolution and disintegration. At all events, both state and church replied with a powerful tightening up of cultural policy.

At the great synod in 1551, the *Stoglavyj sobor,* Groznyj brought up the matter in his third question to the assembly, declaring that the icon painters must be supervised with the greatest care to ensure that they were unimpeachable in taste and virtue, and that they were zealous in training pupils, so that these might unite skill and faithfulness to the traditional models (12). The resolution of the synod fully supported this attitude. The priests were given instructions to supervise the virtue and behaviour of the painters, to prevent mediocre work and to punish skilful painters who misused their talents. The painters were to follow the old models, but by no means to give way to their own fancies and individual inspiration, *samomyšlenije* (13). So far, the Czar and the church were in complete agreement to preserve and defend the existing ideal of art at any cost.

This was naturally fully consistent and fully explicable by the classical alliance between czar and church, which earlier had brought forth the inquisition against undisciplined cultural movements (14). All traditional cultural groupings, however, seem to fall into confusion when the discussion of

---

11. For the Czar's summoning of artists, see *Akty AE* p. 247 A. On western influence, see D. Ainalov: *Gesch. d. russ. Monumentalk.* etc. pp. 51, 105, *Nik. Andrejev:* O "dele d'jaka Viskovatago" = *Seminarium Kondakovianum, Recueil d'Éudes t. V* (Prague 1932) pp. 236 f.
12. *Stoglav,* izdanije *D. E. Kožančikova* (Spbg. 1863) pp. 42 f. French translation in *E. Duchesne: Le Stoglav ou les cent chapitres* = Bibl. de l'Inst. Franç. de Petrograd, t. V (Paris 1920) pp. 27 f.
13. Chap. 43: »*a samomyšlenijem by i svoimi dogadkami božestva ne opisyvali*«, *D. E. Kožančikov ed. cit.* p. 153 = *E. Duchesne op. cit.* p. 135. Cf. the instruction from the close of the century in *D. A. Ravinskij:* Istorija russkix škol ikonopisanija do konca XVII veka = *Zapiski Imper. Arxeol. Obšč.,* t. VIII (Spbg. 1856) pp. 75 ff.
14. According to *N. E. Mneva* (see *I. E. Grabar' op. cit.* p. 583) the new tendencies in painting were a "progressive" movement closely connected with the "democratic" social endeavours. It might have been expected that the official alliance on art policy between state and church, as expressed in "*Stoglav*" would have been discussed in this context, and correspondingly interpreted as the expression of a "reactionary" and "undemocratic" tendency.

policy on art is followed up to the *cause célèbre* started at the initiative of the *d'jak,* Ivan Viskovatyj, one of the most influential of the officials of the Czar's administration.

In the autumn of 1553, Viskovatyj made an official complaint to the Czar of the new tendencies in painting, as expressed in the icons of the Church of the Annunciation and the frescoes of the Gold Salon. For three years he had been seriously concerned at what was here offered to the view of the believers, and could no longer hide his opinion of the blasphemous perversions appearing in this art. He claimed that the known, traditional representations of the Saviour, Our Lady and the saints had been replaced by the painters' own inventions (*mudrovanija*), based on their independent interpretations (*po svojemu razumu*) instead of on the Scriptures—they had even, through western influence, opened the way for pure Roman Catholic heresy (*latynskije jeresi mudrovanije*) (15).

This was apparently also a case of a faithful pillar of society's zealous defence of the good old ideal. But now, unlike the case in 1551, the attack was really directed against the responsible guardians of the good old ideals themselves. As protopope of the Church of the Annunciation, Sil'vestr was responsible for the new icons of the church, and as the Czar's spiritual guide, he had chosen the motifs for the frescoes in the Gold Salon, which he made no attempt to hide when the Viskovatyj case came formally before the synod at the beginning of 1554 (16). Moreover, the Metropolitan Makarij strongly defended Sil'vestr, and obviously also felt himself seriously attacked by Viskovatyj. Makarij declared sternly that Viskovatyj ought not to accuse others of heresy, since he was well on the way to acquiring the taint himself (17). These words were more than a polemical phrase. The humanistic heretic and free-thinker, Matvej Baškin, a little while before, had been tortured until he "screamed with various voices", and "his tongue hung far out of his mouth", till he finally acknowledged his heresy (18). The Inquisition was once more in action, for reasons to be discussed later.

As far as Viskovatyj was concerned, the result of the synod of January 1554 was that his complaint was rejected and that he was declared to have strayed into heresy. The decision, however, meant only a reprimand to the influential *d'jak* in the Chancery for Foreign Affairs. His position in the administration remained unchanged, and the heresy case was not followed up. The result of the case was authoritatively formulated by Makarij, who exhorted Viskovatyj to occupy himself with his duties for the future, and

---

15. *O. Bod'anskij:* Rozysk o bogoxul'nyx strokax i o somnenii sv'atyx, čestnyx ikon, Diaka Ivana Mixajlova syna Viskovatago = *ČOIDR* 1858/II, pp. 7, 11.
16. *Akty AE* p. 247.
17. *ČOIDR* 1858/II, Rozysk etc., p. 2.
18. *PSRL.* t. XIII p. 232 cf. *Akty AE* p. 250 B.

not to "devise sophistries" (*mudrstvovati*) about the sacred icons (19). Considering all the possibilities, Viskovatij got off lightly. The question now is, did he raise the matter relying on his secure position and simply to defend the classical values with his unassailable authority, or did he consider the case so important in a wider, political sense that it was worth taking a personal risk for it.

The answer must probably be that Viskovatyj attached no little political importance to the case, and that he knew that he was running a risk, but that he raised the matter in reliance on his established position. It has already been stated that Viskovatyj's complaint was felt as a direct attack on Sil'vestr and on Makarij. It may, perhaps, be assumed that Viskovatyj was thinking only of Sil'vestr, and had not reckoned with Makarij's standing shoulder to shoulder with the protopope (20). But even if that experienced curator of the kingdom's diplomatic affairs made a tactical error in regard to the Metropolitan, it is at any rate impossible to imagine that he was not aware of the complicated tactical play and the ruthless struggle for power that would inevitably result from an attack on the position of the mighty Sil'vestr. Under no circumstances can Viskovatyj have been so maladroit as to bring himself into a difficult, not to say dangerous position without particularly weighty reasons. He says in so many words that he had considered the matter for three years before raising it, and that he had hesitated because of a certain apprehension (21).

Viskovatyj's reasons for his apprehension are extremely interesting. What restrained him, he maintained, was his consciousness of conspiracy between Matvej Baškin and Artemij—an extreme representative of the *nest'ažateli* (22)—and that Artemij was conspiring with Sil'vestr, which would lead to dangerous intrigues against Viskovatyj. The assertion of heresy in the art of the icons, in other words, was directed against a broad front, ranging from one of the period's most prominent middle class free-thinkers, Baškin, by way of Artemij, whose position was precarious, to Sil'vestr, who occupied a central position among those at the head of affairs (23). By linking these three persons together, Viskovatyj managed first, to identify Sil'vestr with the most dangerous form of heresy, and secondly, to present Baškin as the product of or the instrument of one of the most powerful men in the kingdom. The answer to Viskovatyj's sum must in any case be that Sil'vestr was the root of the evil, that he was dangerous, and that he ought to be removed.

But why was Sil'vestr dangerous? According to Viskovatyj's official com-

19. The judgement: *Nik. Andrejev op. cit.* pp. 195 f., *ČOIDR* 1858/II, Rozysk etc., p. 40, *Akty AE* pp. 245 B–246 A. Makarij: *ČOIDR* 1858/II, Rozysk etc., p. 14.
20. *Zimin Per.* p. 174.
21. *ČOIDR* 1858/II, Rozysk etc., pp. 9 f.
23. *PSRL* t. XIII p. 524, *Materialy* p. 56.

plaint, the answer was that the protopope was a danger to Orthodoxy, since he opened the door to heresy and western influence through art. It is quite evident that Viskovatyj did not—as might be supposed from a present-day point of view—take to the field for a matter of taste. He would scarcely have risked his life for an aesthetic conviction. Icons were not merely art in the church, but valid and binding dogmatic formulations with the same validity and the same effect as words. This, even, is too weak a description, since the icons had more than a symbolic significance as representations of the objects of worship, they were in reality themselves the objects of worship, just as words had more than their intellectual significance when used in the magic of prayer (24). It is characteristic, that one of the accusations against Matvej Baškin when he was condemned as a heretic was that he and his fellows regarded the worship of icons as idolatry (25).

Thus it was not without logical consistency that Baškin was both accused by Viskovatyj of having introduced heresy into the icons and condemned by the synod for doubting their holiness. From a humanisitic and more or less rationalistic point of view, the heretic could naturally not see anything but artistic objects in the icons. There was nothing remarkable, therefore, in his having helped to promote the new icon style, which was of course precisely the expression of individual artistic efforts and a secularizing tendency to let the aesthetic play its own part, independently of the religious (26).

It was this tendency to artistic emancipation that the synod of 1551 called *samomyšlenije* and Viskovatyj in 1553 called *mudrovanije*. The two words mean one and the same thing, an impermissible intellectual individualism, corresponding to *samovolstvo* as the term for an impermissible self-assertion in a political sense. There is hardly any doubt that *samomyšlenije* is a more neutral, descriptive term than *mudrovanije*, which has a clearly pejorative ring of self-conceit and pomposity, in fact is roughly an anti-intellectual word of abuse. As such it played a prominent role in Iosif Volockij's vocabulary in addressing heretics (27), and from then on had a permanent place in the characteristic Iosifist vocabulary. It was in that very year, 1553, that the Iosifist Toporkov warned the Czar against surrounding himself with "all too wise", *mudrejšije,* advisers (28), and Viskovatyj, ironically enough, got as good as he gave from the most prominent Iosifist of

24. The significance of both word and picture, prayer and icon, appears clearly from the circumstance that the icons represent the sacred persons with a gesture of the hand that shows them speaking, notably blessing, and thus completes the magical effect. Cf. *E. E. Golubinskij: Istorija russkoj cerkvi. Period vtoroj, Moskovskij,* t. II/2 (Moscow 1917) pp. 492 ff. On miraculous icons, *ibid.* pp. 600 f.
25. *Akty AE* p. 250 B: "*idoly okojanii narič'ut*".
26. *P. Mil'ukov: Očerki po istorii russkoj kul'tury,* č. II (4. izd. Spbg. 1905) p. 225.
27. *Moisejeva* p. 112 with references.
28. Above p. 53.

the time, when Makarij declared that he ought not to pretend to be wise about things he did not understand.

There was thus something compromising, or at all events, something suspicious in being "wise", *mudryj*, seen from the official, high church point of view. But this view was naturally not shared by the heretics and the *nest'ažateli*, whose endeavours were just in the direction of intellectual clarification, or at any rate, aimed at securing the individual the right to believe and think as he liked. Kurbskij, whose nearest intellectual predecessor was Maksim Grek, thus combined his fundamental view of *svobodnoje jestestvo čelovečeskoje* with the requirement that the ruler should surround himself with *mudryje sovetniki* (29). He never uses words like *mudrovanije* or *mudrstvovati* of his opponents.

Instead, Kurbskij uses another depreciatory term, which also has affinities with intellectual qualities, the idea of "cunning", *lukavstvo*—in adjectival form, *lukavyj*, often intensified to *prelukavyj*. Thus he designates the Iosifists, including Toporkov, and the Czar's flatterers (30). The concept of *lukavstvo* is also used by Kurbskij's opponents, which was natural enough, as the word in itself has a depreciatory meaning. What was not natural was that the depreciatory ring about it was transferred to the original positive concept of wisdom. Thus there is nothing unusual in Groznyj's diction when he speaks of his opponents as acting from "inveterate cunning", *lukavyj obyčaj* (31). The word means a combination of intellectual agility and ethical or moral worthlessness. In Kurbskij's conceptual sphere, it was extremely suitable for the worthless *laskateli* and *man'jaki*, just as wisdom characterized the self-controlled and intelligent noble. To Kurbskij, *lukavstvo* is the direct opposite of "purity of heart", *pravost' serdečnaja*, by which he probably means primarily ethical uprightness (32).

The difference between this diction and the Iosifists' use of the word *mudrovanije* is undoubtedly that this last does not designate an actual ethical judgement but rather irritation at intellectual strivings that do not fit into the accepted system and therefore are dangerous for that system. It is only by artifice—by what may be called an implicative characteristic—that the concept becomes ethically condemnatory: a priori, the system is the highest ethical norm, therefore a challenge to the system is ethically reprehensible and to be exterminated. The same thing could be expressed by putting the sign of equality between *samomyšlenije* and *samovolstvo* and then drawing the necessary disciplinary consequences. The necessary condition for these "satanic syllogisms" (33) was the axiomatic assumption that

29. Above pp. 81 f.
30. *Fennell* pp. 184, 202, 204, 236.
31. *Ibid.* p. 86.
32. *Fennell* p. 184.
33. *Kurbskij* col. 52.

the individual could be right only in virtue of obedience and loyalty to the ruling system.

When the conflict over the icons is viewed against the background of this pattern, it matches very well when Viskovatyj called the new style of icon *mudrovanije*. For it obviously represented a challenge to the ruling system. In the months following Viskovatyj's presentation of the case, both Artemij and Baškin were neutralized, together with a number of other *samomyšlenniki*. It does not match the usual pattern at all, however, that Makarij accused Viskovatyj of *mudrovanije*. That he did so is so strikingly contrary to the actual content of the case that there must have been other reasons for it. Either Makarij must have considered Viskovatyj insincere and moved by ulterior motives, or he himself must have had ulterior motives of a special kind.

The result of the case, as we have seen, was that Sil'vestr and Makarij together rode out the storm, and succeeded in bringing Viskovatyj in an awkward situation, even if they did not succeed in having him removed. Viskovatyj, for his part, achieved the lesser objective of his attack, in that Baškin and Artemij were sacrificed. As far as the relations of personal power were concerned, the match was drawn. As far as the principles involved in the case were concerned, however, the result was paradoxical, in that the new icon style was canonized by the decision of the synod, even though it represented a clear challenge to the prevailing tradition. All in all, Viskovatyj was naturally the loser. His official object was to fight against the new tendencies in painting and to liquidate Sil'vestr. In neither of these objects did he succeed, and it is probably doubtful if the fate of Artemij and Baškin was any great comfort to him. The question that remains is whether Sil'vestr or the new style of painting was the principal object for him. Did he want to purify painting by attacking Sil'vestr, or did he want to attack Sil'vestr by means of the paintings?

Here it must be remembered that Viskovatyj as a trusted *d'jak* had great influence both in domestic and in foreign affairs, and must certainly have viewed the icon conflict as part of the great pattern that was his daily preoccupation. There is no sign of his having had any purely personal convictions at stake in the case, or that he allowed himself to be moved by a quite private dislike of the new style of icon. The sources available give a picture of Viskovatyj as a typical *d'jak*, whose primary interest was the administration of the centralized government and the building up of the Czar's autocracy (34). His loyalty to the Czar cannot be doubted, but must rather be taken as the starting point from which to try to interpret and define his standpoint in the case and at that moment now under discussion.

---

34. *Smirnov* pp. 260 f.

This, together with Viskovatyj's action in the icon dispute, makes it possible to characterize his standpoint as in principle related to that expressed in *"Beseda valaamskix Čudotvorcev"*. Both Viskovatyj and the anonymous author are careful to dissociate themselves from every approach to heresy. Viskovatyj speaks of *mudrovanije*, just as the anonymous author warns against getting lost in all too profound thought (35). Both are absolutely loyal to the Czar, and both—each in his own way—take up a challenging attitude to the leaders of the church, but without being classifiable with the heretics and included in the attacks on them. The anonymous author had undoubtedly a tactical object in positioning himself thus, and the question is whether it was the same with Viskovatyj. He must have realised, at all events, that by meddling in church matters he risked being accused of heresy. Consequently, he must have been very anxious to guard against every possibility of suspicion in that direction. The Kuricyn case must have been to him, as to the anonymous author, a warning example. And perhaps Viskovatyj had a further reason for caution, for he seems to have had some connexion with Baškin at a certain period (36).

On this basis—for as already indicated, Viskovatyj had started a highly complicated tactical operation—it is tempting to go a step further, and to assume that Viskovatyj started his action on the icon style not because his interest in painting was his primary motive but because precisely this case provided him with the most advantageous start-line. In any case, his action was a complicated attack on Sil'vestr, who was brought into connexion with Baškin and Artemij, and a defence of values that the Iosifists, including Makarij, might be expected to feel obliged to defend. A better way of getting Sil'vestr isolated in the circle of power and then overthrown, therefore, is hardly imaginable, if this was the main object of the action. This is the view of *I. I. Smirnov,* who maintains—though on rather slender evidence—that Viskovatyj in his disguised political action against Sil'vestr represented the Zaxar'ins, who thus sought to win more power at the expense of the protopope (37). If this is correct, then Makarij had every reason to regard Viskovatyj as insincere in his religious action and to have other aims in his attack than those given officially.

This, however, does not fully clear up the Viskovatyj case. From the outset, the idea that Viskovatyj had tactical and political aims in his action is so natural and probable that it is easy to allow one's attention to be too much dominated by this alluring explanation. There are factors that indicate that Viskovatyj was really more sincere than might be thought beforehand. To begin with, it is impossible to ignore the fact that there really was a

35. *Moisejeva* p. 171, cf. above p. 107.
36. *Zimin Per.* p. 170.
37. *I. I. Smirnov:* Ivan Groznyj i bojarskij "m'atež" 1553 g. = *Ist. Zap.* t. 43, pp. 162, 165 f.

radical divergence from the normal in the new icons, and that the provisions of the *"Stoglav"* were in fact infringed. And further, there is reason here to turn back to the fact that the ideological content of the new icons had been given a no less striking twist away from the tradition than the style.

The twist, as we have seen, was to a claim for the church of an independent role as a power factor side by side, or over, the state, consequently a claim of *voinstvujuščaja cerkov'*. Sil'vestr had a great share in the responsibility for this ideological campaign. But Makarij, too, had a share of responsibility, if in no other way, then at any rate a co-responsibility from the moment he supported Sil'vestr against Viskovatyj. If Makarij was fully justified in attacking Viskovatyj for exceeding his competence by meddling in church affairs, then Viskovatyj was quite as justified in accusing Sil'vestr and Makarij for exploiting their ecclesiatical authority by meddling in the political affairs of the kingdom. And if Viskovatyj was insincere in choosing religious formulae to combat church meddling in politics, then Makarij was no less insincere when he did exactly the same to gain political power for the church.

When all this is considered, it is clear that a more exhaustive definition of the content of the Viskovatyj case is required than that proposed by *I. I. Smirnov*. Viskovatyj's action was directed against Sil'vestr, and secondarily also against Makarij, in order to limit their influence. But it was not only a political action, disguised in religious formulae. The action was taken to promote one view of the role and position of the church in the community, and was directed against another view of the same question. In order to promote his interests, Sil'vestr had taken up a modern and challenging style of propaganda. He wished to make propaganda for the church as a power factor by means of a form of communication which, with its surprising innovations, was a breach with the tradition of the church. Viskovatyj's action was directed against this campaign, and thereby also against Sil'vestr's person. Which was the more important of these two targets it is impossible, in the last resort, to determine, since the person and his policy can hardly be separated from each other and considered apart.

As far as Makarij is concerned, the case is somewhat different. By defending Sil'vestr against Viskovatyj and accusing the latter of heresy, he identified himself with Sil'vestr's view of the role of the church. But as champion of the form Czarism had hitherto had, and as a representative of Iosifism, he might have been expected to adhere to Viskovatyj's view. Thus the difficulty, in Makarij's case, is not only to distinguish between the person and his policy, but also to distinguish between two fundamentally different political objectives, both of which seem to have had a determining influence on the Metropolitan. If the attempt to distinguish between the person Makarij and the Metropolitan's policy be abandoned—and needs must—it becomes necessary to speak of two Makarijs, of a split personality, and an extremely ambivalent policy.

One Makarij brought up the Grand Prince Ivan to take his place as the autocrat of Russia, had the autocracy's opponents neutralized and executed, took the Grand Prince forward to his coronation as Czar, and saluted the Czar as the true heir of Constantine the Great, St. Vladimir, Aleksander Nevskij and Dmitrij Donskoj. The other Makarij, with increasing zeal and energy, nursed the interests of the church against the crown, fought valiantly for the ecclesiastical estates, and in this fight did not shrink from fetching in arguments from the west (38), he helped to outmanoeuvre the family of the Czar's mother in 1547, he supported the clerical politician Sil'vestr in 1554, he had himself represented on equal terms with the Czar in the Svijazsk Monastery. One was a Iosifist and the Czar's supporter. The other was the advocate of *voinstvujuščaja cerkov'* (39), and as such the Czar's rival.

The Viskovatyj case is extraordinarily interesting and significant as one of the clearest symptoms of the political conditions of the period. It shows how extremely necessary it was to undertake political confrontations and debates within the limits of the religious ideology, and similarly, the great extent to which all those involved were compelled to go beyond these limits in safeguarding their political interests. It shows, further, that the conflicting forces—whether determined by religious ideology or by political tactics— held one another in check in their risky and complicated play. In this sense it was a question of a policy of compromise, as when Viskovatyj and Sil'vestr both left the field with their personal positions intact, or when the synod canonized a style of icon that was uncanonical. This last was not the only example of self-contradictions, unsolved problems, or untenable solutions within the framework of the policy of compromise. It was rather a particularly clear and well defined expression of the situation of the autocracy, which was so tangled as to be almost insoluble.

There was thus a great resemblance between the Czar's political situation in 1547 and in 1554. At first sight, this may seem surprising, when it is remembered that in the course of these years a policy of reform was carried out which had great effect, and that in the same period the Czar's personal position and prestige were greatly strengthened, primarily with the victory

---

38. *F. Dvornik: The Slavs in European History and Civilization* (New Brunswick 1962) pp. 506, 522 with references, *E. E. Golubinskij: Istorija russkoj cerkvi. Period vtoroj, Moskovskij*, t. II/1 (Moscow 1900) p. 800.

39. *Zimin Ref.* p. 320, *Zimin Per.* pp. 78 f. Cf. the account of Makarij's clerical zeal in *E. E. Golubinskij op. cit.* p. 771, where, however, the conflict of interest between Czar and Metropolitan is covered over, cf. *V. Val'denberg: Drevnerusskija učenija o predelax carskoj vlasti* (Pgr. 1916) pp. 289 f.

over Kazan'. This light and fortunate period of reform that Kurbskij talks about, did not give that form of political clarification and modernization that implied a fundamental and durable solution of the pressing problems of the community. It rather left behind it many half-solutions, besides the new problems it brought in itself.

The reform period was prepared by a gradual extension of and change in the *bojarskaja duma,* which came to be dominated by men like Aleksej Adašev. With this new composition, the way was open for a policy the crux of which was consideration for the interests of the new groups in the community, particularly those of the *dvor'anstvo* (40). This development was completed in February 1549, at the epoch-making Diet usually called "The Reconciliation Assembly", *Sobor primirenija.* Ivan Groznyj here acted as arbitrator between the conflicting groups in the community, emphasing the offences of the various parties—though especially those of the *bojarstvo*— and preparing the way for a reconciliation on the basis of a new policy of more equal consideration for all parties (41). *A. A. Zimin* is undoubtedly right in terming this assembly the first real Diet, *zemskij sobor,* and in emphasising that hereafter the most important acts of government began to be done with the sanction of the ruling classes, including among these the *dvor'anstvo.* The new tendency of the crown to rule in consultation with the estates was thus actually to take the form of a sort of representative monarchy (42).

The re-arrangement of the relative strengths of the various influential groups primarily required a financial re-distribution, in other words, a change in land policy. This problem, the need to limit the landed possessions of the church, had already presented itself under Ivan Velikij, and now appeared with renewed urgency. It was part of the policy of reform that the *Stoglavyj sobor* in 1551, in spite of the energetic resistance of the Iosifists, led to a partial victory for the government's classical policy of secularization. And it was a result of the policy of reform that the church replied by compensating for its losses by an intensive exploitation of the estates that were still left to it, which again involved a popular reaction to this worsening of the conditions of the peasants (43).

This began a *circulus vitiosus. A. A. Zimin* formulates the result thus, that the government's attempt to solve the land problem at the expense of the church estates failed, and that a second attempt to carry out the experiment was prevented by the fact that vigorous growth in the reformation movement made it necessary, on the contrary, to support the church, the

---

40. *Zimin Ref.* p. 317.
41. *PSRL* t. XXII pp. 528 f., *Istoričeskij Arxiv* t. VII (Moscow 1951) pp. 295 f.
42. *Zimin Ref.* pp. 325 f.
43. *Ibid.* pp. 391, 404 with references.

fixed ideological foundation of the autocracy (44). It is quite evident that these various effects must have intensified one another. By starting a limited and moderate action against the church lands, the government necessarily brought the church into a state of alarm, besides the church's undertaking financial measures for a harsher exploitation of these estates. The state of alarm involved increased church intolerance towards all heretical tendencies, and thereby a new wave of the inquisition, while the heretical tendencies only grew stronger under the impression of the harsher conditions for the peasants. When these effects began to be felt seriously, the situation became so difficult for the government to control that there could no longer be any question of taking stronger measures on the lines followed hitherto. For ideological reasons, the government could not risk a struggle for power with the church. For economic reasons, however, it had to solve the land problem—but at the expense, therefore, of others than the church.

Logic pointed to two possibilities: the *bojarstvo,* and an extension of the land of the state. The first was limited by the policy of compromise, which assumed collaboration between the Czar and the boyars. The second was limited by the military power of the kingdom, the growth of which was completely dependent on the solution of a number of political, economic and administrative problems. The two possibilities were closely connected, for the boyars traditionally formed the nucleus of the military system of the kingdom. Whichever alternative was chosen, consequently, would mean an attack on the boyars' prerogatives, with the main emphasis on either the political or the financial effect.

To the boyars, there were points of conflict in all the reforms, in the modernization of the military system, in the regulation of the legal system on the basis of the new *"Sudebnik"*, in the normalization of the monetary system. It was a logical consequence of these endeavours and a natural part of the reforming government's programme of efficiency, that after his return from the Kazan' campaign in 1552, Ivan gave orders for the planning of a revision of the *kormlenije* system (45). This form of decentralized local administration, which gave the magnates great liberty of action in their areas —also to take a sizeable reward for their administrative efforts—from a reformist point of view was primitive and out of date.

A. A. Zimin emphasises the purely practical reasons in favour of abolishing the old system, which prevented the centralization of local administration, and the improvement of the efficiency of the military system. It was

---

44. *Ibid.* p. 406.
45. *PSRL* t. XIII p. 529: *"o kormlenijax sideti"*, cf. *Smirnov* p. 265, *Zimin Ref.* p. 418. On *kormlenije* in general, see *Očerki* p. 122, *Vernadsky: Russia at the Dawn of the Modern Age = A History of Russia* Vol. IV (New Haven 1959) pp. 102 f., *N. Rožkov: Proisxoždenije samoderžavija v Rossii* (Moscow 1906) pp. 71 ff.

not, therefore, in itself an expression of the struggle between the *dvor'anstvo* and the *bojarstvo,* that the authorities took steps to modernize the system (46). Yet in its effects, the reform was one of the most fundamental encroachments on the traditional position and powers of the boyars, and was thus necessarily felt to be the expression of a political fight against them. On the long term view, therefore, the reform of the *kormlenije* system appears as a portent of the stiffer attitude to the rights of the boyars that was expressed in the reform policy from 1555 to 1560, and which was the result of the failure of the attempt to solve the land problem by secularizing the church estates (47). The development pointed clearly towards a state of things where the sting of the reforms was directed against the boyars, and where, consequently, the balance achieved under the policy of compromise since 1549 was seriously threatened.

The policy of reform, as started in 1549 was an attempt to make good the deficiencies of the policy followed hitherto, which is best described, perhaps, as a policy of improvisation. It was this policy the inadequacy of which stood revealed by the dramatic events of the summer of 1547, when all parties were more or less compelled to admit the necessity of a political strategy to replace the haphazardness that had hitherto prevailed (48). Its combination of chaotic intrigue and actual physical danger must have made the situation intolerable to the newly crowned Czar. It is evident, however, that he had no cause to find the situation clear and the problems solved in the course of the fifties, either, let alone feel that he was master of the situation. The reform policy was based on the compromise agreed to at the *Sobor primirenija.* Compromise means half-solutions, but the state of affairs required whole ones.

One can try in theory to imagine the conditions required to enable the half-solutions of the compromise to lead to the full harmonizing óf the problems by a calm and balanced development, canalized, perhaps, through a more influential and more consolidated *zemskij sobor.* This has little interest, however, compared with the evident fact that the policy of compromise little by little was largely assuming the character of a renewed policy of improvisation. The boyars improvised, in that some of them accepted the reform policy and others opposed it. Makarij improvised, his attitude determined—or, his attitudes determined—by the landed interest of the church. Viskovatyj improvised in his struggle with Sil'vestr. And faced with all this, the Czar himself must also improvise, whether he wanted to or not.

On top of these political conditions, which must have greatly contributed

---

46. *Zimin Ref.* p. 440.
47. *Ibid.* p. 470 f.
48. See above pp. 99 ff.

to a feeling of uncertainty and confusion, now came the accident of the Czar's apparently mortal illness in March 1553, producing the succession crisis. Faced with the Czar's demand for an oath of allegiance to his son Dmitrij, then only four months old, a number of magnates chose to propose the Czar's adult cousin, Vladimir Starickij, as his successor instead. After two days of negotiation under pressure the magnates gave up their proposal and took the oath to Dmitrij, thanks not least to the energetic efforts of Viskovatyj. In the long run, the crisis was completely ended, for Groznyj recovered and his son died early (49).

In his account of the matter, eleven years later, Groznyj speaks of the crisis as part of the boyars' conspiracy against him and against the new Czardom, the continuity of which was to have been secured by the succession of his son. He claims further, that the boyars intended to kill both him and Dmitrij (50). It has been shown, however, e. g. by *A. A. Zimin,* that the accounts of the crisis do not support the view that it was a question of a revolt or a conspiracy by the boyars, but that these betray a split or disagreement within the administration with regard to political objectives (51). From the account in *"Carstvennaja Kniga"* it appears that Sil'-vestr and Adašev's father refused to acknowledge Ivan's son as the next Czar, which can hardly have been due to their participation in a boyar plot, but rather to the fear of the political consequences of what would really have been an empty throne, just as during Ivan's minority twenty years before. On the other hand, Andrej Kurbskij complied with the Czar's demand, which at any rate does not confirm the traditional judgement of his political attitude as a typical boyar—and otherwise shows nothing except that Kurbskij did not baulk at the idea of a Czar on the throne who was a minor.

It is not possible, therefore, to speak of a clear division between the adherents of Ivan and the Czardom on one side and their opponents on the other (52). It is obvious that this division existed. It is also clear that for that matter there could very well have been some kind of conspiracy among the boyars hostile to the Czar at such a favourable moment as during the Czar's illness. But it is certain that a refusal to accept Dmitrij was not necessarily a sign of hostility to the Czar or of friendliness towards the boyars, any more than the acknowledgement of Dmitrij was necessarily an expression of faithfulness and loyalty to the Czardom. Fedor Adašev refused on the explicit argument that with an infant on the throne, the country

---

49. *PSRL* t. XIII pp. 522–526.
50. *Fennell* pp. 62, 94, 192.
51. *Zimin Ref.* p. 414.
52. For a detailed discussion of the crisis, see *Zimin Ref.* pp. 410–417, *Smirnov* pp. 277–298, *I. I. Smirnov* in *Ist. Zap.* t. 43, pp. 150–181, *A. N. Al'šic* in *Ist. Zap.* t. 25, pp. 266–292.

would be ruled by the Zaxar'ins (53). Sil'vestr seems to have thought the same, and perhaps Makarij also (54). This attitude was more hostile to the boyars than it was to the Czar. And Fedor Adašev added, as an explanation of his fear of government by the Zaxar'ins, that during Ivan's minority the country had suffered enough under boyar rule. In the light of Adašev's judgement of the situation, the logical conclusion might very well be drawn that the most subtle form of treason against the Czar would be to put Ivan's infant son on the throne and a boyar group into the seats of power.

But not all the adherents of Groznyj and the Czardom shared Adašev's view. Kurbskij was loyal in the face of Groznyj's demand without its being possible to ascribe to him such a degree of subtlety that he wanted thereby to promote his alleged boyar interests. Rather, he saw no other alternative to supporting the regular heir, since the only other possible heir, Vladimir Starickij, could just as well have involved the re-establishment of the boyars' *camarilla*.

As far as Viskovatyj is concerned, his purposeful activity on behalf of Dmitrij can, of course, be set to the account of the theory of his alliance with the Zaxar'ins (55), but here, too, there must be a reservation—that Viskovatyj's real motive may have been just the fear of the alternatives rather than any preference for government by the family of the Czar's wife. As a central figure in the administration, Viskovatyj may well have been extremely worried by the power of Sil'vestr or Adašev, or by the influence of Makarij and the church on the government of the country, especially if these groups got the opportunity to gain even greater influence in a collaboration with the weak Vladimir Starickij—while, on the other hand, he may have felt a certain confidence in the possibility of the administration being able to carry on the political line of the Czardom during Dmitrij's minority, supported by the increasing influence of the *d'jačestvo* and the *dvor'anstvo*. In other words, he may have felt that times had changed, and that history would not repeat itself, even though the situation of 1533 should arise again.

It would have been understandable if Groznyj himself had expressed great concern at the possibility of a repetition of the situation that was so disastrous for his own childhood and upbringing. There is, however, no hint of such concern. Ivan chose to go all out, in this tense situation, for the only solution that could be imagined that would prevent the Starickij branch of the dynasty from winning an easy victory in the longstanding rivalry for power. Nor had Ivan any other alternative than to maintain the formal demand for direct succession, which his father had also maintained

53. *PSRL* t. XIII p. 524.
54. *Ist. Zap.* t. 43 (*Smirnov*) pp. 171 f.
55. Cf. above p. 119.

in his will (56). Whether, at the same time, he bitterly remembered the admonition that Vasilij III addressed to the magnates before his death, "Stand fast, so that my son may become the ruler of the kingdom and *pravda* endure in the land" (57), and the chaotic confusion after his father's death—that we can never know. If Groznyj had energy and leisure to utter more differentiated judgements in those critical days, these have not, at any rate, found their way to the one-sided and tendentious account in *"Carst-vennaja Kniga"*.

But if there are obvious explanations of Groznyj's obstinate insistence on the succession in those critical days, there are traits, however, in his account of the crisis written in 1564 that cause surprise. Certainly, it is to be expected that his account would be extremely one-sided and subjective, since it forms part of a polemic. The Czar's aim is to reveal the boyars' fundamental perfidy and criminal plots, and the crisis could serve as a very good argument. But it is to be remembered that the polemic is primarily directed against Kurbskij, whose attitude during the crisis was completely correct and loyal to the Czar. Apparently Groznyj had not realised that in reality he had thus weakened his own argument. Not even at that late date, eleven years after the succession crisis, does he seem to have clearly understood the intricate possibilities and the paradoxical truth of the matter. On the contrary, his account is an exact repetition of his attitude while the crisis was upon him and he was preparing himself for death.

He still maintains the inherited succession as the only acceptable solution, but also maintains at the same time, with a fixed order of succession, the unnecessary and out of date requirement of an oath of fealty, *krestnoje celovanije,* and thus gives official blessing to an untenable compound of dominal and feudal state practice. With that role that Groznyj in his messages otherwise gives to *krestnoje celovanije*—a role more sacral than juridical, more moral than political (58)—Groznyj further brings himself into the untenable situation that his politico-religious argumentation is riddled through and through by the actual facts: an arrant oath-breaker and *krestoprestupnik* like Kurbskij has got safely away and saved his life, while other magnates did not even escape the Czar's terrorism by acquiescing in the oath of fealty (59). In short, Groznyj lets slip the opportunity of making a consistent settlement with the past and a resolute consolidation of his own position in the sense of political theory.

Groznyj's insistence on a traditional formalism may probably be explained, to some extent, at any rate, by the fact that ideas on politics and

56. *PSRL* t. VI pp. 270 f.
57. *Ibid* p. 271.
58. Cf. above pp. 68 f.
59. Cf. above pp. 69 f.

theory of the state were in his kingdom so little clarified. But this particular problem cannot be brushed aside with merely that explanation. It must be remenbered that Groznyj wrote his message to Kurbskij a few months before the abdication crisis at the end of 1564, when he faced the magnates and the estates with his *après nous le déluge*. It is hardly conceivable that Ivan's ultimatum was the result of a hasty improvisation. His later question to Queen Elizabeth on the possibility of asylum in England, should it become necessary (60) shows a tendency, at any rate, to consider all possibilities, even the most extreme, in good time. It is most likely that in the summer of 1564 Groznyj had abdication in mind as a theoretical possibility, and that this possibility had given him occasion to ponder on the problems of the succession crisis. In the last resort, the crises had the same content, the question of what would happen if the Czar left the throne, involuntarily or voluntarily.

Just as the succession crisis of 1553 could give occasion for undertaking a comparison with the conditions for the succession in 1533, so in 1564 there was every reason to see the tactical possibilities for a successful course for the abdication crisis in the light of the experiences of both 1533 and 1553. That, all the same, Groznyj gives not the slightest hint of a direct contribution to the elucidation of the succession crisis, is probably because his thoughts ran in quite another direction than would be expected from the previous course of events. It is quite true that there was little clarification of ideas in politics and state theory, but in this connexion the problems were so concrete that their significance in principle could not have gone unperceived by Groznyj's clear intelligence. It is also quite true that there might be tactical reasons why he was silent about any realistic considerations when he formulated his message, but such a subtle display of cunning as that he should have deliberately covered himself by a repetition of the official, stereotype evaluation, is hardly conceivable, either. On the other hand, the message contains many signs that in the course of the previous years Groznyj had come to a fundamentally new evaluation—not of his own tasks and his own position, but of the political possibilities open to him, and that on this basis he wanted to break with a past that he himself also shared.

Hitherto we have followed the premisses for this revaluation. It appears from Groznyj's personal, autobiographical argumentation in the message of 1564, that the events connected with the fire at Moscow have played no

---

60. The proposal was made in 1567, and was formally based on a mutual right of asylum as part of a treaty. Elizabeth was rather astonished by the proposal, and for her own part not at all interested in such a precautionary measure, but was willing to receive Ivan if it should become necessary: *Early Voyages and Travels in Russia and Persia by Anthony Jenkinson and Other Englishmen*, ed. E. D. Morgan and C. H. Hoote, Vol. II = The Hakluyt Society No 73 (London 1886) pp. 238, 241.

little part in the formation of his ideas and his evaluations, so that it is also natural to assume that his actual deliberations took him right back to the situation at that time. This, as we have seen, consisted in a general breakdown of the system of government prevailing until then, and of an extremely confusing mixture of tendencies and manoeuvres, during which the Czardom's fixed buttresses seemed to give and to give way, or at any rate to be unreliable. It has been further emphasised that the policy of reform, which was intended as the answer to the breakdown of the policy of improvisation, was largely reduced to resting on a set of untenable compromise solutions, the interplay of which led to a renewed form of improvisation policy. After having attained a climax of prestige by the conquest of Kazan', Ivan found during his illness that the whole of this delicately balanced system could be overturned by his death. And finally, the ring closes with the Viskovatyj case, of which the far-reaching perspectives in cultural and power politics indicated conditions of a similar kind to those of the crisis of the summer of 1547.

In principle, the content of the Viskovatyj case, as the Czar saw it, was that he was formally and officially responsible for the compromise solution (61), which left behind it an undecided struggle for power between his most distinguished *d'jak,* possibly in alliance with the family of the Czar's wife, and his dominating adviser and spiritual director, who was supported by the Metropolitan himself. There were, without doubt, repercussions of the succession crisis in the Viskovatyj case, as is maintained especially by *I. I. Smirnov* (62). This can only have strengthened still further the Czar's feeling of an utterly ambivalent situation, where on the one hand he sat enthroned as autocrat and God's vicar on earth, and on the other hand was reduced to manoeuvre with the others in complicated play between a purposeful administration, socially critical heretics, a high church that was primarily interested in preserving its worldly goods, a spiritual director who exalted himself as a grey eminence, a nobility of birth fighting for its privileges and a service nobility demanding land.

On the way from the observation of the premises to the investigation of Ivan's conclusion, it may be assumed provisionally that on the one hand the Czar was clear about his responsibility for the policy of reform, insofar as he both desired and willed the attempt of that period to deal with the tasks and problems of the government, but, on the other hand, that he would not accept the condition that the opposing forces prevented a definitive solution. Kurbskij praised him for the first active role. Groznyj deliberately repudiated responsibility for the reform policy from the latter, negative motive. He felt his conditions as a Gordian knot, and worked his way forward to the only possible solution. To slash it through.

---

61. *ČOIDR*. 1858/II, Rozysk etc., p. 1.
62. *Ist. Zap*. t. 43 p. 186.

VII

The Czar's State within the State

So far, it has been maintained that Groznyj's repudiation of the reform period was not so much the expression of arbitrariness or inconsequence as a reply to inconsequence, and that his attitude, taken as a whole, seems to be the expression of a determined effort to clear up the situation. Hence it follows that Ivan Groznyj made his change of system in 1565 deliberately, and in order to free himself from a complicated, ambiguous situation. This conjecture runs counter to the classical assertion of the Czar's change of character or fall into sin, put forward first by Andrej Kurbskij and continued down the centuries by others (1). For practical reasons, we may speak of a "theory of simplification" versus a "theory of change".

In principle, of course, there is nothing to prevent these two assertions, as presented here, from being combined. Perhaps precisely because it was a question of a process that went on for years and was carefully thought out, it may be that Groznyj's settlement with his situation was so radical that for him personally the final result was equivalent to a change of mentality or outlook. And if the change is to be accounted a fall—that is to say, a change that was injurious both for himself and others—that is a matter of a value judgement, and irrelevant to a descriptive and analytic essay. Still, it seems necessary to make a closer examination of the tenability of the two conjectures and of the possibility of combining them, first because the theory of change seems to have quite fundamental weakness and errors, and secondly because it will hardly be possible to derive a tenable characterization from a combination of the two approximations.

It has previously been maintained that Groznyj's ideological standpoint and political programme contain no point on which there is a fundamental break with the traditional positions of the Muscovite state, either religious or political. There is no basis for calling Groznyj insincere, let alone hypocritical, in his repeated confessions of faith. There is a tendency to secularization in his way of thinking, but this, too, can be put in relation to tendencies of the same kind in the Iosifist tradition. In political matters, Groznyj betrays an attitude and a conceptual world that is extremely traditional. He does

---

1. Cf. above pp. 21 f.

not think out in principle such concepts as *ot'jezd* and *krestnoje celovanije,* but condemns the actions of the boyars concretely. On the other hand, he shows no clearer understanding of the new political forces regarded as categories, than, for example, Kurbskij does.

When it is considered that Groznyj's ideological and political manifestos originated in the time shortly before the change of system and in the years that followed, and, moreover, that no decisive changes in principle can be observed from one message to the next within that period, two things stand out clearly. First, Groznyj's writings indicate no decisive change in his fundamental religious and political views when these are compared with what is known of his traditional background. There is nothing that shows any form of change in outlook, any kind of religious or intellectual conversion, any change of mentality. Secondly, there is no basis for the assumption that Groznyj's writings—including especially the very full message of the summer of 1564—give expression to the Czar's views from the period previous to any decisive change in mentality of views. They are rather evidence of unbroken continuity right from Groznyj's youth to his old age, from the inheritance he took over to that he left behind him.

This in itself must be considered a quite serious weakening of the theory of change. But there is the further fact, that this theory in its various forms contains the quite invalidating self-contradiction that Groznyj's change showed him as he really was, constitutionally. This self-contradiction in Kurbskij's formulation is in itself more acceptable than in later formulations. Kurbskij talked of man's constitutional weakness, which could be combated only by one's own piety and others' guidance, and on this basis he drew the logical conclusion that a man as a ruler had a very special obligation to practise piety and to allow himself to be guided by wise advisers, both for his own sake and for the sake of his subjects. In Kurbskij's view, Groznyj's change consisted in his abandoning his piety and getting rid of his wise advisers, which inevitably led him to destruction and abuse of power, and led his subjects into slavery and terror.

In other words, Groznyj was changed from a Czar who was only a man to a Czar who was more human that he had any right to be. Hitherto, it has been argued that it is indefensible to call this attitude "reactionary" in contradistinction to the "progressive" attitude of Czarism and Iosifism. This interpretation is a value judgement, and can be maintained only by the acceptance of the axioms of the absolute autocracy. Kurbskij's political foundation was not even decidedly traditional or conservative. Even though his formulations to a very large extent were founded on a mediaeval view of the state, the substance of his thinking, however, was so penetrated by a humanistic philosophy that it may be said, with equal justice, that his foundation was related to the reasoning lying behind every form of constitutional monarchy or parliamentary democracy. But, at the same time, it must be insisted upon that Kurbskij's judgement of Groznyj is also a value judgement, which, as it stands, cannot be used in a descriptive and analytic essay.

Kurbskij took it for granted that the change of system was due to Groznyj personally, and that it could have been avoided if he had refrained from exchanging good advisers for bad ones, and thus allowing evil to gain the upper hand of itself. He assumed, in other words, that the community, and thereby Groznyj's political working conditions, were in principle fixed and unchangeable magnitudes. But as we have seen, this is precisely what they were not. Had Groznyj been able to understand Kurbskij's way of thinking and to use his method of expression, he could justifiably have answered that the problem did not turn at all on his retaining true piety and wise advisers but on mastering a situation where all important political groups and forces were severally doing their best to get into positions where they could behave more humanly than they had any right to. In his indirect and involved manner, he managed to say this, when he declared that personal piety was one thing and the business of a ruler another, and when he accused the magnates of boundless self-assertion, *samovolstvo*.

We leave Kurbskij's formulation of the theory of change by noting that he regarded the Czar's working conditions as unchangeable, but his government and his morals as changed. The first was an error, which led directly to a distorted interpretation in the second. In its further development, the theory of change has been given a constantly more subjective and psychological stamp, especially in the writings of the romantic historian *Karamzin,* where he speaks of a sudden, devilish inspiration in Groznyj (2), but also in the psychologically stressed studies from the end of the 19th Century. Here again we have the self-contradiction between the assertion of constitutional characteristics and of a process of change, this time in the form of the assertion of innate psychical weaknesses, and the final break-through of these weaknesses in the years round the change of system (3). The psychiatrist, *P. I. Kovalevskij* glosses neatly over the self-contradiction by operating with four possibilities, innate psychical health and ill-health, and healthy or unhealthy external conditions. In his opinion, Groznyj was an example of the most unfortunate combination, since he was both psychically unhealthy and had an unhealthy adolescence, which inevitably in the end must turn him into a paranoic and a monomaniac (4).

---

2. *N. M. Karamzin: A Memoir on Ancient and Modern Russia. The Russian Text* ed. by Richard Pipes (Cambridge, Mass. 1959) p. 12.

3. *V. O. Kl'učevskij: Sočinenija*, t. II (Moscow 1957) p. 198.

4. *P. I. Kovalevskij: Ioann Groznyj i jego duševnóje sostojanije* (Kharkov 1893) pp. 8 f., 94 ff., 110, 202.

Behind all this argumentation, however, there lies in the last resort the same error as Kurbskij's, for although unfortunate conditions during puberty have been taken into account, the political conditions in which Groznyj had to rule have not been considered at all. In a way, all that has been achieved is a neutralizing of the discussion of constitutional or milieu determined psyche, but no explanation of the fact that Groznyj made his change of system on the basis of a conscious and fully consistent political manifesto. From a historical point of view, no progress can be made by operating with psychological theories of this kind. The most that can be said is that the man who started these psychological attempts, Cesare Lombroso, naturally had weighty arguments for the defence of his thesis of the existence of *l'uomo delinquente* at all levels of society. But in a historical context, this says no more than the banal observation that numerous rulers in the history of the world ought to have been sent to a psychiatric clinic. But this gives no specific explanation of Ivan's way to the change of system.

There are thus extremely narrow limits to the possibility of using psychological observation as a means of analysing Groznyj's ideas and actions. If the attempt must be made, the best way would appear to be to disregard the general observations that can be made of any inherited tendencies or of the conditions under which he grew up, and instead to concentrate on Groznyj's known, actual situation politically, and on this basis to consider the probable psychological reaction of the man at the centre of the situation.

As will be evident from what has been said hitherto, Groznyj's political situation was ambivalent. His ideological views and the structure of the state he ruled over singled him out as the inviolable autocrat. But in his function as ruler, he met with an extremely capricious play of reactions from all the forces in the kingdom, the effects of which appeared in a manner quite incalculable. That the Czar found himself in this situation appears from a historical and political analysis. And perhaps there is reason to try to get an analysis of the Czar's reactions under such conditions elucidated by asking psychology or psychiatry whether conditions of this kind release a specific and foreseeable psychical reaction.

An authoritative answer—if such can be given—would assume a profound collaboration between the consulting and the answering parties. It can hardly be considered unreasonable to assume in advance that the answer, to some extent at any rate, must take the form of a reference to the psychical mechanisms, the study of which was begun, with such great results, by I. P. Pavlov. It is almost impossible not to think of the animals used by Pavlov in his experiments when reading Groznyj's complaints that in his childhood he did not get his meals at fixed times, or that he was not shown that respect he had been taught to require (5).

---

5. *Fennell* pp. 74–76.

The British psychiatrist, *William Sargant,* has occupied himself with the resemblances between the reactions of men and of animals under conditions of this kind when these lead to an acute situation (6). Such situations where men are involved are known in connexion with what is called brain-washing, the result of which is a deep, but by no means definitive change in the person's intellectual reactions, manifested by the assumption of a new set of convictions of a political kind. They are also known, to an even greater extent, from religious conversions, the result of which is similarly a fundamental, though not always permanent change in the person's intellectual and emotional constitution (7). Where the experimental animal reacts with a nervous breakdown, the human being reacts by simplifying a situation that, in one way or another, has become intolerably complicated and uncontrollable. The simplification may, formulated in religious terms, consist in the individual's self-surrender (8), or, in psychological terms, it may consist in the refusal to participate in the situation in question (9).

It cannot be doubted that at various periods of his life, Ivan Groznyj was exposed to even very drastic experiences of the kind that predispose to an unbalanced state of mind and an acute conversion. It can be understood that the masterful Sil'vestr must have used powerful, psychological means of influencing his pupil, when both Groznyj and Kurbskij mention his use of supernatural horror images in young Ivan (10). The strain during the fire crisis of 1547 and the succession crisis of 1553 may have exercised a powerful influence on Groznyj's attitude, not least because they both appeared in strong contrast to previous climaxes of effort and triumph, the coronation as Czar and the conquest of Kazan'. Finally, it seems a reasonable conjecture, that the death of his son Dmitrij in 1553 and that of his wife Anastasija in 1560 produced powerful reactions. In the case of Anastasija, he maintained that it was a question of a plot against her life on the part of the boyars, either with sorcery or with gross wantonness—and he states expressly that her death brought a change in his way of life (11).

A change in way of life, however, is by no means equivalent to any form of conversion or change of mentality, and this it clearly was not, in Groznyj. His statement may be understood in two ways, first as a reason for the executions after Anastasija's death, and secondly as an explanation for the dissolute life for which Kurbskij reproached him (12). It is, of course, quite

---

6. *W. Sargant: Battle for the Mind. A Physiology of Conversion and Brain-washing* (London 1957) pp. 22 ff.

7. *Ibid.* pp. 139 ff.

8. *William James: The Varieties of Religious Experience* (London 1902) pp. 211 f.

9. *W. Sargant op. cit.* pp. 223 ff.

10. *Fennell* pp. 202 cf. 120, 140, *Kurbskij* col. 9.

11. *Fennell* pp. 190–192, *Kurbskij* col. 100, *Akty AE* p. 329 B.

12. *Fennell* p. 8.

impossible to use the Czar's private life to explain his political acts and way of thinking, since we have no direct evidence of any such interaction. And as to the executions, certainly no weighty argument can be adduced to support the view that these revealed a fundamentally new trait in Groznyj's way of thinking or acting. Neither in word nor in deed does Ivan appear as an essentially changed person after 1560, when the question is judged on the basis of a political analysis. On the other hand, it seems natural to speak of a constant piling up of psychical stresses and strains which, without leading to any demonstrable acute state of breakdown or conversion, yet regularly found release in particular political behaviour with tendencies to simplification of the situation.

This brings us back to the "theory of simplification", which it is to be hoped can now be seen in a clearer light. The starting point was the study of Groznyj's ambivalent political situation. On the one hand, he was absolute autocrat by virtue of the prevailing ideology and the formal system of state, but on the other hand, he was the object of the capricious and incalculable counter-play of a set of forces in the community. It is tempting to see this situation further elucidated by means of the psychiatric observations just discussed: the religious and political ideology that formed the foundation of the autocracy gave the autocrat a conditioned reflex, and the capriciousness of the play of political forces, which seemed to defy all rules and groupings, brought the frustration that naturally predisposed to nervous breakdown or to refusal to participate in a situation.

Professional psychologists would certainly call this illustration an example of popular psychology. In defence of what is perhaps a rather rash parallel, however, it must be said that it is used in order to turn the discussion away from another popular psychological manifestation, which has largely dominated the study of political phenomena, the theory of the pure need of power as a motive for action. This theory will hardly account for even so apparently simple a phenomenon as the terror and the executions. In the first place, this would require the ascription to Groznyj of a completely cynical insincerity in respect of religion, when he ordered the executions in the name of God and with the declared object of ensuring the salvation of the souls of those executed (13). From a human point of view, the matter is even more horrible, in that he obviously was both honest and serious in this. And in the second place, it can hardly be doubted that Groznyj, in executing his adversaries, really felt that his back was to the wall. He refused to take part in a situation that had grown too complicated for him, and consequently either he had to disappear or he had to get rid of his adversaries. Either of these was a method of simplification.

So far, the argument has aimed at showing crucial weaknesses in the

---

13. Cf. above p. 61.

"theory of change" and at supporting the "simplification theory". It remains to evaluate the possibility of combining the two in a collected analysis of Groznyj's pattern of action. It was stated above that from a theoretical point of view there is nothing to contradict the possibility that a process, well prepared and taking years to accomplish, should have so profound an effect that in the end the result must look like a change in the Czar's mentality and outlook. This possibility was, however, denied beforehand, as it was considered that the resulting characteristic of the present subject would not be tenable.

A policy that appears as the manifestation of a change of mentality in the person initiating it, must be revolutionary in one way or another. But Groznyj's policy was never at any moment revolutionary. It was a more or less consistent following of principles and objectives, with varying choice of tactics and methods, that at certain points had already been realised by his grandfather and his father. This is not to say that Groznyj lacked independent judgement or creative capacity as a political leader and planner—as has been maintained from time to time (14), but simply that his acts— however profound their effects—were a continuation of inherited objectives and intentions, the accomplishment of tasks given to him, so to speak, in the cradle, and which he now had identified with himself. Moreover, his policy—as will appear from what has already been said, and as will be maintained in what follows—to a very high degree was based on an administrative apparatus which underwent neither a change of mentality nor a change of outlook. To this banal observation comes the circumstance that an individual conversion may very well have led to great spiritual renewals, but seldom if ever to immediate, political structural changes. That it may do so indirectly, as for example, in the case of Mohammed, is another matter. Politics is a heavier machine than both art and religion, literature and philosophy. *Zōon politikon* cannot be converted.

As to Groznyj, it may be added that he seems to have been endowed with an exceptionally great power of resistance to the influences and stresses that might predispose him to nervous breakdown or to any form of personal conversion. It is obvious that he adhered to his fundamental principles, his religious faith, and his political convictions through all the situations of strain already mentioned, and more besides. It is natural to suppose that he had been gifted with that form of strong and permanent conviction, of that mental toughness, that according to the psychiatrists is the best condition for resisting pressure and escaping a breakdown (15). In a political sense, it is not difficult to discover in what this capacity for resistance consisted.

---

14. *Karamzin* t. IX p. 435, *N. Kostomarov: Istoričeskije monografii* t. XIII (Spbg. 1881) pp. 217, 237, *V. O. Kl'učevskij: Sočinenija* t. II (Moscow 1957) p. 196.
15. *W. Sargant op. cit.* pp. 229 f.

Groznyj did not feel as an individual, when he acted, but as an institution. He had been appointed ruler by God, and as ruler, he was answerable only to God. This was the principle on which he based the whole of his axiomatic argumentation, which stamped every motion of resistance as *samovolstvo*—inpermissible egoism and self-assertion of the individual—and permitted him to punish and reward according to his pleasure. His strength lay just in the immobility inherent in the substance of a political institution.

Moreover, it can be observed that, as already stated, Groznyj reacted with the other form of effective resistance to strain, by refusing to collaborate in a situation (16)—the phenomenon that, in a political sense, has been termed simplification. This is not to say that Groznyj carried out his action, or performed the acts that followed in consequence of the change of system with imperturbable coolness. The simplification was the answer to a strain. Groznyj's two Livonian "Commissioners for War", Taube and Kruse, report that after the change of system he appeared *"mit solcher vorkerter und schleunigen Vorenderungk seiner vorigen Gestalt, das er auch von vilen nicht hatt megen erkandt werden ... kein Hare auffem Kopfe und im Bart behalten, welches ihm alles der Zorn und innerlich tirannisch Hertz weckgefressen und vortilligt"* (17). This is not, however, evidence of a change of personality, but of an intense psychical strain in a crisis. Groznyj had played high, and bore the mark of it.

We have hereby rejected the "theory of change" and maintained the "theory of simplification" alone. With this as the starting-point, the discussion of the pattern of Groznyj's actions will now be taken up again at the point where it was interrupted with the assertion that in 1564, the Czar had reached a fundamentally new evaluation of the existing political possibilities, and on that basis wanted to revise the situation that had prevailed for a number of years (18). The question now is whether any indication of this alleged new evaluation can be found in the message of 1564, or whether the assertion must fail.

This discussion must be carried on with the course of the external events in the decade from 1554 to 1564 in mind. The abolition of the *kormlenije* system and the turning of the policy of reform against the interests of the boyars led to a strengthening of the military possibilities of the kingdom,

---

16. *Ibid.* pp. 226 f.

17. *Johann Taube & Elert Kruse:* Sendschreiben an Gotthard Kettler, Herzog zu Kurland und Semgallen = *Beiträge zur Kenntnis Russlands und seiner Geschichte, herausgegeben von Gustav Ewers und Moritz Engelhardt*, Bd. I, Heft 1, (Dorpat 1816) = *Sammlung Russischer Geschichte*, Bd. X, Stück 1 (Spbg. 1816) pp. 195 f. It is not certain that this description is based on anything but a report from a third party, since the first evidence that Taube and Kruse were in Groznyj's service and could make independent observations is from 1566, cf. *Epstein* p. 258.

18. See above p. 128.

to the conquest of Astraxan' in 1556, and in the next few years to a new, great initiative in foreign policy with the attack on Livonia in 1558 (19). If the increase in military strength was gained at the expense of the boyars, since they had had to give up their traditional monopoly here, the attack on Livonia was a further challenge to their interests, as will appear later from the discussion of the situation in foreign policy. Provisionally, it may be said that the Baltic War was carried on with increasing tension within the government. In 1560, Adašev and Sil'vestr were overthrown, and the relation between Groznyj and the boyars deteriorated violently, which found expression in a number of defections and intrigues (20). All this culminated in 1564, with the defection of Andrej Kurbskij and his flight to Lithuania on 30 April, with Groznyj's great message in July, and with his preliminary step towards the abdication crisis by leaving Moscow on 3 December.

Exactly a month later, on 3 January 1565, Groznyj sent two messages to Moscow. The first was addressed to the clergy, the princes, the boyars, the civil servants and the service nobility, and announced that the Czar was abdicating (*ostavil svoje gosudar'stvo*) because of the opposition he had met from all these classes. The second was addressed to the population of the capital, to be publicly proclaimed, and emphasised that the Czar's decision to abdicate was not in any way due to dissatisfaction or anger with the people. The reply was a joint appeal from clergy, nobility and from *černyje l'udi* to the Czar to remain on the throne. The appeal was complied with, after Groznyj had obtained by negotiation the assurance that he could rule with authority to carry out his programme, the introduction of a Czar's state within the state: *opričnina* (21).

To judge from the account of it handed down to us (22), the message of 3 January to the governing classes closely resembled the main content of Groznyj's great message to Kurbskij of July 1564. The reasons why the Czar had abdicated and why his wrath (*gnev*) and disgrace (*opala*) had fallen on these classes can be set under four heads: first, the treason of the magnates right from the time of Vasilij and through Ivan's youth, secondly, their greedy efforts to enrich themselves and their ruthless taking the law into their own hands in the same period, thirdly, their disobedience in respect of foreign relations, particularly during the Baltic War, and fourthly and finally, the obstruction of all these groups to the Czar's disciplinary measures. No details of these accusations are given, but it is quite evident that this skeleton corresponds very closely to the corpulent figure visible in the message of 6 months earlier.

---

19. Cf. *Zimin* Ref. p. 449.
20. Cf. *Očerki*, pp. 300–302.
21. *PSRL* t. XIII pp. 392 ff.
22. *Ibid.* p. 393.

The first two points stand as a list of contents of Ivan's autobiographical account in the July message, where he gives his personal reasons for his hate of the magnates and the necessity of the autocracy (23). The third point corresponds to the main content of Groznyj's political justification and his argumentation for reasons of state (24). The fourth point corresponds to the requirement in principle that the Czar must have the right to reward and punish according to his pleasure, without his subjects meddling in the matter, let alone permitting themselves to have a different view of it (25).

There can be no doubt that this last point was the crux of the matter. In the account of the discussions after the receipt of Groznyj's message, we learn that the classes to which the message was addressed decided to ask to Czar to rescind his decision to abdicate and his declaration of his anger and displeasure, and in return he was to govern and to punish at his pleasure (26). The reply sounds like a contract. Corresponding to the formula that Ivan *položil gnev* and *opalu*, it was decided to ask that the Czar should revoke his denunciation (*otovratiti gnev, opalu otdal*) and show clemency (*milost' pokazati*), which must be understood as the restoration of normal collaboration between ruler and subjects. The introduction of the concept of mercy or clemency, *milost'*, was not meant as an attempt to limit the Czar's freedom of action towards his subjects, at most an attempt to propitiate him as far as possible. He got full authority to exercise his will as ruler (*gosudar'skaja vol'a*) on all who were guilty of treason (*izmennyje dela delali*) without, apparently anyone attempting to define the concept of treason. In other words, the ruler could himself define it, and what that definition would be was known from the July message: all opposition to *gosudar'skaja vol'a* was synonymous with *samovolstvo*, and *samovolstvo* was treason (27).

Everything indicates that the message to the ruling classes was intended as a formal denunciation of the compromise formula of the *Sobor primirenija* of 1549 (28), and that it was thus understood. As we have seen, the compromise formula had been constantly undermined, and now it was to be abolished. But if this is correct, then we must also necessarily conclude that the compromise formula had in reality been denounced six months before, with the issue of the July message. It may be added that it had ceased to be effective long before, as is shown not least by the defection of the reformist Kurbskij. But in this context, the crucial point must be that the

23. See above pp. 28 ff.
24. See above pp. 26 f.
25. *Fennell* pp. 66, 106.
26. *PSRL* t. XIII p. 394.
27. See above p. 35.
28. See above p. 122.

action of January 1565 was based in principle on the message of the previous July, since in that message there is not even the slightest indication of loyalty to the compromise formula, but on the contrary, emphasis on its ineffectiveness in face of the self-assertion of the boyars (29), and at all decisive points the message annuls it.

Neither the author nor his public could have cherished any illusion that a publication that maintained the irresponsibility of the ruler to any earthly power and his right to punish at his pleasure could serve as a basis for any sort of compromise. The July message is Groznyj's prolegomena to the change of system. Considering the traditional nature of the ideas contained in the message, it may be further added that in the last resort, the change of system was the logical consequence of the traditional foundation of the Muscovite Czardom. The question is, however, what was the interplay of circumstances that dictated the moment for the change of system and its announcement. On the basis of what has been adduced so far, it will be assumed that the July message and the January action were two links in the same chain, and consequently the circumstances surrounding the great message to Kurbskij will be discussed first.

Formally, the appearance of the message was due to chance, and in any case not due to Groznyj's initiative, since it is formed as a reply to Kurbskij's letter of renunciation of allegiance, and thus comes as the Czar's reaction to the initiative of the fugitive. On this point, it has several times been pointed out that the formal reason is not to be taken too seriously, but rather as the opportune occasion for issuing a declaration that would in any case have been made at about that time. Thus *J. S. Lur'je* maintains that according to the superscription the message is addressed to the whole kingdom, and that the text betrays a wider address than merely Kurbskij by changing the form of address from singular to plural, directed to the boyars as the treasonable group (30). From this point of view, Groznyj had a topical, political reason for issuing the message—a reason stronger than given by the case of Kurbskij.

Against this it may be urged that it is hardly permissible to take the superscription as a more important indication than the text of the message. As to the text, the collective form of address can hardly be taken as a proof that the message was not directed to Kurbskij as an individual person, since a close analysis of Groznyj's method of argumentation shows that he has a marked tendency to undertake that mental operation that was earlier termed collective identification by means of an implicative characteristic (31). Finally, it may be pointed out that the often extremely colloquial style of the

---

29. *Fennell* pp. 86–88.
30. *Posl. Grozn.* pp. 470–474.
31. See above pp. 34 ff.

message and the very frequent use of invective and personal attack do not, at any rate, support the theory of the purely official character of the message. These observations are not intended to repudiate the idea of the official function of the message and in return to approve the formal explanation of its cause, but simply to justify the conjecture of a somewhat more complicated set of circumstances.

It seems quite evident that Groznyj would not have found it compatible with his dignity to send his voluminous and passionate message to an inferior and indifferent person, or to issue that message to the public on the occasion of the act of an inferior and indifferent person. That person would not have been worth either of these things. It cannot even be imagined that Groznyj would have done so in the case of the defection of a boyar, however distinguished, who belonged to the traditional, anti-Czar wing. It has been argued earlier for the view that Kurbskij did not belong to this category, but that, on the contrary, he was a sincere adherent of the policy of reform, a trusted helper of the Czar within the framework of the policy of reform and the compromise formula, and moreover a person of distinguished humanistic and religious culture. Kurbskij did not represent the traditional boyar line at all. He rather personified a reformist loyalty to the Czar—but with a condition for that loyalty, the requirement that the individual should be secure against arbitrary terrorism (32).

To Groznyj, the crucial point was to win for himself the right to exercise arbitrary terrorism. This appeared from the change of system. But it was also evident earlier, after the fall of Sil'vestr and Adašev, when Groznyj turned to the executions mentioned by Kurbskij in his first letter to the Czar. The policy of compromise was thenceforward gradually wound up, and Groznyj tried more and more to get out of his ambiguous, unclear situation, away from the ennervating policy of improvisation, by making what was termed above a simplification. There can be no doubt that this development was due to Groznyj's initiative. It is true that the sources report various personal influences—one speaks of the strong influence of Ivan's second wife, Marija Temgr'ukova, another on promptings from the boyars Vasilij Jur'jev-Zaxar'in and Aleksej Basmanov (33)—but none of these reports gives more than the conjecture, in itself quite obvious, that Groznyj did not, to a greater extent than any other autocrat, exercise his power alone, or alone invented good ideas for maintaining its effectiveness. Helpers or no helpers—Groznyj took the initiative. In this question, only one thing is certain. Kurbskij was not one of the Czar's helpers in these matters.

It has been maintained previously, that Kurbskij represented a moral and ethical alternative to Groznyj's autocracy, but not a concrete, political alter-

---

32. See above Chap. IV and pp. 50, 90, 102, 125 f., 132
33. *Epstein* p. 20, *Materialy* pp. 76, 146, *Fennell* pp. 8–10.

native. If the attempt be made to extract a political programme from Kurbskij's principles, it would probably be the requirement of the maintenance
of the representative monarchy that seemed to have been founded by the
introduction of the popular assembly, called together somewhat irregularly,
the *zemskij sobor,* which to some extent, at any rate, could canalise the
desires and interests of the various groups of the community. The idea that
there would be continuous rivalry between the traditionally privileged classes
and the new ambitious classes, did not frighten Kurbskij. But it is quite
evident that Groznyj could not tolerate the idea of such a continuation of
the compromises and improvisations of the reform period. The experiment
had been tried, and he had rejected it as a failure. For Groznyj, it was now
a matter of branding all such aspirations as useless, harmful, even criminal,
and of legitimizing his alternative—absolute discipline under the autocracy
—the only viable alternative.

Under the surface of the formalities, the initiative lay with Groznyj. He
had taken the step to a political development that left no room for Kurbskij's
standpoint. As it gradually became clear that not merely the extreme traditional boyar standpoint, but also more differentiated and moderate views,
were regarded as criminal, Kurbskij must have felt that the basis for his
work had disappeared. We cannot know if he had reason to feel that his
life was really in danger when he decided on flight. But it is clear, at all
events, that there was no room for him and his type in the future. And
it is also clear that Ivan Groznyj needed to mark and to justify his standpoint with a view to consolidating and securing the victory of his principle
of discipline over the principle of representation. Consequently it is vain to
discuss whether the message of 1564 was directed to Kurbskij or to the kingdom. It was directed to Kurbskij as the personification of that kingdom, or
that part of the kingdom, that Groznyj would no longer recognize.

Both Kurbskij and Groznyj argued for an absolute requirement, and
neither of them showed any inclination to take into consideration the social
and political differentiation offered to the view of an objective eye. The idea
behind Groznyj's implicative characteristic and collective identification was
that all who were not with him were against him. He was not interested in
emphasising the merits of one class rather than another. He uttered not a
word in favour of the service nobility or the civil servants or the citizens,
whose interests coincided so widely with those of the centralized Czardom,
and disposed them to be the Czar's indispensable political supporters. All
alike, noble and cleric, official and citizen, were met with the general requirement of absolute discipline. There was consequently no room in the
July message either, for discriminating considerations on the background of
the succession crisis, on the justification of the fear of a new oligarchy under
a child-prince. Groznyj maintained that the situation, in itself hopeless, at

the prospect of his death offered only one possibility, unshaken adherence to the mechanical succession by inheritance, that is, unconditional loyalty to the Czar as an institution.

Here, without doubt, lies the reason why Groznyj attached so little importance to a tactical comparison between the crisis over the succession and that over the abdication. To him, there was one crucial difference in principle between the two situations, that in the latter he still existed after the abdication, which meant that, with his full capacity for action unimpaired, he faced the population with the choice between the institution and the vacuum that would be left behind. His deliberations here were different from those connected with the succession crisis. He had to decide what was the prospect of the leading elements of the population choosing the institution and him, or choosing the vacuum with the free play of the various forces in the community. As we have seen, it was one of the main arguments in the July message that the alternative to the absolute autocracy would be precisely this free play of the forces in the community, chaos, in fact, with the struggles of rival groups, internal division of the kingdom and externally, weakness leading to destruction (34). Thus he prepared the population for their choice. His own deliberations undoubtedly must have centred on a comparison with the situation during the crisis over the fire in 1547.

In such a comparison, Groznyj had every reason to expect that the coming choice would fall more favourably to him than the situation in the summer after he had been crowned as Czar, seventeen years before. The strong man Makarij had died in 1563, and Afanasij had succeeded him as Metropolitan. The reform policy had left its mark on the Russian community, and increased Groznyj's prestige with the new forces in that community. Political publicists had long been maintaining views that to a very large extent supported Groznyj's demands, perhaps had even inspired him to form his demands as he did—and in any case, formulated them earlier than Groznyj himself did (35). He no longer needed to fear a commons that reacted in blind panic and in fact allowed themselves to be used by rival groups, as had happened when the populace trooped out to Vorob'jevo in 1547. In the July message, then, Ivan could speak, apparently deliberately, of *narod xudožajšix umov* as a covert warning to the *černyje l'udi* not to behave so simple-mindedly and foolishly another time (36).

In his message, Groznyj could also intimate that he was not dependent on any group in the community, but that he always had the helpers he needed. Though formulated in quotations from the Bible, he plainly told the traditional participants in government that their position depended on their

34. See above pp. 25 ff.
35. Cf. above p. 108.
36. Cf. above p. 95.

acts, and was not given at birth, and that true helpers could be fetched from anywhere, merely on the condition that they showed themselves willing to do what was required of them. Abraham's children were to be known by their deeds only, and consequently God could raise up children unto Abraham from stones (37). This has been taken to be a threatening warning of the coming change of system (38), and it has been added that the lack of more precise indications of the coming order may be due to the fact that the plans for *opričnina* had not taken concrete form at that date (39).

It is striking, however, that Groznyj also at another place in the July message says something similar, and in words that may seem to have a subtle secondary meaning. In connexion with his demand for the right to punish and reward his subjects at his pleasure, Groznyj declares that he has not—as alleged by Kurbskij—exterminated his army leaders. On the contrary, he has, by the help of God, a multitude of them, even excluding the traitors (40). Thus Groznyj declares here once more that he is not dependent on the traditional ruling class of privileged magnates, but that he can obtain his helpers in sufficient numbers from other classes of the population. He does so with an ironical allusion to Kurbskij's description of the traditional leader group as "those given by God" (41). In other words, God has not given the Czar a particular group of the population as his helpers, and consequently the Czar is not obliged to listen specially to the advice of this group—God has simply given him a population of subjects, and the authority of the ruler is not limited with regard to the merits of one class or another. Consequently, neither could the service nobility or the civil servants count on any kind of privileged position. The only group that required special definition in relation to the Czar was that of the traitors, who were named by exclusion. It seems more than mere chance, that the expression used for exclusion is *oprič*—the root, in fact, of the word *opričnina*. It is hard to believe that, when he wrote this, he did not have fairly clear ideas about his coming action.

It was asserted above that Groznyj would scarcely have been so cunning that he deliberately concealed his realistic, tactical considerations about the succession crisis by giving the misleading, traditional and simplified account. It has also been stated that Groznyj may be supposed to have had quite different ideas about the succession crisis than might have been expected beforehand. It is a far cry from this, however, to the assumption that Groznyj would have given comparatively concrete information or indications in

---

37. *Fennell* p. 150, *John* VIII, 39, *Matt.* III, 9.
38. *V. O. Kl'učevskij: Sočinenija* t. II (Moscow 1957) p. 170.
39. *J. S. Lur'je* in *Posl. Grozn.* pp. 476 f.
40. *Fennell* p. 66.
41. Cf. above p. 21.

his July message had he had precise plans for his coming action—or to the opposite conclusion, that in July he had no precise plans. Even though he refrained from subtle, misleading manoeuvres, he had no need to blurt out his plans before the time.

There is nothing to show that Groznyj was a worse tactician than a propagandist. His abilities in this latter respect have already been discussed (42). It is natural to assume that on both tactical and propagandist grounds, Groznyj found it advisable to prepare the way for his action psychologically. Kurbskij's defection was an appropriate occasion and a suitable excuse. With his great message to the traitor, Groznyj could undertake his general settlement without needing to do so ostentatiously. The formal addressee could be used as a scapegoat or symbol, and by allowing the message to leak out to the homes of the population it could simultaneously serve its real purpose—to clarify theoretically both the situation and its possibilities. The Czar translated the situation into abstract terms to prepare his public for the concrete choice. In the course of the six subsequent months, the message could sink in, and the ground be prepared as he desired. In the sixth month, from 3 December to 3 January, the psychological pressure was increased by the Czar's departure from Moscow, with a conspicuously large train and an inexplicably abundant equipment. And after a month's increasing bewilderment among the people, came clarity like a thunderbolt from the hand of the Czar.

On this view of the matter, there can be no doubt of the circumstances that determined the timing of Groznyj's action. He issued his July message at a moment that, for several reasons already mentioned, was ripe for a break. Groznyj had long ago made his evaluation—and revaluation—of the political possibilities. The issue of the message was the first step in the action as planned. The nature of this preliminary step required that in order to obtain the desired effect, a certain time should elapse before the next step was taken. On the other hand, this period must not be so long that the effect of the message should be diffused or weakened, or that indiscretions might leak out concrete plans to the public. The last month's absence—which included the Czar's family and immediate entourage—served both purposes. In July, then, the alarm-clock was set going. And it was its inner mechanism that determined when the final signal should be given.

It is striking, but on the basis of what has been stated hitherto, not at all inexplicable, that Groznyj directed his proclamation of *gnev* and *opala* to all the leading classes in the kingdom, princes and boyars, the clergy in all the ranks of the hierarchy, to the service nobility and to the civil servants. We have already seen that even though the July message was formed

---

42. Cf. above pp. 33, 44.

primarily as an attack on the *bojarstvo,* there was no question of emphasising the merits of other groups as a contrast to the born traitors, or as examples of what the Czar supported and was supported by. In the July message, *dvor'anstvo* and *d'jačestvo* simply do not exist. There are only traitorous subjects and obedient subjects. Groznyj carried this line further in his proclamation with complete consistency, which did not make the situation unclear or confused for him, but on the contrary, completely clear and unambiguous. Nobody, not even the representatives of Iosifism, was to feel that he was superior to the seriousness of the situation or secure against a fall. All these leading groups were to feel at one, though they were incompatibles: they were all to feel that they were in the same boat, though they would never be able to agree to steer in the same direction: they were to feel, one and all, that without the captain's authority and their own subjection, they would be lost.

During the absence of the Czar, the Metropolitan, Afanasij was regent, but not a regent who could fill the Czar's place and stand as an alternative to Groznyj. It was to him that the proclamation of wrath was sent, and automatically he had to function as the intermediary of the situation: on the one hand, as the deliverer of Groznyj's decision, and on the other hand, as the receiver of the representations, expostulations and proposals of the various groups in this panicky situation. Moreover, it was he, who—in spite of his reverend position—also belonged to those denounced by the Czar, that had to receive the deputations from the *černyje l'udi,* from citizens, merchants and foreign colonies who in Groznyj's second proclamation had been given a certificate to say that they had not lost the Czar's favour and grace. These people demanded that the Metropolitan should help to persuade the Czar to rescind his decision to abdicate, and they did so with the express reason that they did not wish to stand defenceless for the leading groups, "the wolves" and "the mighty". In other words, Afanasij had to receive the people's intimation that he and his like were not wanted, and that the Czar and his unlimited power, on the other hand, was wanted. Thus the situation developed as planned: the voice of the people demanded the capitulation of the leading groups: the leading groups were themselves panic-stricken: Groznyj, therefore, could present an already defeated delegation with an ultimatum, which included a completely worked out project—formulated with the precision of a truce agreement, to judge from the account in the chronicle (43)—of the division of the kingdom into *zemščina* and *opričnina.* The arrangement was accepted, and Ivan rescinded his abdication.

The question now is, Was Ivan's victory absolute and universal? He had

---

43. *PSRL* t. XIII pp. 394 f.

denounced the compromise formula, and demanded unlimited power. He achieved approval of the terror and the establishment of *opričnina*. This fact, however, does not mean that a sign of equality can be put at once between what was demanded and what was agreed to.

According to the formulation in the chronicle, Groznyj resumed the government by delegating power to a group of his trusted followers, who were to reside in Moscow and, according to his orders, govern his kingdom on the lines hitherto followed (*po svoim prikazom ... prav'at jego gosudar'stvo po prežnemu obyčaju*). From his seat outside Moscow, he himself dealt with the administration of the new, special sphere, on the formula that he was organizing it with a view to his full personal maintenance (*na ves' svoj obixod učiniti osobno*). These two formulations undoubtedly cover the negotiators' definitions of the two spheres of which the kingdom was henceforth to be composed, and it cannot be far wrong to take these two as the central and crucial formulations in the agreement, or, at any rate, reflections of them. If they be taken as contractual provisions and interpreted as such, the result must be that to the one hand, Groznyj resumed the responsibility as ruler of the kingdom in general, and that he bound himself to govern in accordance with practice hitherto through the usual instances and institutions, as far as concerned the *zemščina,* i. e. that part of the kingdom that did not fall within the special arrangement, but that, on the other hand, in his special sphere, the *opričnina,* he could exercise his full, personal power, in the manner and through the instances that suited him.

With Western, mediaeval constitutional practice in mind, this arrangement looks quite normal and comparatively moderate, a sort of compromise and a demarcation of the spheres of *iura regni* and *iura nostra*. Nor, on Russian ground, was the concept of *opričnina* a new invention. It had been used in former times to designate a special area of an estate set aside for a particular purpose, a dower house, for example, though without being so extensive as to acquire political significance (44). Formally, the arrangement seems to involve a renewed compromise, which meant only half a victory to Groznyj: he got a free hand in the special area, but in the ordinary part of the kingdom everything remained as it was. Further, the special area was established by a formula that actually meant a revival of old ways of thinking, and rather betrayed Ivan's dependence on tradition than was the expression of a revolutionary new creation. Such dependence on tradition has already been mentioned in other contexts.

---

44. *I. I. Sreznevskij: Materialy dl'a slovar'a drevne-russkago jazyka*, t. II (Spbg. 1895) col. 694, *A. Presn'akov:* Udel'noje vladenije v kn'azom prave Velikorossii i vlast' Moskovskix gosudarej = *Dela i Dni*, t. I (Pbg. 1920) pp. 16 f.

The result of the crisis is most accurately evaluated by comparing the two parts of the account, where there are traces of a contractual style and a stamp of formula from the negotiations. The first part, formulates the basis of the request to the Czar to annul his decision to abdicate. The condition was that the Czar should revoke his *gnev* and *opala* and show *milost'*, and in return he might freely exercise his *gosudar'skaja vol'a* against traitors, and in reality define "traitor" as he wished. The second part formulates the agreement as the result of the negotiations just concluded. The kingdom in general will be governed as the Czar's *gosudar'stvo* and *po prežnemu oby-čaju*, while the special area was established *na svoj obixod osobno*. It is evident that the two parts—preamble and result—do not agree. The pre-amble indicates a solution for the whole kingdom as one unit, and implies a surrender to the Czar's provisional demand in his message of 3 January, the demand to be allowed to use terror. It is true that the result maintains as a whole the Czar's right to punish traitors, but limits, in reality, his liberty of action to the special area, while in the ordinary part of the kingdom, the usual practice is to continue.

There are two ways of taking this divergence. Either the accused negotia-tors managed to get access to discussions with Groznyj on the basis of a vaguely worded capitulation, which they then succeeded in turning into a precise agreement in the course of their negotiations on a compromise be-tween government practice hitherto and the Czar's personal absolute power. Or the negotiators went to the Czar with a capitulation he neither wanted nor had any confidence in, and therefore rejected in favour of a division arrangement, the principle and the formulation of which came as a surprise to Groznyj's opponents. In the first case, the Czar's victory was, of course, limited, since the negotiators went back with concessions they had won. In the second case, there is no question of a limited victory, since the Czar had achieved precisely what he wanted to achieve.

On the basis of the previous discussion, the second interpretation must be considered the more probable. It is difficult to imagine that Groznyj had not prepared the organization of the special area even six months before the crisis. In the first place, his argumentation in the July message seems to point in the direction of this arrangement (45), and in the second place, the account of the details of the arrangement as given in the chronicle, has all the marks of a well prepared project, one so complicated that it could scarcely have been produced as an improvisation on the spur of the moment during the negotiations. Since the crisis was started by Groznyj and came as a surprise to his opponents, the fully fledged project must have originated from the Czar and not from any other party to the negotiations.

---

45. See above pp. 143 f.

And there is the further indication, that *opričnina* in its concrete formulation turned out to correspond closely to the interests of the Czar, but to be catastrophic for his opponents. This argument cannot be countered by a conjecture that, after he had been forced to accept a division of the kingdom, he had succeeded in taking his opponents by surprise by giving the special arrangement a character quite different from what had been expected. From the start it was clear that the division into two areas meant a profound change in conditions in the special area, including the expulsion or transfer of undesirable elements of the population from particular quarters of Moscow and from the districts that came under *opričnina*. Even if the name of the area and the contractual formulation of its legal basis seem extremely traditional, this does not obscure the fact that the new institution got—and was planned to have—a far more original form than might have been expected from its traditional background. It was a question of a state within the state, governed with the help of a picked *élite* banded together like conspirators under an absolute discipline, symbolized by a common oath which seems to have bound them to have no intercourse with *zemščina*, a sort of uniform based on the black habit of the monks, and common badges (46). This corps of *opričniki* was to enforce the Czar's will in every detail, administer his punishments and prevent resistance by terrorism.

The new system meant a tautening and an improvement in the efficiency of the Czar's government. It is not necessary to dwell on the fact that this tautening was at the expense of *zemščina,* and that the terror was administered with a senselessness and a ruthlessness that horrified not only the cultivated Kurbskij in his exile, but also the certainly less squeamish adventurer Heinrich Staden, who was in the centre of these events (47). In this connexion, it is more important to note the significant fact that Groznyj gave up the idea of tautening and efficiency in the whole kingdom. And that he considered that to be impracticable must be because his ressources of power were inadequate for such a task. We have already seen that both in his July message and in his abdication declaration he had rejected the whole of the kingdom's leaders and administrators *en bloc,* from the boyars and the Metropolitan to the service nobility and the civil servants. This was obviously a tactical move, but it may be added that the making of this move at all was obviously because he did not consider it possible to govern satisfactorily by means of even the most loyal branches of the administration. There must first be a tautening or simplification, so that a completely loyal *élite* could be obtained from the loyal branches by an appropriate sorting or purging.

That the resources of power were too small meant that administratively

46. *Epstein* pp. 21, 43, *J. Taube & E. Kruse op. cit.* (see p. 137) pp. 197 f., 202 f.
47. *Epstein* pp. 38, 48 ff., 156.

the kingdom was too large. In another context it has been noted that the kingdom was too small, when the growing service nobility was to be rewarded with land. This paradox gave rise to two domestic tasks: first, to intensify the exploitation of the land and the peasants' labour by a redistribution in favour of the service nobility, as was done within the special area (48), and secondly, to deal with an administrative powerlessness of the government in local administration that had defied all measures and all efforts. It is typical that, as late as towards the end of the seventies, the Danish ambassador, Jacob Ulfeldt, could report how on the one hand he was assured of the Czar's absolute power, but on the other hand that out in the country people refused to obey the Czar's orders unless compelled to do so by whips and blows (49). Consequently, there is nothing surprising in the fact that Ivan abandoned the idea of efficiency in the whole kingdom and chose, instead, to concentrate on certain vital parts, the complete mastery of which gave him the key to the direction of domestic developments and allowed him to pursue his objectives in foreign policy. Thus Groznyj's simplification of his position as ruler was given not only a clear, political but also a tangible territorial definition.

The disciplinary nature of this simplification inspired many of Ivan's contemporaries and many interpreters since to see in his action a devilish inspiration, a fall from grace, a change. But behind this action, however, there were urgent and permanent administrative and economic problems, which certain foreign observers had perceived even in his own days (50), and which have since taken a prominent position in the evaluations of historians, where these do not confine themselves to changes of personality and psychological mysteries (51). It is precisely in these tangible motives behind Groznyj's acts and decisions—or, if you will, in their character of justified political "necessity" viewed in relation to the objective—that we must find the explanation why the system of government by terrorism did not call forth only horror and hate but also the support in principle of the traders and the craftsmen (52), and, in his helpers, their ecstatic devotion.

---

48. *P. A. Sadikov: Očerki po istorii opričniny* (Moscow-Leningrad 1950) pp. 50 f

49. *Jacob [Ulfeldt]: Hodoeporicon Ruthenicum* (Francofurti 1608) p. 26. On the loc.al weakness of the central administration, see *P. Mil'ukov: Očerki po istorii russkoj kul'tury,* č. I (5. izd., Spbg. 1904) pp. 187 ff., *N. Rožkov: Proisxoždenie samoderžavija v Rossii* (Moscow 1906) pp. 76, 162 f.

50. *J. Taube & E. Kruse op. cit.* pp. 199–202. In addition to these observations by adventurers who had been in Groznyj's service, we have particularly the impressions of an English diplomat, based on reports, see *Giles Fletcher: Of the Russe Common Wealth = Russia at the Close of the Sixteenth Century,* ed. by E. A. Bond, The Hakluyt Society No. 20 (London 1856) pp. 33 f.

51. *S. M. Solov'jov: Istorija Rossii* (2. izd., Spbg. 1860) t. VI, pp. 436 ff.

52. *P. A. Sadikov op. cit.* p. 60.

Of this last, we have a clear witness in the imprisoned *opričnik*, Vasilij Gr'aznoj, and his self-effacing humility and self-sacrificing obedience to the Czar, who in his eyes stands in the place of God (*aki bog*) while he himself is only the slave, whose only value is his usefulness (53). This is not piety, but idealism, not the worship of God, but the cult of personality. The Czar is compared with God, he is not identified with the divine. But Groznyj is identified with a political object. Thus it happened that Groznyj's system could be called by some a hell, and a kingdom of light by others (54).

There was madness in Groznyj's system—the madness that manifested itself in the unlimited exercise of power by means of terrorism. There was logic in his system—the logic expressed by the determined pursuit of political plans, even when adverse circumstances make almost superhuman demands of tactical ingenuity and political strength. There was method in his system—and the method was simplification. First, simplification by refusing to go on ruling in a situation that did not permit him to rule in his sense of the term. Then, simplification in that by his ultimatum he faced his subjects—with what may appear to be subtle irony—with a chaotic situation, the only possible solution of which was the relief of simplifying everything by laying everything in the hands of the Czar. And finally, simplification by concentrating all his ressources on his state within the state, and refusing to have serious dealings with the rest of the situation.

Lastly, there was also continuity in Groznyj's actions through all fluctuations and changes of system. It was a continuity that was based on a fixed ideological conviction of the mandate and the task of the Czar, but also on the stubbornness of an administrative apparatus when it has once established itself and gained a view of the practical functions of the government. The question then is what were the relations between these ideological convictions and these practical functions in the system that Groznyj erected.

---

53. *Ibid.* pp. 534 f.
54. *Ibid.* p. 62. "The kingdom of light" (*car'skaja svetlost'*, *gosudarevaja svetlost'*) see *ibid.* pp. 146 f. with references, *Istoričeskij Arxiv*, t. III (1940) pp. 170 f., 242. "Hell", see *Fennell* p. 214. Kurbskij's pun *kromešnik/opričnik: ibid.* pp. 204, 242, *Kurbskij* col. 109, 111, 140 f., 145, 147, 156, 163, 190 etc. Cf. the discussion on "light" and "dark" even before the introduction of *opričnina*, *Fennell* pp. 2, 44–46, 104.

VIII

The Strength and Security of the Realm

Ivan Groznyj claimed as his mandate that he was Russia's Czar and autocrat by the grace of God and by God's command, for the benefit of the true faith and the security of the Russian kingdom. God's grace and God's command were two sides of the same thing. His subjects could not question his right to the throne since he occupied it by virtue of grace, *Boga milost'*, manifested in the right succession. And he himself had no right to act otherwise than as Czar and ruler, since that was what he was by virtue of the command, *Božije povelenije,* and thus was responsible only to God. On the basis of this axiom, Groznyj claimed his monopoly of deciding what was right and what was wrong, and what was required in regard to the two highest values, the true faith and the Russian realm. Conflict between these two supreme considerations did not exist, any more than he foresaw the theoretical possibility of such a conflict. There was no defined boundary of difference between the two concepts—they were consequently as one.

This does not, however, prevent there being two different phenomena behind this observation. Let us compare Groznyj's view of the state to a spectrum. The difference between the faith and the realm manifests itself clearly in the outer fields of the spectrum, which on the one side represents the Czar's relations to the church authorities and religious dogmas, and on the other, the Czar's concern with national affairs in relation to the world round about. Using this picture of Groznyj's view of the state, it will be seen that the two outer fields—the religious responsibility and the imperial responsibility—have this in common, that they lie beyond the Czar's sphere of sovereignty and yet face him with categorical demands. Those parts of the spectrum that lie between the outer fields, that is to say, all forms of domestic policy, lie, on the other hand, completely under the Czar's authority, since here he represents, so to speak, the categorical demands of the outer fields for the population. There is consequently a resemblance between the outer fields insofar as they perform a more or less identical function in relation to the field at the centre. At the same time, however, there is the crucial difference that the religious requirement, on the one side, represented a moral or ideological limitation of the Czar's sovereignty, but on the other side, the imperial faced him with the physical limitation of power politics—that which in the last instance is identical with the fortune of war.

So far, we have seen how Groznyj administered his mandate in relation to one outer field, his religious responsibility. He exploited the ideological support of the church after having first ensured its political reliability. In those cases where the church failed him on this point, he did not shrink from interpreting the requirements of the true faith himself. In other words, Groznyj did not allow himself to be guided by given, unchangeable, in-appellable ideological principles rooted in the church authorities, but de-manded, however, that his subjects—including the church authorities— should do so in relation to himself. He utilized his religious mandate to assume liberty of action in politics, but acknowledged no political obligation to his subjects within the framework of religious requirements and com-mandments. This freedom of movement in relation to the religious outer field he achieved, from an ideological point of view, by distinguishing be-tween personal piety and political piety and by postponing his religious re-sponsibility till Doomsday.

We have also seen how Groznyj, in relation to the central field, that is, in his domestic policy, consistently endeavoured to exploit his mandate and his freedom of action as much as possible, and especially by getting rid of hindrances and possible checks by that form of political tactics that may be called simplification. Groznyj's simplification was a method, not an end. On the grounds explained earlier, Groznyj had no difficulty in justifying his method in relation to the religious responsibility. We must now turn our attention to the other outer field, which could limit the Czar's freedom of action in a more tangible manner, by concrete force. The facts of foreign policy were not to be shaken like the church's articles of faith.

Here, Groznyj's axiomatic way of thinking and lack of clear political ideas in politics and in intellectual concepts must play a decisive part in any evaluation of his motives.

By his demonstration of the unfortunate consequences in foreign policy of the internal weakness and division of a kingdom (1), Groznyj in reality bound himself to the only tangible form of responsibility—which means the only form of political obligation—in the whole of his system: that his govern-ment should mean security and progress for the kingdom. This was the only decisive test here on earth and before the Day of Judgement. It is hardly necessary to mention that this *ultima ratio* was not a unique or a particularly characteristic trait of Ivan Groznyj or his Russia, or, for that matter, of his period. But it must be remembered that such a reason of state, also in Groznyj's case, meant that he connected his only clear, political responsibil-

---

1. Cf. above pp. 25 f.

ity with precisely that aspect of his political activity that, in the most concrete sense, lay outside the field of his sovereignty. Moreover, by introducing the fortunes of war motif as proof of God's grace and favour (2)—a motif, again, not peculiar to him—he made his religious mandate more or less dependent on that form of political success the conditions for which were given by foreign powers and depended just as much upon their strength or weakness as on his own skill or authority.

If these traits were not peculiar to Groznyj, they yet had special significance within his system because of their connexion with a tradition that was unique. Ivan's role as Orthodoxy's Czar was historically rooted in the conception of Moscow as the Third Rome, and thus inseparably connected with what was originally an eschatological conception of Russia as the last and only orthodox kingdom, but with constantly increasing stress on power politics. The Czar's responsibility for the true faith and the Russian realm was thus not only in regard to domestic politics a single combined concept that excluded the possibility of conflict between religious and political considerations, it was also in regard to foreign policy a fixed, closed whole, an amalgam of ideology and power. A loss of power by the kingdom meant a set-back for the only true faith. A gain in power for the kingdom was progress for the true faith and consequently a victory for Our Lord and the whole of humanity.

In his July message, Groznyj reproached his adversaries, and primarily Kurbskij, that by their dilatoriness and passivity during the Baltic War, they had prevented what would otherwise, with the help of God, have been achieved in the course of a year, the conquest of the whole of Germany for the true faith (3). It obviously did not occur to him that by his remark about Germany and the true faith he was putting a highly critical query by his own appeal to a religious mandate. If a heavenly desire to see Germany also brought to the true faith, and if the help of Heaven to achieve this desirable result could really fail, or be defeated by the evil efforts of the traitors and oath-breakers despised by the Czar and rejected by God, then the fortunes of war motif could not be so valuable as Groznyj maintained it was. His absent-mindedness reminds one of the village parson who announced that there would be a service the following Sunday "if God will and nothing happens to prevent it".

There was nothing, of course, that prevented Groznyj from giving his accusation against Kurbskij and the other army leaders great weight, even though he had kept his argumentation to the purely political. In view of the imperial requirement, it would be a heavy moral responsibility that would rest on the generals if they could justly be accused of having let slip

---

2. Cf. above pp. 75 f.
3. *Fennell* p. 120.

a favourable opportunity of extending the kingdom by conquest. Groznyj, however, would not be satisfied with this temporal argument. Whether he realised at all the temporal consequence of his argument may be a matter for discussion—and will be discussed later. To him, quite obviously, the main point was to link the concrete military problem with the highest religious considerations and obligations. Thereby he would make his argument authoritative and inappellable—but by mixing the two he managed only to render his religious mandate vulnerable and arguable.

A corresponding inconsequence showed itself also in Groznyj's actions compared with his ideological principles. He claimed to hold his office as Czar by virtue of an inviolable order of succession, and an imperative *Božije povelenije,* but all the same disobeyed God's command by abdicating in 1565. Faced with this argument, Groznyj might have replied that his refractory subjects had prevented him from carrying out God's will as Czar, so that he was justified in refusing to act as ruler over godless subjects. This reply, however, would not have served in 1575, when he put Simeon Bekbulatovič on his throne and disguised himself as his subject (4). Finally, it might be mentioned that his confidence in the divine grace was not quite absolute, since, as stated earlier (5), he thought it advisable to make sure of Queen Elisabeth's hospitality, just in case.

Such examples cannot be taken as proof that in religion Groznyj was a hypocrite, or that he was intellectually backward. Groznyj's obvious sincerity in his faith was simply reserved for personal, individual piety, while he took the full consequence of the justification by reason of state for extensive operational freedom both ideological and practical, when it was a question of public affairs. He utilized religious arguments to reduce his opponents, but he simply did not accept the possibility that the same arguments could be turned against himself. These arguments could naturally be turned against the Czar himself, as already shown by indications of a possible polemic against Groznyj's argumentation, and as Kurbskij actually did in connexion with the fortunes of war motif (6). But it is impossible to find in Groznyj's writings any convincing sign that he lacked intellectual capacity, and that this was the reason why he thus laid himself open. The reason must be taken to be quite different, that his approach was not intellectual at all but emotional, not analytic but synthetic (7).

It may be imagined that Kurbskij would have accepted the figurative comparison of Groznyj's conception of the state to a spectrum divided into

---

4. *Istoričeskij Arxiv* t. VII (Moscow 1951) p. 226.
5. See above p. 128.
6. See above p. 76.
7. On the formal expression of this, see pp. 34–39.

various fields: but Groznyj himself would never have done so. It would have been more acceptable to him to compare the system to a lens, which caught the heavenly light and the burning point of which was the divine exercise of power through the Czar, that is, the existence of the faith and the kingdom in one, indivisible whole. Spreading outwards, there would be a series of concentric circles, differentiated by the diminishing influence of the burning point, a constantly lower degree of inspiration and receptiveness. Actions and arguments, insofar as they were just and true, came from the burning point as the common centre. What came from outside, represented ungodliness and treason.

It was because of Groznyj's centric conception, that he did not acknowledge ecclesiastical instances as a religious control institution, and that he did not accept domestic power groups as fellow players in his system. This he must have done, if he had a spectral conception and viewed the various fields as in themselves defined magnitudes in a mutual functional relation. Clearly, the same attitude marked Groznyj's conceptions in foreign policy. The last circle in his concentric system is the frontiers of the realm, which subjects are not permitted to cross—either in person or by correspondence—except on official business (8). What lies on the other side of the frontier is heathendom and hostility and unwholesomeness. The Germans are not proper Christians, the Poles are in the throes of political dissolution (9). The relation with this foreign world must be either that it is converted by a successful war, or that it is exploited to the utmost by treaties on trade, by calling in technical, military or scientific experts (10), or by diplomatic intrigue.

It is true, of course, that neither war, nor the conduct of commercial interests, nor efforts at technical modernization, nor participation in the diplomatic game were characteristic of Groznyj or his government or his country, as compared with others. Just as his reasons of state and his appeal to his divine favour were, from an ideological point of view, common property in Europe, so his practice in foreign policy was largely of the same character as that of his fellow players in high politics. There is thus nothing surprising in the fact that Groznyj officially started the war against Livonia in order to enforce a demand for sovereignty over the country that had been put forward since his grandfather's time (11). None the less, there are other circumstances that serve to throw a peculiar light on Groznyj's practice in

8. *H. Fleischhacker: Die staats- und völkerrechtlichen Grundlagen der moskauischen Aussenpolitik* = Jahrb. f. Gesch. Osteur., Beiheft 1 (Breslau 1938) p. 34, cf. the sureties against *ot'jezd* in *SGGD* t. I, pp. 458, 475, 477, 487 ff., 537 f., 558 ff., 565 f.
9. *Fennell* pp. 16, 26, 154.
10. *S. F. Platonov: Moskva i zapad* (Berlin 1926) pp. 9 ff.
11. See *Epstein* pp. 244 ff.

foreign affairs, just as the theory of Moscow as the Third Rome gave his ideological foundation a quite special character.

In 1558, Groznyj caused reproaches to be sent to Copenhagen because the Danish King had addressed the Czar as "brother". This form of address, it was claimed, had never been customary (12). In fact, it had been the custom since the days of Ivan Velikij. *R. Wipper* observes that what Moscow maintained was not true, but adds in explanation that Groznyj and his diplomats had not forgotten anything or confused their terms. They had simply decided to change their tone to Denmark and to be more arrogant in their treatment of that country. What it all meant, then, was that the Russian potentate would not be addressed as an equal by a little king. This case does not prevent the Russian historian from talking about Groznyj's incomparable mastery of the art of diplomacy. A less ecstatic admiration for Groznyj and a more traditional view of the art of diplomacy would dictate a preference for calling this an inappropriate piece of clumsiness, to be explained only by the Czar's view of himself as the administrator of the only true religion and the only righteous realm. It was, so to speak, a centric reaction against the periphery. But from the outside it could only be considered as a gross breach of etiquette, which Groznyj otherwise punctiliously insisted on.

With irritation that sometimes rises to desperation, most foreign diplomats describe their difficulties in working with the Muscovite government. The Dane, Jacob Ulfeldt, complained of the bad treatment of his mission, in that the most necessary material wants could hardly be supplied, and about the Russian technique of negotiation, which seems to have consisted mainly in ignoring the other side's arguments and repeating their own until the other side was softened up (13). The English ambassador to Moscow in 1568, Thomas Randolph, complained about this treatment under five heads: first, that he was not allowed to make contact with his fellow-countrymen in Moscow; secondly, that during his stay there he was kept shut up in his quarters like a prisoner; thirdly, that dispatches from Queen Elisabeth were kept back and read by the Russians with the help of an English agent; fourthly,

---

12. *C. Schirren: Neue Quellen zur Geschichte des Untergangs livländischer Selbständigkeit. Aus dem dänischen Geh. Archive zu Kopenhagen*, Bd. I = Archiv für die Gesch. Liv-, Est- und Churlands. Neue Folge, Bd. IX (Reval 1883) p. 90. Cf. *R. Wipper: Ivan Groznyj* (3rd edn., Moscow 1947) p. 175.

13. *Jacob [Ulfeldt]: Hodoeporicon Ruthenicum* (Francofurti 1608) pp. 26, 35 f.: "*Quam barbari hi se esserant vel ex hoc potes colligere, quod omnia quae dixerint, rata et firma esse existiment et quod magis est, contradici sibi in tractationibus non patiantur,...ea considerantes quae ipsi in medium adduxerint, quod si quicquam dictum fuerit illis non conveniens, absurdum esse nihilque ad rem pertinere ajunt, atque ita de se solum bene existimantes, prae se alios pro nihilo ducunt, ut merito hinc dici possit: Inter bonos bene agier, inter malos male.*"

that his dispatches home to London were likewise intercepted and censored; fifthly, that immediately after he had taken leave of Groznyj he was sent out of the country headlong, without being given time to make the most necessary preparations (14). This last must have annoyed Randolph particularly, since he had had to spend seventeen idle weeks under strict supervision, before the Russians found that the time had come to present him before the Czar (15). Complaint could be piled upon complaint in this manner. Even if it may be supposed that many complaints have been exaggerated in order to justify poor diplomatic results, the fact remains that to be accredited to Moscow was not the dream of every diplomat.

It should be added, however, that though such evidence is specially abundant in Groznyj's period, it is not necessarily more typical of him than of the traditional Russian system. The plenitude of cases could very well be due to the enormous extension of relations between Russia and Western Europe in the middle of the sixteenth century. Moreover, cases of Muscovite arrogance and quibbling can be found long before Groznyj took over the government. During Ivan's minority, the boyars maintained the formal autocracy, personified in the child prince, so as to obtain a diplomatic advantage over the Polish-Lithuanian negotiators (16)—but not, as we have seen, because they were faithful guardians of the Czardom in a general and domestic sense. It was diplomatic opportunism—and meant that, in spite of inner divisions and conflicts, they held fast to the might and superiority of Russia in foreign relations.

The foreign service seems to have been so rigid and its methods so inflexible, that it is not possible to observe fundamental changes in consequence of the transition in the leadership from the arrogant and often self-willed *bojarstvo* to the loyal and disciplined *d'jačestvo*. The same atmosphere that marked the diplomacy of the boyars during Ivan's minority seems to have surrounded Ivan Viskovatyj also, in his functions as Keeper of the Seal and Head of the Foreign Department. Heinrich Staden reports that Viskovatyj was so proud that one must consider oneself fortunate if one could get a case dealt with by him in a month (17). And when, in 1561, Anthony Jenkinson came to Moscow as Elisabeth's ambassador, he had a serious clash with Viskovatyj, who demanded the ambassador's letters so that he might read them before the ambassador could be allowed to present his credentials (18).

---

14. *Early Voyages and Travels to Russia and Persia by Anthony Jenkinson and other English-men*, ed. by *E. D. Morgan* and *C. H. Coote* = The Hakluyt Society No. 72–73 (London 1886) Vol. II, pp. 277 f.
15. *Ibid.* p. 247.
16. *H. Fleischhacker op. cit.* pp. 51 f.
17. *Epstein* p. 18.
18. *Early Voyages and Travels* etc., Vol. I, p. 123.

It is clear, then, that just as Groznyj's ideological principles were founded on the national, church tradition of the Third Rome, his practice in diplomacy and foreign policy also showed faithfulness to a tradition in the attitude of Russia to the rest of the world. It may be added that naturally, ideology and practice are here inseparably connected, since the second was based on the first, and both originate in the Byzantine tradition. The diplomatic behaviour was the ideology manifested in act and the tradition realised at the moment. Moreover, it must be remembered that Groznyj's diplomatic practice was quite obviously founded on a purely administrative tradition of institutional permanence. He did not create a foreign service or a fundamental attitude in foreign policy. He took over both from previous generations.

We have seen what was Groznyj's imperial principle, and that the prerequisite for this principle was the complex of ideas round the theory of Moscow as the Third Rome. We have also seen that his administration of this imperial idea rested on a diplomatic tradition which in its outer form largely corresponded to the ambition to represent the inheritance from the Byzantine Empire. The question now is whether the substance of his foreign policy was also dominated and conditioned by this ideology.

It may be asserted beforehand, that it would be extremely surprising if it really were so. It is quite obvious that no matter how clear might be the idea of a continuation of the inheritance from the Byzantine Empire, the actual conditions and problems of the Russian kingdom in its foreign relations must of necessity compel an approach to what were in principle new situations with what were in principle new objectives. It is only apparently a paradox that Muscovite foreign policy became more and more independent in just the century after the fall of Constantinople, when, from the traditional point of view, the Byzantine inheritance ought, on the contrary, to have enjoined the heir to pursue a programme in foreign policy that was both narrow and preconceived. In reality, the main point was that Russia in that period—among other reasons, precisely because of the fall of the Byzantine empire—moved out on to the stage of high politics and was compelled to play its independent part as a great power on the basis of quite different economic, geographical and military conditions from those of its predecessor.

The chief of the new conditions was Russia's ambivalent relation to Western Europe. Ideologically, the Russians felt themselves superior, which found abundant expression in Groznyj. The Western European countries, it was true, believed in Christianity, but only in forms that, in his opinion, were so perverted that these populations must be classed with the heathen. Further, their political systems looked, to Groznyj, like pure dissolution and confusion. But in technology, he was reduced to allowing himself to be taught. The taking of Kazan' was not carried out by Groznyj alone with his generals, but also by a foreign expert named Razmysl' (19)—probably a Danish engineer named Rasmussen (20)—who knew the art of exploding a bomb under the defences of the besieged town. Both contempt and respect for the foreigner were thus intimately connected with vital interests, and it was necessary to act in conformity with both feelings.

Similarly, the attitude of Western Europe to Russia was also ambivalent. Russia was courted, with appeals to both vanity and common sense, in order to draw the new Eastern European great power into a European coalition against the Turks. Had Russian foreign policy been purely ideologically motivated, Russia must have seized the chance to represent the Byzantine tradition in so concrete a way. Neither Ivan Velikij, Vasilij III, nor Ivan Groznyj did so, however (21). To them, the anxieties of Western Europe about the Turks were less important than the activities in commercial policy in the Baltic area. While the aspirations of the neighbouring countries were aimed at controlling the lines of communication to the Russian market, and cutting off the Russians from independent trade with Western Europe (22), Russian efforts were primarily directed to these last objectives, beginning with the legal claim to Livonia under Ivan Velikij, and continued by Groznyj's Baltic War.

Compared with these vital interests—which, essentially, comprised the maintenance of East-West contact on equal conditions with the Western European states—the Turkish problem, or any wish to re-establish the sway of Orthodoxy at Constantinople, were matters of indifference (23). Seen from Moscow, the various European invitations to join an anti-Turkish alliance must have looked like a trap, the object of which was to get Russia to pull the chestnuts out of the fire for the other states, while these, in return, could skim the cream off the Baltic trade and exploit Russia as a backward country. The Baltic towns' traditional restrictive policy, which had its roots in the Middle Ages but which by this time was no longer tenable, consequently provoked a justified but violent Russian drive towards the Baltic, and in a longer perspective, towards the Atlantic (24).

---

19. *PSRL* t. XIII, pp. 209, 215 f., 505, 511 f.
20. *S. F. Platonov: Ivan Groznyj 1530–1584* (Pbg. 1923) p. 86, *S. F. Platonov: Moskva i zapad* (Berlin 1926) p. 12.
21. See, e.g. the reply to the Western appeals to Vasilij, *Sbornik russkago istoričeskago obščestva* t. 53 (Spbg. 1887) pp. 97 ff. He preferred to maintain the demands in the Baltic area, rather than enter a holy alliance against the Turks.
22. *Artur Attman: Den ryska marknaden i 1500-talets baltiska politik* (Lund 1944) pp. 239 ff., 434.
23. *N. S. Čajev:* "Moskva – tretij Rim" v političeskoj praktike moskovskogo pravitel'stva XVI veka = *Ist. Zap.* t. 17, pp. 22 f.
24. *Sven Svensson: Den merkantila bakgrunden till Rysslands anfall på den livländska ordensstaten 1558* = Skrifter utgivna av Vetenskaps-Societeten i Lund Vol. 35 (Lund 1951) pp. 48 f. 93 ff. 164 ff.

The Russian imperialism that was thus taking shape, was certainly provoked, but it was also provocative. And so the other aspect of the attitude of the Western European countries to Russia was uncertainty and fear. The Muscovite form of diplomacy, which even under auspicious constellations put great strain on mutual understanding, did not inspire others to grasp the fine nuances behind Moscow's actions. The lack of Russian interest in the Turkish danger that was threatening Europe plus the Russian drive in Livonia made a very simple sum, with the clear answer that besides the Turkish danger there was also a Russian danger. Consequently it was both unwise and criminal to cultivate intimate connexion with the Russian kingdom. This view, strongly held by Lübeck, meant that Russia ought to be cut off from all technical assistance from the West (25). Thus cause and effect melted into one: isolation provoked an explosion, which, from outside, it was thought could be neutralized by further isolation.

Heinrich Staden cannot be accused of drawing the same conclusion. He declared clearly that he considered that Groznyj had far-reaching plans of aggression in Europe, first to get control of Poland, in order to exert direct pressure on Germany (26). He did not make this statement, however, until he had been an *opričnik* under Ivan for many years. Nor until he had found it advantageous to leave the Russian service. Staden, like Taube and Kruse, is undoubtedly an unreliable witness where the fundamental objectives and views of Groznyj and the Russians are concerned. These foreign adventurers serve first and foremost as good examples of another Western attitude to Russia. Impressed by Russia's growing power and importance, and tempted by the personal chances that seemed to lie open in that strange country, they entered Groznyj's service, only to leave it later, when both the personal chances and the victorious progress of the Russian realm looked like coming to nothing. And in return, as will be discussed later, they advocated a policy of Western conquest in Russia.

In the whole of this complicated play of Russian-Western European relations, it is quite evident that Groznyj and his government were primarily actuated not by ideological motives but, on the contrary, by particularly concrete, practical interests. And yet, at the same time, it is equally evident that this general statement must be taken wih a certain reserve, as long as the view of Groznyj's designs on Europe expressed by Staden and others have not been definitively invalidated.

With the knowledge of Groznyj's political outlook that can be deduced from his statements, it may be taken for granted that any plans of drastically extending his power into Europe must be intimately connected with a

---

25. *Materialy* pp. 249 ff. *S. F. Platonov: Moskva i zapad* (Berlin 1926) pp. 10 f.
26. *Epstein* pp. 93, 95, see moreover the list of examples of Russophobia *ibid.* p. 93, note 42.

politico-religious messianism. They would not only be logical consequences of Groznyj's ideologically based, imperial responsibility—the sole Orthodox realm would be more secure by the extension of the sole true faith to other countries—but they are hardly conceivable without just this imperative, which was the Czar's alpha and omega. The only authentic declaration, in the nature of a manifesto, however, is that cited previously, that, under certain circumstances, the whole of Germany could have been won for the true faith in the course of a year.

Groznyj charges his opponents in the administration with the responsibility for the failure to achieve this result, and has thus clearly and unambiguously declared that he considered that result desirable. This statement is usually regarded as a confirmation of Staden's interpretation of Groznyj's imperialist plans (27). To this must be added as confirmatory indications, first, the imperialist ring in Filofej's phrase about the sole, Orthodox, great Czar in the whole world, and secondly, Groznyj's tactical endeavours to make use of the vacancy in the *Rzeczpospolita* to become himself the Polish-Lithuanian King. The plan was then said to be to get through Poland—by peaceful means or otherwise—to Germany, the heart of Europe and the focus of the Lutheran heresy.

It must also be stated that the evidence against this interpretation may appear to be very weak. Groznyj's intentions cannot be deduced from his actions, for the very good reason that he did not succeed in conquering Livonia, but was stopped after a quarter of a century of war. He could not, therefore, carry out more extensive plans of conquest, even if he had such plans. The lack of conquests is no proof of the lack of intention to conquer. It may also be asked how much proof there lay in Groznyj's statement to the Papal Legate, Antonio Possevino, that beyond the current Livonian problem he had no territorial demands, and that he was not so great a sinner as to aspire to world dominion (28). This kind of assurance has been given, believed and broken both before and since. Moreover, in all probability, the statement was not meant as a general assurance (29) at all, but rather as a neat rejection of Possevino's call to attempt, with the support of Western

---

27. See above p. 154. *Stählin* p. 159, *Epstein* p. 97.
28. "*Božijeju blagodat'ju došli jesm'a soveršennogo vozrastu, p'atdes'at let s letom nam ino mne nekoli už peremen'atis' i na bolšoje gosudarstvo xoteti; my v buduščem vosprijatija malogo xotim, a zdešnego gosudarstva vseje vselennyje ne xotim, čto budet ko grexu popolznovenno*". See *Pam'atniki diplomatičeskix snošenij drevnej Rossii s deržavami inostrannymi*, t. X (Spbg. 1871) col. 301. In Possevino's account: *Vides, inquit, mihi quinquagesimum iam annum agenti, non adeo diuturnum vitae spacium superfuturum: ea porro in religione me educatum, quae vera christiana, quaeque mihi mutanda non sit...*". See *Possevino: Moscovia* (Antverpiae 1587) p. 135. In principle the Russian text ought to be taken as authoritative for Groznyj's utterances, and Possevino's for his own.
29. Thus *I. Ševčenko* in *Harvard Slav. Stud.* II (1954) p. 162.

Christendom, to set up the Czardom in Constantinople (30)—and so the case is naturally quite different: if it is a question of an assurance, it is an assurance only to the Turks.

However obvious the facts of the case may seem to be, there are modifying and differentiating factors that must be taken into consideration here.

The value as evidence of Groznyj's candidature for the Polish-Lithuanian throne should not be exaggerated. It is true that the Czar's tactics meant that he tried to become the head of the state in the country most decidedly hostile to his own, by means of the political support of groups in the nobility that had Muscovite sympathies (31). But Zygmunt III Wasa, in return, did something quite similar, later, in Moscow, when Polish troops under Stanisław Zółkiewski in 1610 controlled the Russian capital, and the boyars were prepared to swear allegiance to a Polish Czar (32). In principle, therefore, there are no grounds for regarding the candidature for the throne as evidence of special tendencies in Groznyj.

It has been stated that, in connexion with the election of the king of Poland-Lithuania, Groznyj made use of a very special device to promote his own candidature, by formally setting Simeon Bekbulatovič on his own throne and himself figuring as his subject from 1575–1576, after Henri Valois had left Warsaw. If the object of this was to stand free and disengaged, even innocent and harmless in the eyes of the electors (33), it is, of course, obvious that he took enormous pains and sacrificed much prestige to deceive the neighbouring country, and it does not need a very lively imagination to see what would have been the consequences for that country if such a stratagem had really succeeded. Perhaps Kurbskij's chief motive in writing *"Istorija o Velikom Kn'aze Moskovskom"* was to warn against the election of Groznyj (34). The conjecture of this odious stratagem, however, must be taken with extreme reserve, since Groznyj in writing to the electors

---

30. Cf. *N. S. Čajev op. cit.* p. 9. In the Russian report (*Pam'ati* etc. col. 300) Possevino says: *"a ty V(elikij) G(osuda)r' budeš' s Papoju s Grigor'jem, i s cesarem s Rudelfom i vse gosudari v l'ubvi i vo sojedinen'je, i ty V. G-r' ne tokmo budeš' na praroditel'skoj vot čine na Kijeve, no i vo carstvujuščem Grade Gosudarem budeš', a Papa i cesar' i vse gosudari velikije o tom budut staratca".* In Possevino's report: *"eo apud Deum lucro ut serio sperare quoque possis, fore ut certioribus, quam hactenus factum est, insignibus, ac titulis, Orientis Imperator non ita multo post appellaris, si in Orientem Orthodoxam, & Catholicam fidem promoveris; ad quam rem non deerunt Principes Christiani, qui aliis ex partibus tibi opem sedulo ferant"* (*Possevino op. cit.* p. 138). In Possevino's account, the invitation comes after the reply, which must be due to a lapse of memory, since Groznyj's reply has no logical meaning without an invitation.

31. *Historia Polski, red. T. Manteuffel*, t. I, cz. II (Warsaw 1958) pp. 259 f.

32. *Ibid.* pp. 528 f.

33. Cf. *P. A. Sadikov: Očerki po istorii opričniny* (Moscow-Leningrad 1950) pp. 43 f., 136 f.

34. See above p. 85 with references.

signed himself as Czar with the full, official intitulation, during this same period (35). There is thus not much left of the case, beyond the not surprising fact that the Czar took his place in the queue for the Polish-Lithuanian throne like other potentates and princes.

The second ideological indication, in Filofej's imperialistic manifesto, must be taken with a grain of salt. In the first place, it is not, in the last resort, absolutely clear what Filofej actually means by his phrase—and there is perhaps some reason to doubt whether he himself attached a clear idea to it. His mention of "the one, Orthodox, great, Russian Czar on earth" (*jedin pravoslavnyj velikij russkij car' vo vsem podnebesnoj*) does not clearly show whether he means that the Russian Czar is and remains the only great ruler in the true faith among all the other rulers on earth, or that the Russian Czar, in virtue of his special merits, ought to be lord of the world (36). And in the second place, this declaration by an ideologist in enslaved Pskov—however it is to be understood—cannot be taken as a binding expression of the Czar's intentions. *Ihor Ševčenko* puts it very emphatically, declaring that Filofej was a quisling, whose exaggerations are not authoritative (37). The notion of Groznyj's ideologically motivated aggressiveness must therefore be deprived of its most important evidence, and consequently must stand or fall with the interpretation of the simple facts, that is to say, Groznyj's own statement in the July message.

Neither is this statement really so unambiguous as it might appear. Whether Groznyj means "Germany" by the word *Germanija* is extremely uncertain. Kurbskij had certainly, in his first letter to Ivan, spoken of the German towns (*grady Germanskije*), which, thanks to the Czar's generals, had fallen into Russian hands, and by these he meant, of course, the Baltic towns of Narva, Dorpat, Fellin, and so on, that were taken by the Russians in the first years of the Livonian War (38). In his July message, Groznyj countered this by declaring that not only would these German towns have fallen into the hands of the Russians, but even more, in fact, the whole of the country of Germany, if only the generals had been active and efficient (39). In other words, Groznyj stamps Kurbskij's claim as ill-timed boasting of a result that in reality, comprised only a fraction of what could very well have been achieved.

Now it is, of course, inconceivable that Groznyj would have considered it an effective counter-stroke to Kurbskij's argument to declare that the extremely modest results in Livonia—modest, that is, in a territorial and

---

35. *SGGD* t. V p. 157 (January 1576).
36. See above pp. 48f. with references.
37. *I. Ševčenko* op. cit. p. 161.
38. *Fennell* pp. 2–4.
39. *Ibid.* p. 120.

imperialist sense, though important enough from the point of view of commercial policy—could have been extended to the conquest of the whole of the German nation in the course of a year, if only the generals had been more energetic. To speak of the whole of Germany would be so grotesque as a higher bid that the whole polemical point would be lost—unless it is taken as an ironical exaggeration, in which case the statement is not to be taken literally. It was not at all unreasonable, however, though undoubtedly quite contrary to the actual military possibilities, if he maintained that it could have been a question of conquering the whole of the territory within the boundaries of which these towns lay. Kurbskij talked of German towns, and so Groznyj replied by calling this territory Germany. Kurbskij meant towns in Livonia. And by "Germany", Groznyj may also, in this context, have meant Livonia.

In his second letter to Kurbskij, in 1577, Groznyj returns to the same usage. He again speaks of the capture by the Russian forces of *grady Germanskije,* alluding thereby again to the towns in Livonia and to Kurbskij's expression in the first letter (40). It is quite evident that in his diction, Groznyj was strongly bound to that of his opponent. There has earlier been occasion to emphasise that it is typical of Groznyj that he seizes and takes over Kurbskij's expressions and polemical figures in order to strike back with his opponent's own weapon (41). And we have seen that this technique can set Groznyj off at a tangent, as in his treatment of Kurbskij's expression *soprotiv,* where the Czar, surprisingly betrays a secularising way of thinking (42). It might be claimed, of course, that the same applies in the case of *"Germanija",* where in that case Groznyj, as ill luck would have it, revealed his secret, imperialistic ambitions and intentions. There is a crucial difference, however, between the two cases. In the first, it was not the word *soprotiv* itself that gave the twist to the meaning but the connexion with the object to which Groznyj changed over, from "orthodoxy" to "reason". The twist occurred on his own initiative, so to speak. But with the word *"Germanija",* Groznyj retained Kurbskij's usage, and merely extended it from an adjectival designation of part of the whole—to cover the whole in substantival generality. It was a question of a quantitative not a qualitative change. In all probability, Groznyj had not the remotest idea that by this he could be taken to have intruded upon *Das heilige römische Reich deutscher Nation.*

---

40. *Ibid.* p. 194.
41. See e. g. the following reminiscenses of Kurbskij's terminology in his first letter: *"pravoslavii presvetlomu",* Fennell pp. 22, 44, 90, 92; *"sil'nyx vo Izraili", ibid.* pp. 64, 66, 68, 102, 104, 156; *"mučeničeskimi", ibid.* pp. 36, 64, 66, 92, 100, 102, 104, 110, 112; *"dobroxotnyx tvoix", ibid.* pp. 62, 64, 66, 70, 72, 78, 82, 92, 102, 104.
42. See above p. 27.

In other words, there is no solid basis for any other assumption than that Groznyj was primarily interested in conquering Livonia, and thereby improving Russia's position in the Baltic area. It must be added, however, that this does not include the assumption that Groznyj would have confined his efforts in Europe to this objective under any circumstances. Let it be supposed, for the sake of the argument, that Groznyj had succeeded in conquering Livonia, and that he really had been elected King of Poland-Lithuania with power to maintain his special view of the royal power. Under such circumstances, Groznyj would have taken over new objectives on behalf of all his kingdoms, and there is no reason, at any rate, to suppose that the new objectives and the extended radius of action would have meant a static foreign policy towards the rest of Europe—unless Groznyj were compelled to stand where he was by outer pressure. The fact is, however, that he did not reach these forward positions, and there is no evidence of serious consideration of a policy on this basis.

On these grounds, it cannot be maintained that Groznyj, driven by a politico-religious messianism, had plans of far-reaching extensions of his power in Europe. The case is perhaps best expressed by saying that Groznyj's undoubted ideological disposition in this direction had not the opportunity to take effect in practice. That Groznyj made efforts to strengthen the Orthodox Church in Livonia where it already existed (43) was only a natural result of his function as Orthodoxy's Czar.

With this we have given up speaking of clearly defined and definitive plans, and instead must deal with conditions and possibilities, with degrees and nuances. The question then is, what was Groznyj's attitude in foreign policy in relation to the non-European countries. This question is inseparably connected with another, the question of Groznyj's attitude to rival opinions of foreign policy in Russia and in the Muscovite administration.

In principle, Muscovite foreign policy had necessarily, and for a hundred years, directed its activities and interests in several main directions at once, but primarily in two directions, towards the north-west and towards the south-east. The efforts of Western Europe to get Russian activity canalized in a south-easterly direction and thus away from Europe, had been resisted. But at the same time, active efforts had been made to clear up the unclear and dangerous situation in relation to Kazan', Astraxan' and the Crimea. The Muscovite administration found itself in a permanent situation of choice, and when circumstances required a major effort, this situation was bound to develop into a dilemma, since it was necessary to concentrate on one of these tasks and to neglect the other. This was an absolutely unavoidable condition. It was not to be taken for granted, of course, that all the interests

---

43. See *Epstein* p. 160 with references

in the administration were always agreed on the choice of the task on which all efforts were to be concentrated.

In this dilemma, the attitude adopted might be dictated by ideological, primarily religious, motives, or by practical, that is to say, economic, motives —or possibly by both at once. If from ideological motives, it was considered that efforts must be concentrated on securing the kingdom against the Mohammedan Tartars, this meant that in spite of everything, the Christian, European kingdoms were considered to be closer to Orthodox Russia than the heathen Khanates. If, on the contrary, the Papists and the Lutherans were considered to be just as ideologically unworthy and dangerous as the Mohammedans, or even worse, since they were arrant heretics, then it was possible to make a choice without regard for the classical, ideological objective in the direction of Constantinople, with practical interests as the first consideration, such as the Baltic trade.

This alternative, however, involved other problems, closely connected with those already mentioned. In the first place, concentration in a south-easterly direction inevitably meant an important change in the north-western engagement, however quiet that may have been left. The conquest of Kazan' and Astraxan' gave the Russians control of communications to Central Asia, which the Russians wanted to exploit in commercial collaboration with the English, and which naturally brought the question of control of the Baltic lines of communication right into the foreground at Moscow (44). The solution of one problem thus immediately required the solution of the other also. And here there was a problem of ideological and political character, balancing out sympathy with the disciplinary and strongly centralized government of the Turks and the Czarist repulsion and contempt for the Western tendencies to division of power. It was characteristic that the publicist Peresvetov emphasised the efficiency of the Turks as an admirable virtue, and as God's reply to and punishment of the degenerate Byzantines (45). And on the other hand, boyars with a traditional outlook can hardly have been other than unwilling to see the connections with Poland and Lithuania destroyed by war. It was a question of political systems that they were more in sympathy with than with Czarism, and of territories in which they often had personal connexions and interests. Pressure from them was consequently directed towards the south-east (46).

It is on the basis of these general conditions for an imperial policy that many dark and paradoxical factors must be understood. It has already been

---

44. *Sven Svensson op. cit.* pp. 76 ff.
45. *D. Jegorov:* Ideja "tureckoj reformacii" v XVI v. = *Russkaja Mysl'* 1907, No. 7, pp. 1–14, *Claude Backvis:* Les slaves devant la ,,leçon" turque à l'aube des temps modernes = *Revue de l'Université de Bruxelles*, t. VII (1954–1955) pp. 137 ff. Cf. above p. 105.
46. Cf. *Zimin Ref.* pp. 471 f.

observed that the policy of reform was to a large extent made necessary by military reasons and reasons of foreign policy, and the requirement of a more modern and effective administration. The first years, which showed the results of these reforms in foreign policy were comparatively problemless, for the conquests of Kazan' and Astraxan' were at once in perfect accord both with the requirements of the religious ideology and with those of the security of the kingdom against attack by the Tartars. But it was precisely these years of Groznyj's triumph, when Makarij saluted him as a new Constantine, that had in them the germ of a conflict in domestic politics on the subject of foreign policy.

Here it is well to remember that Viskovatyj was a principal character in the design and execution of Muscovite foreign policy, and that the Viskovatyj case on the icon-paintings started in 1553, after the conquest of Kazan' (47). To this must be added a peculiar statement by Heinrich Staden, in which Viskovatyj is described as an enemy of the Christians and a friend of the Tartars—the latter to such an extent that he would have liked to see the Khan of the Crimea ruling in Moscow (48). The English, however, acknowledged that Viskovatyj showed great sympathy for them (49), which does not seem improbable, even though he had had a clash with Jenkinson over a matter of form. At the same time, Sil'vestr was not only Viskovatyj's enemy and the object of his attack in the paintings case, but also—as was Adašev— an opponent of the Baltic War, which must be considered one of the main reasons for the fall of these two political leaders in 1560 (50). If Viskovatyj, then, was pro-Turk and anti-Christian, Sil'vestr was anti-Turk and disposed to peaceful relations with the Western, Christian states.

It is quite obvious what is implied by Staden's description of Viskovatyj. The records of the Viskovatyj case show that the attitude of the Head of the Foreign Service was strictly Orthodox, and he warns against heresy and tendencies to reformation. Viskovatyj was anti-Christian in the sense that he detested the Christian countries outside Russia, or in other words, those that called themselves Christian but in his eyes were not Christian. To a man like Viskovatyj, whose principal task was—as Makarij told him— political planning, and not religious matters, the consequence of his detestation of the Christian countries must be the conclusion that Russia should

47. See above pp. 114 ff.
48. *Epstein* p. 18, refers at the same place, to a similar Russian declaration, cited by Paul Oderborn.
49. In November 1955, George Killingworth, the Russian Company's representative at Moscow, asked that letters from London should be sent through Viskovatyj, *"whom we take to be our very friend"*. See *Richard Hakluyt: The Principall Voyages, Trauailes and Discoveries of the English Nation* (London 1589) p. 301.
50. See Groznyj's accusation *Fennell* p. 118, cf. *Očerki* pp. 375 f.

not cultivate too friendly relations with them unless there were quite particular advantages in doing so. His hostility to Sil'vestr implied, among other things, that he considered the most important political task to be the concentration of efforts on the drive to the Baltic and the promotion of the strategic and economic interests involved in this. There was no reason to allow ideological considerations to interfere. On the other hand, commercial policy indicated that it could be advantageous to collaborate with the English.

Because of the dilemma, Viskovatyj's attitude to the Tartars must quite logically be the opposite. As an undoubtedly sincere and consistent adherent of Czarism and the autocracy, he could, like Peresvetov, feel more attracted by Asiatic discipline than by Western European dissolution and slackness. As a decided adversary of the forms of religious observance in Western Europe, he cannot have felt ideological distaste for efforts to establish peace or perhaps even a *modus vivendi* with the Mohammedans, who were no worse than heretics. As an alert and zealous guardian of the imperial interests of the kingdom, he must have found it necessary, in his efforts to establish peace to the south-west, to display a certain amiability in that direction, as towards the English. That he should have cherished a desire to see the Khan of the Crimea on the throne in Moscow is probably pure fantasy. If this rumour originated from a well-informed source, it should hardly be taken as the explanation of Viskovatyj's execution, together with that of a number of other prominent leaders, in 1570 (51), but may rather be explained by the not unfamiliar fact that a terrorist government often gets rid of its faithful helpers at a critical moment—and must just as often find some absurd explanation or other for this absurd act.

With Viskovatyj's end we have anticipated developments, and must return to the fall of Sil'vestr ten years earlier. Then it was undoubtedly Viskovatyj's line that was victorious. And that it was victorious meant that it was identical with Groznyj's. What Sil'vestr's line was is less clear. Viskovatyj's attempt to get him classed with the heretics in 1553 was undoubtedly based on the fact that Sil'vestr was comparatively close to the *nest'ažatel'* wing. And this was connected with a much greater tolerance of other Christian observances than was shown by the *iosifl'anstvo*. Thus *R. Wipper* is probably right when he conjectures that Sil'vestr had certain plans of a closer collaboration with the Roman Catholic Church, perhaps even an actual revival of the idea of union with a view to a common front against the Turks (52). If Viskovatyj's political and religious observance can be said

---

51. See *Epstein* p. 40, with references.
52. *R. Wipper: Ivan Groznyj* (3rd edn., Moscow 1947) p. 73. Cf. *Nik. Andrejev* in *Seminarium Kondakovianum, Receuil d'Études* t. V (Prague 1932) pp. 217 f.

to have been decidedly centric, then Sil'vestr's have obviously been marked by an inclination to recognize other confessions in Christendom as buttresses for the faith against its enemies, and to regard the security of the faith as the main point.

It has been maintained earlier that Sil'vestr, by calling in the West-Russian icon-painters, utilized a modernist means of propaganda to glorify the central position of the church and the faith in the community (53). We have seen that this act had consequences in domestic politics. But it is obvious that it also had certain implications in foreign policy. Novgorod and Pskov, whence these painters were fetched, were the starting points for the infiltration of Western ideas into Russia, and at the same time they were the main centres in the traditional commercial connexions with Western Europe, connexions based on the intermediary, independent status of the towns. This status, which did not give power enough to compel the assertion of Russian interests in the Baltic trade, was completely destroyed by Moscow's centralizing policy, first under Ivan Velikij, last and definitively by Groznyj's terrorist action at Novgorod in 1570 (54). Thus a double reaction was directed against Novgorod and Pskov, first the high church dogmatic and counter-reformatory, and then the imperial and commercial policy of the administration. Sil'vestr did not fit into this pattern.

He did not represent the dogmatic, Iosifist, high church interests, but rather opposed them by his modernist dispositions. And he did not support the plans for an energetic drive westward, which required a strict disciplining of the West Russian towns and a hostile attitude to Europe, at any rate, to Russia's European neighbours. The probability is that he maintained the classical line in foreign policy, the main object of which was to secure the kingdom against the Tartars and ultimately to make a drive towards Constantinople. With this line, conditions would be more favourable for a continuation of the policy of reform without the serious disciplinary tautening and without the increasing mobilization of the church in the service of the state, which must be the inevitable consequence of the imperialistic drive to the west.

If this was Sil'vestr's line, it was temporarily victorious over Viskovatyj's policy by the decision of the synod in 1554. And the victory was due, as we have seen, primarily to Makarij's help. The reason for this peculiar situation must certainly be found in the fact that the metropolitan found himself increasingly on the defensive as the representative of a high church that of course supported the Czardom, but also had its own vital interests to defend. Makarij does not seem to have shown much interest in or sym-

---

53. See above, p. 120.
54. *Očerki* pp. 310 f., *Sven Svensson op. cit.* p. 58.

pathy for the policy of reform. The interests of the church as a landowner were his concern. And he did what he could to consolidate the church's active and normative role in the community. This became increasingly difficult in collaboration with a Czardom that demonstrated its will both to exploit the church's legitimation for its own purposes and to collaborate closely with new forces in the community that were foreign to Iosifism. The prospect before Makarij was a constantly more and more secularized—or modernized—state, where commerce and technology predominated over the time-honoured, traditional values. He chose to support the line that was nearest to the high church's old objective in foreign policy, the continuation of the inheritance after the Byzantine Empire in the strict, classical sense. This would give him the best chance of throning side by side with the Czar in common triumph on behalf of the true faith. His programme was that presented to view in the icon *"Cerkov' Voinstvujuščaja"*.

At first glance, Viskovatyj's attitude might seem to be the one most ideologically motivated. His centric maintenance of the church dogmas and norms was formally stricter than both Sil'vestr's and Makarij's. And yet it is clear, in the context of foreign policy at any rate, that Viskovatyj, more than his opponents, represented a purely worldly, practical weighing of interests and possibilities, both economic and military. He cherished no sentimental feelings for the notion of a Russian mission against the Turks and the Tartars for the spread of the true faith—or its inclusion in one single realm. He was interested in the strength and security of the Czardom, its power for the sake of power, its progress for the sake of progress, its greatness in an economic, military and political sense, more than in a religious one. His line was realistic, logical and consistent. Reason of state was his alpha and omega. And Viskovatyj's aims and interests were also Groznyj's. How much one got from the other we cannot know. Probably they were both such powerful personalities that they simply supplemented each other. But that they were agreed appears from the outbreak of war in 1558 and from the fall of the compromise government in 1560. Thereby not only was Sil'vestr's role played out, but also, in the long run, Makarij's.

The object and the justification of the state's exploitation of the religious mandate for its own use, its breaking of *svobodnoje jestestvo čelovečeskoje* according to its own will, its domestic reforms and modernizations, was the strength and security of the kingdom. The imperial requirement and responsibility was the main point. Sil'vestr faded out because, in spite of everything—especially in spite of his own active participation in the government—he wanted to maintain an autonomous spiritual power by the side of the temporal one, a conscience independent of the exercise of power. And Makarij's triumph in the coronation of the Czar turned into defeat, because he had to abandon his attempt to maintain the position of a secularized church as an equal power factor side by side with the crown. In the struggle to maintain even the semblance of a *sacerdotium* by the side of the *regnum*, the latter won and took over the mandate of both parties. What was originally a religious mission in a national and imperial framework developed into a national and imperial self-assertion with a religious definition.

Strictly speaking, the fortune of war motif with Grożnyj needed no religious justification. He could very well have appealed to reasons of state alone as the justification of his measures for securing political and military efficiency and success. As we have seen, he used both justifications. But the worldly justification got its particular weight from the fact that it brought Groznyj into line with the new forces in the community, with the service nobility, the civil servants and the citizens of the towns. By his simplification under *opričnina* he broke forever the power of the boyars as the bearers of a traditional system of society. For a time, he gathered all the threads into his own hands—the domestic by means of the terror, the commercial by means of monopolies granted to foreign companies—and concentrated all his efforts on the decisive military drive that was to secure the power and position of Russia in Europe. The Czardom in this form, however, he succeeded in carrying through only for a time, his own time, since by playing the fortune of war as a trump, he laid himself ominously open to military nemesis.

The two directions that together caused the dualism in Muscovite foreign policy were inseparably connected in more than one sense. In the first place, activity in one direction necessarily involved passivity in the other. The less the results gained by the activity, the greater the risk implied by the passivity. And in the second place, those very results won in one direction brought the need for new results in the other, since Russia was the middle-point and was to remain the middle-point in the trade routes. And finally, hostility in one direction and hostility in the other direction must have a double effect on each wing, when the enemies, to some extent at any rate, co-ordinated their offorts, if not in an actual alliance, yet by exploiting points and periods of weakness whenever the opportunity offered. By choosing the western drive, which took a quarter of a century of fruitless warfare, Groznyj opened the way for the Khan of the Crimea, Devlet Girej, to make his victorious advance right in to Moscow in 1571 and the following year (55).

In the later part of his correspondence with Ivan Groznyj, therefore, Kurbskij could appeal with great effect to military nemesis, not only by giving a drastic sketch of the Czar's panic flight during the invasion of the

---

55. *Očerki* pp. 385 f., *PSRL* t. XIII, pp. 300 f., *Istoričeskij Arxiv* t. VII (Moscow 1951) p. 225.

Crimean Tartars (56), but also by taunting him with his constantly adverse fortune in the Baltic War (57)—all of which was ascribed to the rejection of worthy and qualified generals in favour of the Czar's useless and terrorist *opričniki*. Kurbskij was not the only one who reacted in this way. Heinrich Staden reports that it was forbidden to mention the hated word *opričnina* after the critical years during the invasion (58), and as the fruit of his varied experience, could advise the Emperor Rudolf to undertake the conquest of the Muscovite kingdom, which he judged—undoubtedly wrongly—would surrender without bloodshed in order to be rid of Ivan Groznyj's rule (59).

Ivan Groznyj imposed on his kingdom a heavy-handed solution of the problems of domestic politics which did not last, in order to secure the carrying out of an imperial task that had to be left to posterity. And thereby he also left it to posterity to ponder over the question of what would have happened if he had been able to concentrate his forces and his power on the creation of a durable solution to the inner problems of the kingdom.

---

56. *Fennell* pp. 204–206, cf. 228.
57. *Ibid.* p. 234.
58. *Epstein* p. 77 with references. The Bekbulatovič episode, however, was possibly an attempt to carry further the *opričnina* system. Cf. *Posl. Grozn.* pp. 482 ff.
59. *Epstein* pp. 156 f. Staden's judgement was not confirmed during Devlet Girej's invasion in 1571, nor, under similar conditions, in the Polish invasion in 1610.

IX

Conclusion

In the previous chapters, the attempt has been made to elucidate the formation of Muscovite Czarism under Ivan Groznyj by considering the fundamental decisions and actions of the period in relation to ideological and practical motives. In almost all the concrete cases concerned it has had to be admitted that a clear line between ideological and practical motives cannot be drawn. Moreover, it has been found that as far as the ideological motives are concerned, it is extremely difficult to distinguish between a religious and a political ideology, since it is only occasionally that political thinking appears openly, for it is usually clothed in the formulations of religious ideology. In consequence of this, no attempt has been made to give a definitive answer to the general question of whether the individual actions or the policies of the period as a whole were determined by ideological requirements or by practical needs in such a manner that one was predominant.

The attempt has been made, however, to the greatest possible extent, to ascertain what were the conditions, both ideological and practical, of the individual situations in which a decision was taken or an action begun. There has been no conjecture beforehand as to whether the decisive factors were ideological or practical, but it has been assumed that there might be both stimulating and inhibiting circumstances of both categories, and that the individual choice-situation has in principle been subjected to extremely various influences from this pattern of tendencies and forces. We have considered it an impermissible simplification to assume that in any situation, the autocrat might have ruled as an autocrat in the sense that he was absolutely free to pursue and realise his ideas. But we have considered it possible, to some degree, at any rate, to follow the threads in a pattern of decision and action, where both ideas and conditions were clearly manifest.

A summary of the observations and interpretations in the previous chapters must consequently take the form of a general review of the politico-ideological pattern of the period, the forces that manifested themselves and either dominated or were dominated during the shaping of Czarism in Groznyj's time.

It is one of the paradoxes of the period that what beforehand would appear to be most markedly ideologically determined and determinant, in reality were the most markedly practical. If one may begin by assuming, as a principal rule, that actions that are in accordance with the accepted requirements of an ideology but in conflict with obvious practical interests, are ideologically determined, then it is not possible to maintain that the Orthodox Church, dominated by *iosifl'anstvo,* was ideologically determined in its political actions, or in its political influence on the Czar's government. The church sacrificed its ideological integrity and sovereignty in order to keep economic privileges and political influence, which in principle had nothing to do with its ideological nature. It surrendered its inmost being to be used at the pleasure of the crown, for a role that in principle belonged to the nature and essence of the temporal power.

If, on the other hand, it is assumed as a principal rule that actions that are in conflict with the requirements of an accepted ideology but in accordance with obvious practical interests, are practically motivated, then this very formulation can be applied to the Iosifist dominated church. It is beyond discussion that in its struggle for its lands, the church was safeguarding obviously practical interests, but it may reasonably be maintained further that in doing so it did things that were in conflict with the requirements of the accepted ideology. This ideology never completely abandoned its weak and vaguely formulated demand for an independent and sovereign position side by side with the state, but in practice it consistently sacrificed this principle. Moreover, it concentrated the whole of its energy and prestige on combating those who opposed the church's worldly commitment, both in regard to economic privileges and to political support of the crown. It turned its practical opportunism into a pseudo-ideological *credo,* and did so with a ruthlessness and a zeal that showed the crown the way to rule by means of terrorism and to turn that terrorism also against the church.

This last point is naturally the reason why the church as a political phenomenon was really more ideologically determinant than determined. What is meant by this is that the church as a whole gave up the possibility of promoting decisions and actions by the crown that could be said to serve specially the interests of the faith, but on the other hand, played the part of an indispensable support and legitimation for the crown, no matter what decisions or actions the crown wanted to take or perform.

This gave rise to the paradoxical situation that the church left to the crown the legitimation of the faith, and in return the crown tolerated interests that were those of the church but not necessarily those of the faith. It was this confusion of the church with the faith that the heretics and the *nest'ažateli* wanted to combat, but which the church with the help of the crown carried through by force. By its campaign against all tendencies to intellectual sifting and clarification and independent and original thought, the church undertook the role of ideological rectifier, which did not make it culturally valuable but politically useful. When the last word of the faith had been said for the advantage of the crown, further discussion was not only unnecessary but also impermissible. Thus the church played an important part as an ideologically determinant factor in political life.

It was urged initially that it was not possible to found observations on an assumed distinction between idea and act, ideology and practice, opinion and exercise of power. And the subsequent investigations have not given rise to a revision of this claim. It has not been possible to show any case where a decision or an action of a political nature has been made to depend on verification or legitimation in relation to a programme of ideas. Nor has it been possible to find cases where a programme of ideas represented by a group opinion has exercised a controlling influence on political practice represented by the exercise of power. The Metropolitan Filip tried something like this, but could not carry it through. The explanation is that for a generation, his church had shown almost complete passiveness with regard to the role that otherwise ought to have been obvious, which was, in fact its primary role—but had been extremely active in repressing every tendency to the formation of independent opinion.

A portrait of the Orthodox Church must take the character of the head of Janus. To worldly and political life, it turned the face of the faith and divine inspiration. The Czardom maintained its position and drew its legitimation from the gracious smile of this face. The Czardom could not do without this legitimation, and in consequence, political life was certainly ideologically determined. But the other face, that of worldliness and political opportunism, the church turned inwards to its own affairs, and in this harsh face may be read the practical motivation of the decisions of the hierarchy. The policy of the state, therefore, may well have been ideologically determined in that it was dependent on the support of the church, but the conditions for that support were of a character that was not determined by the church's ideology, but rather was contrary to it.

This equivocal position was of disastrous significance during the reform period. The Czar could not free himself of his dependence on the church's ideological legitimation, and ultimately had to act in accordance with the church's requirements, which had little to do with ideology. Had it been possible for the state to justify its actions in purely temporal terms—to appeal to reasons of state in purely secular phrases, it would not have been reduced to conforming to the church requirements to the extent that it actually did. But this was impossible. The result was that the church largely kept its economically privileged position, and in return became even more important as the politico-ideological justification of the acts of the state. These, again, had to be directed with correspondingly greater force against the other hitherto privileged group in the community, the *bojarstvo*.

The boyars did not represent any form of ideological opinion or ideological pressure against the Czarist state. They have not left behind them any trace of a coherent political programme, nor do their actions bear the stamp of defined political tactics or objectives. There is nothing that indicates a conflict of principle between the boyar group and the Czar over the structure and character of the government, but plenty of evidence of diversity in the reactions of the boyars to the new tendencies, ranging from clear recognition of the need for reform to overt maintenance of purely egoistic and individual interests. The boyars were a social group, but their political engagement was infinitely various. Some were loyal helpers in the service of the Czar. Some even became dreaded tools in Groznyj's system of terror. Others sought to oppose the policy of reform as far as they could, especially those parts of it that involved a limitation of their prerogatives.

This last attitude acquired decisive importance by raising points of principle, which approached, at all events, the character of a politically determinant, ideological factor. In foreign policy, many boyars seem to have held as a principle the desirability of peaceful relations with the neighbouring states to the west, and thus directed against Groznyj's Baltic action. This standpoint, however, can be read only indirectly from the numerous cases of flight to Poland and Lithuania. More important is the factor in domestic politics that comes to expression so clearly in Groznyj's autobiographical account of his experiences with the magnates. Here he gives the reason for his hostility to the boyars, which bears a clearly empirical stamp. Here Groznyj does not seem to have adjusted his account of his experiences in accordance with an anti-boyar idea and conviction, but rather to give an account of the genesis of this idea. He explains how the idea of a concentration of power by terrorism gradually ripened as he grew up, and was strengthened by his experiences as an adult ruler.

The idea was consolidated by the political influence of the *dvor'anstvo*. The justification of the existence of this group lay in its services to the state, and the condition of its existence in the rewards it received for these services. Consequently the relation between the state and the service nobility was that of mutual dependence. No reward, no service—and so the state had to find sufficient land for the maintenance of the service nobility, with the consequences this involved in relation to the church, the aristocracy and neighbouring countries. And no service, no forces—which meant that the state would be unable to cope with its imperial tasks, with the result that the country would be extremely vulnerable to its traditional enemies to the south-east, and reduced to passivity in commercial policy to the north-west. Out of this relation of dependence, there arose automatically an opinion, the demand and objective of which was that the administration should be made modern and efficient, so that both the economic and the military problems could be satisfactorily solved.

The influence of the service nobility thus had a decidedly practical turn. It is true that when the publicists present the views of the service nobility, they have a strongly ideological stamp, but this is very largely only a concession to the prevailing church ideology and a tactical use of it. Peresvetov's religious formalism only scantily covered his real intentions, which were to give practical solutions for the problems of the community by rationalization, standardization and modernization. In religious terms he formulated an extremely worldly objective for all endeavours, success in foreign policy, to be achieved by a disciplined administration, a *volnoje carstvo,* under a *volnoj car'.* Success in war was the aim and the yardstick for *pravda* in domestic politics.

In this, as generally in the manifestos of the service nobility, there was a defined and palpable standpoint, but not an actual ideology, if that is to be taken as a set of principles that are determinant for decisions and acts, and in relation to which decisions and acts may be judged. An indication of practical methods of achieving efficiency and emphasis on success in war as the end of all endeavour, is not an ideology. It is characteristic that as soon as really ideological questions arose, there was disagreement and discrepancy between the spokesmen of the service nobility. One held fast, in spite of everything, to certain humanist principles of man's natural rights, while another obediently followed Iosifism and preached the limitation of independent thought to the minimum. In the face of questions beyond the purely practical and immediate tasks and interests, there was uncertainty, and to some extent, indifference.

Something similar seems to have been largely true of the *d'jačestvo.* Even in a case so ideologically involved as Ivan Viskovatyj's action against Sil'vestr, the motives for the action were quite obviously dictated by the practical tasks and interests of the administration. It was a matter of combating the church's tendency to play an independent ideological-political role in the community, and to support the church's traditional role as the legitimation of the Czar's power. Moreover, political motives, both domestic and foreign, were also involved, motives which, to Viskovatyj, were in accordance with considerations of practical efficiency and the requirement of expediency in imperial policy. In the face of these requirements, consideration for ideological aims played only an insignificant role. Viskovatyj showed no interest in the traditional, ideologically formulated, objectives in foreign policy, but brushed them aside to promote more concrete interests. The actions and decisions he administered were determined practically and not ideologically.

Viskovatyj and his like did not represent a social or political group, in itself exercising power and influence in the Muscovite society. The position of the civil servant was in no way privileged and secure, but on the contrary, from the point of view of the individual, extremely uncertain and exposed to the ruler's whims. On the other hand, they exercised an influence of another kind—an influence it is difficult to overestimate—that of experience and professional efficiency. It was an influence that could not be defined by a group, but in a more abstract manner, by a function. If the service nobility was indispensable as a military instrument, the civil service was indispensable as the Czar's administrative instrument, and as the bearer of continuity in administrative practice. It was this—together, of course, with personal ability and efficiency—that enabled distinguished officials like Viskovatyj to maintain their positions in otherwise dangerous, ideological conflicts. Such cases indicate their importance to and their influence on the government.

The service nobility and the civil servants were the government's only connexion with the common people. From them, especially from the traders and craftsmen of the towns, came the demands and manifestations that reappear in the writings of the publicists of the reform period. The need for a uniform legal system, a standardized monetary system, an incorruptible local administration, corresponded to the wishes of the daily champions of efficiency. From the beginning of the reform period, the tendency in the government's course was largely to satisfy these needs. Since Ivan Groznyj's first meeting with the *černyje ľudi,* where the two confused parties stood facing each other, hostile or at any rate uncomprehending, he had moved himself and them forward to a point where they could meet in a joint demand for a political change of system. Groznyj had managed to position himself as their personal guarantee against "the wolves" and "the strong", which means that in the eyes of the people he represented order and consolidation against arbitrariness and injustice. Once the change of system had been carried out, the Czar's hands were free.

Only from one quarter was the Czar presented with a requirement that can be said to be ideologically determined and to aim at an ideologically determined policy, and that was from *Andrej Kurbskij.* Here also, as with the church, we have a paradoxical case, seen against the background of the traditional evaluation. According to this, Kurbskij represented the anti-Czarist part of the boyar group, or actually was the spokesman of the boyar group in general. A role of this kind can hardly be said to be ideologically determined, since it would be synonymous with the advocacy of economic and political prerogatives from an unprincipled, egotistical standpoint. The fact is, however, that originally Kurbskij was in reality the loyal servant of the Czar, and an open adherent of the policy of reform with its satisfaction of the obvious need for practical changes in the social system. In this capacity, he gained a distinguished position as statesman and general. He broke with the Czar on the ground that the policy of reform had been abandoned in favour of arbitrary terrorism and the infringement of certain fundamental human rights.

Kurbskij represented an ideological alternative to Czarism in the form given to it by Groznyj. According to this alternative, a policy could not be forced through by means of terrorist repression of its opponents, e. g. by forcing them to take an oath under the threat of death, or by exterminating potential opponents by whole families. The government must govern in collaboration with qualified counsellors, whose position must be sufficiently secure to guarantee their freedom from bias and their freedom of thought. There must thus be assumed some form of contractual relation between prince and counsellors with a view to ensuring harmonious and satisfactory collaboration in the exercise of power, which must be limited by certain fundamental, inviolable principles, symbolized in the concept of *svobodnoje jestestvo čelovečeskoje*. These requirements were purely ideologically determined and were formulated on a humanistic-religious basis, but had remarkably little connexion with concrete political problems, and in no way represented a political alternative to the policy of Ivan Groznyj.

For this reason, Groznyj as the wielder of *samoderžanije* could afford to ignore Kurbskij's ideological requirements and conditions. There was no group or force in the kingdom behind this ideology. Groznyj did not even need to take up its principles and rebut them in his polemic with Kurbskij. It is an open question whether he understood at all what these principles meant and implied. Considering the fact that posterity has not displayed understanding of Kurbskij's intentions either, but has misinterpreted him, Groznyj's attitude is perhaps not particularly surprising. In Groznyj's kingdom, Kurbskij's ideology was not merely on foreign soil but on stony ground, to which it could not be transplanted. Consequently Groznyj had no difficulty in disposing of this ideological challenge. It could be neutralized by propaganda.

Neither the people in general, the civil service, nor the service nobility presented the Czar with defined requirements or conditions for the exercise of power or the character of his government. He was faced with a highly complicated set of practical problems that had to be solved—but that could be solved only by the liquidation of the policy of compromise. There were certainly fundamental and principal influences and impulses that had their effect on him, but these were primarily in the nature of a maintenance of administrative continuity and emphasis on the priority of the tasks in foreign policy over those on the home front. The Czar had to function, so to speak, as the intermediary of a dynamic pressure in the direction of a drive in high politics, which gave his general imperial responsibility particular significance and weight. With the publicists, this pressure took the form of a consistent appeal to the Czar to carry out complete political discipline and uniformity in the name of the autocracy. This demand was conditioned by practical tasks and objectives, not by an ideological requirement. On the contracy, it was a denial in principle of all ideological obligations and limitations.

Thus from no quarter—nor from the boyars—were there canalized standpoints of principle that could take the form of an actual programme of domestic policy, of an attempt to mark out the way towards a balanced solution of the problems of society. The solution consisted only of the concentration of power. And the concentration of power was intended to carry out imperial tasks. On this basis, the Czar had no choice but to concentrate his resources on the solution of the problems of foreign policy, and to justify his exercise of power and his methods by the need for successes in foreign policy, or simply by success in war. The only apparently ideological impulse towards this choice and all that it implied was the blessing of the church, which may well have functioned ideologically, but in reality originated in opportunist motives.

With this we have returned to the great paradox in the politics of the period—and to the explanation of why Groznyj's manifestos fluctuated between axiom and empiricism, between reasoning and postulate. Ivan Groznyj's upbringing, conditions and situation compelled him to rule on the basis of a religious axiom, and his concrete tasks urged him to liberate himself from that religious axiom. He left no room for doubt that in action, at any rate, he put practical, political considerations above all considerations of religion and conscience, if there was conflict and he had to choose. And in his statements of principle, he clearly showed how far he had moved towards a secularised way of thinking. With this amalgam of idealism and realism—not a fortunate amalgam, since responsibility was diffused and neutralized—Groznyj and Russia moved into the modern world.

Abbreviations

Akty AE = *Akty sobrannyje v bibliotekax i arxivax Rossijskoj Imperii arxeografičeskoju ekspedicijeju Imp. Akad. Nauk*, t. I (Spbg. 1836).

Budovnic = *I. U. Budovnic: Russkaja publicistika XVI veka* (Moskva-Lgrd. 1947).

ČOIDR = *Čtenija v Imp. Obščestve istorii i drevnostej rossijskix pri Moskovskom universitete* (Moskva 1846 ff.).

Epstein = *Heinrich von Staden: Aufzeichnungen über den Moskauer Staat*, herausgegeben von *Frits Epstein* = Hamburgische Univ., Abhandl. aus dem Gebiet der Auslandsk., Bd. 34, Rh. A: Rechts- u. Staatswiss., Bd. 5 (Hamburg 1930).

Fennell = *J. L. I. Fennell: The Correspondence between Prince A. M. Kurbsky and Tsar Ivan IV of Russia, edited with a Translation and Notes* (Cambridge 1955).

Ist. Zap. = *Istoričeskije Zapiski* (Moskva 1937 ff.).

Karamzin = *N. M. Karamzin: Istorija gosudarstva rossijskago*. 4. izdanije (Spbg. 1834).

Kurbskij = *A. M. Kurbskij: Istorija o Velikom Kn'aze Moskovskom*. Izdanije Imp. arxeografičeskoj kommissii (Spbg. 1913).

Lur'je = *J. S. Lur'je: Ideologičeskaja bor'ba v russkoj publicistike konca XV – načala XVI veka* (Moskva-Lgrd. 1960).

Materialy = *Materialy po istorii SSSR. II. Dokumenty po istorii XV–XVII vv.* (Moskva 1955).

Migne gr. = *J.-P. Migne: Patrologiæ cursus completus. Series græca* (Paris 1857 ff.).

Migne lat. = *J.-P. Migne: Patrologiæ cursus completus. Series latina* (Paris 1844 ff.).

Moisejeva = *G. N. Moisejeva: Valaamskaja Beseda – pam'atnik russkoj publicistiki XVI veka* (Moskva-Lgrd. 1958).

Očerki = *Očerki istorii SSSR. Period feodalizma konec XV v. – načalo XVII v. Pod red. A. N. Nasonova, L. V. Čerepnina, A. A. Zimina* (Moskva 1955).

Posl. Grozn. = *Poslanija Ivana Groznogo*. Podgotovka teksta *D. S. Lixačeva* i *J. S. Lur'je*. Perevod i kommentarii *J. S. Lur'je*. (Moskva-Lgrd. 1951).

Posl. Volock. = *Poslanija Iosifa Volockogo*. Podgotovka teksta *A. A. Zimina* i *J. S. Lur'je* (Moskva-Lgrd. 1959).

Prosvetitel' = *Prosvetitel' ili obličenije jeresi židovstvujuščix. Tvorenije pre-podobnago oca našego Iosifa, Igumena Volockago,* izdannoje v Pravoslav-nom Sobesednike (Kazan' 1855).

PSRL = *Polnoje sobranije russkix letopisej* (Spbg. 1846 ff.).

RIB = *Russkaja istoričeskaja biblioteka izdavajemaja Imp. arxeografiče-skoju kommissijeju* (Spbg. 1872 ff.).

SGGD = *Sobranije gosudarstvennyx gramot i dogovorov xran'aščixs'a v gosudarstvennoj kollegii inostrannyx del* (Moskva 1816–1894).

Smirnov = *I. I. Smirnov: Očerki političeskoj istorii russkogo gosudarstva 30–50ˣ godov XVI veka* (Moskva-Lgrd. 1958).

Soč. Peresv. = *Sočinenija Ivana Peresvetova.* Podgotovil tekst *A. A. Zimin* pod red. *D. S. Lixačeva* (Moskva-Lgrd. 1956).

Stählin = *Karl Stählin: Der Briefwechsel Iwans des Schrecklichen mit dem Fürsten Kurbskij* = Quellen und Aufsätze zur russ. Gesch., III (Leipzig 1921).

TODRL = *Trudy otdela drevnerusskoj literatury Instituta russkoj literatury (Puškinskogo Doma) Akad. Nauk SSSR* (Moskva 1934 ff.).

Zimin Per. = *A. A. Zimin: I. S. Peresvetov i jego sovremenniki. Očerki po istorii russkoj obščestvenno-političeskoj mysli serediny XVI veka* (Moskva 1958).

Zimin Ref. = *A. A. Zimin: Reformy Ivana Groznogo. Očerki social'no-eko-nomičeskoj i političeskoj istorii Rossii serediny XVI v.* (Moskva 1960).

Index of Terms and Titles

Index of Names

Errata to the 1964 edition

Page 21, line 14 from above: "Groxnyj", read "Groznyj"
" 28, " 19 " " "twenty", read "thirty"
" 52, " 3 " " *"mnneije"*, read *"mnenije"*
" 61, " 9 " " "conservations", read "conversations"
" 76, " 18 " above: "repitition", read "repetition"
" 77, " 4 " " "Help", read "help"
" 83, " 2 " below: "80-182", read "180-182"
" 85, " 15 " above: "then", read "than"
" 139, " 12 " " "to Czar", read "the Czar"
" 139, " 16 " " *"otdal"*, read *"otdati"*.
" 168, " 5 " below: "1955", read "1555"
" 181, " 3 " above: "contracy", read "contrary"